Cultural Change and
the New Europe

Cultural Change and the New Europe

Perspectives on the European Community

EDITED BY

Thomas M. Wilson
and M. Estellie Smith

Westview Press

BOULDER • SAN FRANCISCO • OXFORD

Copyright © 1993 by Westview Press, Inc.

Published in 1993 in the United States of America by Westview Press, Inc., 5500 Central Avenue, Boulder, Colorado 80301-2877, and in the United Kingdom by Westview Press, 36 Lonsdale Road, Summertown, Oxford OX2 7EW

Library of Congress Cataloging-in-Publication Data
Cultural change and the new Europe: perspectives on the European
  community / edited by Thomas M. Wilson and M. Estellie Smith.
     p. cm.
  Includes bibliographical references and index.
  ISBN 0-8133-8517-2
  1. Regionalism—European Economic Community countries.
2. Ethnicity—European Economic Community countries.
3. Nationalism—European Economic Community countries.   4. Europe
1992.   I. Wilson, Thomas M.   II. Smith, M. Estellie, 1935–   .
JN94.A38R4334   1993
940.55'9—dc20

92-31972
CIP

Printed and bound in the United States of America

(∞) The paper used in this publication meets the requirements
      of the American National Standard for Permanence of Paper
      for Printed Library Materials Z39.48-1984.

10   9   8   7   6   5   4   3   2   1

Contents

PART THREE
Boundaries and Identities

Preface

This book had its beginnings in a panel on "The Anthropology of the European Community," organized by John Cole and Thomas Wilson, at the annual meetings of the American Anthropological Association in Phoenix in 1988. The panel's discussants that day were Charles Gullick, M. Estellie Smith, and Joan Vincent. Wilson and Smith drank gallons of coffee at the meetings while discussing the possibilities of putting a volume together on the anthropology of the EC's "1992," which would be ethnographic, comparative, and speculative. This book, which addresses issues in cultural change in a reconstructing New Europe of the EC, is the result.

The completion of this volume has been a long process, and we have many people and organizations to thank. We gratefully acknowledge the support of Ioannis Sinanoglou and the Council for European Studies, who awarded Wilson a Workshop Grant enabling the contributors to this book to participate in a two-day conference on "The Anthropology of EC Integration in 1992," which met in New York City in October 1991. We also thank Jane Schneider and the Department of Anthropology of City University of New York's Graduate School and University Center, who were our hosts for this conference. Many of the participants in that session presented follow-up papers on a panel, which was also organized and chaired by Wilson, at the annual meetings of the American Anthropological Association in Chicago in late 1991. We thank all who participated in both events.

We also would like to thank the following colleagues who shared their views on the EC by commenting on earlier versions of contributors' chapters: Hastings Donnan, Vincent Geoghegan, Paul Hainsworth, Edward Hansen, Miriam Lee Kaprow, Michael Kenny, Carl Lankowski, Graham McFarlane, James McLeod, Elizabeth Meehan, Edward Moxon-Browne, Liam O'Dowd, and Elizabeth Tonkin.

Thomas Wilson would also like to thank Elizabeth Tonkin and the faculty and staff of the Department of Social Anthropology of The Queen's University of Belfast for their support and collegiality, and Anthony Sheehan of the Faculty of Arts Computing Unit of QUB, without whom the final manuscript of this volume could not have been prepared. Finally we thank our editors at Westview Press, particularly Kellie Masterson, whose appreciation of wider contexts for anthropology helped to get this project off the ground, and Ellen McCarthy.

Thomas M. Wilson
M. Estellie Smith

About the Contributors

Martin J. Bull, lecturer in politics at the University of Salford, is the author of articles on the politics of the European Left, the communist parties of Western Europe, and Italian politics. He is a visiting fellow at the European University Institute in 1992-1993.

Janeen Arnold Costa, an anthropologist, is assistant professor of marketing in the David Eccles School of Business, University of Utah. Her research interests include cross-cultural consumer behavior and the impact of tourism and migration in Greece and Mediterranean Europe.

Charles J. M. R. Gullick, lecturer in anthropology at the University of Durham, has conducted research on the interface between management and anthropology. He holds a D. Phil. in social anthropology from the University of Oxford and a M. A. in management from the University of Leeds.

Alexandra Jaffe is assistant professor of intercultural communications at Bryant College, Rhode Island. Her field research in Corsica in the summer of 1991 was her fourth trip to the island. Her future research plans include a comparison of regional language practices and attitudes on Corsica and Sardinia.

André Jurjus is preparing his Ph.D. thesis for the Department of Economic Anthropology, University of Nijmegen, on the role of farmers' organizations and national agrarian policies in European regional development. He currently works in the Department of Development Cooperation of the Dutch Ministry of Agriculture.

Gary W. McDonogh is Katharine E. McBride Visiting Professor and Director of the Growth and Structure of Cities Program at Bryn Mawr College. His books include *Good Families of Barcelona* (1986) and *Black and Catholic in Savannah* (forthcoming).

Susan Parman is associate professor of anthropology at California State University, Fullerton, and is the author of *Scottish Crofters: A Historical Ethnography of a Celtic Village* (1990).

Mark T. Shutes, associate professor of anthropology at Youngstown State University, has carried out fieldwork in rural Ireland and Greece. His publications have been concerned with social change and agricultural production strategies.

M. Estellie Smith is professor of anthropology at State University of New York, College at Oswego. She is the author and editor of numerous books and articles in economic, political, and urban anthropology. Her most recent volume is *Perspectives on the Informal Economy* (1990).

Hervé Varenne, professor of education and anthropology at Teachers College, Columbia University, is the author of many books and articles on aspects of everyday life and education in the United States, including *American Together* (1977), *Symbolizing America* (1986), and *Ambiguous Harmony* (forthcoming).

Thomas M. Wilson is senior research fellow in The Queen's University of Belfast's Department of Social Anthropology and Institute of Irish Studies. He is the coeditor (with C. Curtin) of *Ireland From Below: Social Change and Local Communities* (1989). His current research is on border cultures in the EC.

1

An Anthropology of the European Community

Thomas M. Wilson

Contrary to a great deal of media-inspired popular expectation throughout the world, at the close of business on 31 December 1992, Europe, or to be precise, the twelve member states of the European Community (EC), will not be transformed into a "New Europe." But the EC's impetus towards the completion of its Internal Market (IM), which began in the dark aftermath of a long European World War, will be at a symbolic threshold. The EC's "1992" project, initiated in 1985 through the efforts of the European Commission and inspired by the political leadership of its then and current President, Jacques Delors, has motivated the EC's twelve members (EC12) to accomplish its most impressive administrative and legislative achievements to date. In five short years the EC bureaucracy and national governments have agreed to the most wide-ranging changes in the structure and function of the EC itself. This has all occurred with one short-term goal – the achievement of a true barrier-free common market among the EC's members – and many other contested long-term goals in mind. For most European decision makers these long-term goals include an eventual EC economic and monetary union (EMU), with a common European currency; for many others they include a redefinition and reconstruction of member nation states themselves, based in large part on nationalism and regionalism; and for some their goal is the ultimate political integrationists' dream, a United States of Europe. The "1992" project of the EC, however, is but one part of the diplomatic agreements of the 1980s and 1990s which are driving the European member governments, if not their constituent states, to greater economic and political integration.

With an enthusiasm rarely seen in European diplomatic and governmental affairs, the EC12 had adopted the Single European Act (SEA) by 1987. This not only spurred on overall EC forces of economic integration but set the legislative goals of the economic components of the IM (alternatively known as the Single European Market, SEM). Leaving the enthusiasm of a small number of Eurocrats, national civil servants, and national governments aside, however, a common EC market will not be achieved until 1993 at the earliest. In fact, "1993" has crept into the EC lexicon as a corrective to the optimistic notion that "1992" would signal the attainment of a new order of economic cooperation in Europe. In other words, in Euro-speak "1992" cannot happen until 1993. But the forces of integration set in motion by the creation of a European Economic Community (EEC) in 1957 will carry the EC12 well beyond this level of achievement, to perhaps such heights, or, in the eyes of their critics, such depths, that the IM may shrink in importance to the status of a modest but necessary step on the way to a supranation of an EC18 or an EC24.

One thing is clear to the people of the EC who are living through these processes and who, at least in the six founding countries, have experienced EC-building since the 1950s: the EC, in its attempt to create a New Europe, in part to compete with the United States and Japan, and in order to complement, accommodate, or rival the new central and eastern Europe, is transforming aspects of society and culture at every level of local, regional, national, and international integration and interaction. Whether stated as its goals or not, whether unconsciously adopted or in the realm of latent function, the 1992 drive to a common market, in conjunction with the Maastricht initiatives of December 1991 (which are being debated throughout Europe as this book goes to press because of the Danish rejection of the Maastricht treaty in the June 1992 referendum) are requiring all of the EC's people to question the basic tenets of their sociopolitical lives.

The New Europe of the EC is reconstructing its societies into a myriad of smaller but no less complex "new Europes," sociocultural groupings and configurations which face the tensions between tradition and change as well as the disconcerting choice of whether, or how, to influence, curtail, or stop the processes of EC political and economic integration. The democratic elements to the EC are often lost to its citizens by the time the words and images filter down to local communities (it is still surprising for me to hear people in England and Ireland talk about "joining" or "entering" Europe, when that decision was reached, perhaps for them rather than by them, twenty years or so ago) so that their own political choices, or the strategies open to their governments to affect the course of EC events, are obscured. The EC directives connected to the 1992 project are often seen by the EC's citizens to be imposed edicts, an impression fuelled in the UK by politicians' debates about threats to a traditional and vaunted British – or is it English – sovereignty. Still other Europeans are bewildered by the numbers and varieties of EC initiatives to complete the IM, a barrage of legislation and public relations that often appears to be chaotic. But many businesses, interest groups, political parties, cities, regions, and state governments claim to recognize the patterns in the chaos, and they are eager to exploit these perceptions in *their* New Europe. Thus, much of the popular debate in Spain, Portugal, Greece, and Ireland regarding the agreements in Maastricht revolve around the proposed Cohesion Funds, the financial aid guaranteed to the peripheral economies of the EC which should help them attain levels approximating the EC core. Irrespective of their own identification with local community and culture, all Europeans of the EC12 must adapt to the changing economic contexts which will result from the completion of the IM, an economic reorganization on such a massive local, national, and international scale that the politics, societies, and cultures within and without the EC will be utterly changed as well.

This book is a beginning in what may be termed a sociocultural anthropology of the EC; it offers anthropological perspectives on the transformations of European culture and community which both result from the processes of EC integration and which may affect those same processes. It takes as a principal focus the 1992 project of the completion of the EC12 common market, but only as one of many ways of looking at the dialogical and dialectical relationships between and among the EC's peoples, communities, regions, nations, governments, and the central EC institutions. The contributors to this volume hope not only to suggest the relevance of anthropological models and insights for a more complete understanding of what the EC may *mean* in the lives of Europeans – who after all are the people who constitute this "New Europe" – but to engage other scholars in an area which remains largely undocumented in social science and in the humanities, namely the impact of the EC on the everyday lives of its residents and its citizens.

An Anthropology of the EC's 1992

It is an understatement to suggest that the sociocultural anthropology of Europe has not kept pace with the startling developments in the EC over the last decade. In fact, there has been a remarkable absence of EC-related research and writing in anthropology since the original EC was formed. With very few, and very recent, exceptions (Giordano 1987; LiPuma and Meltzoff 1989; Shutes 1991; Wilson 1988, 1989), the EC has not figured in the ethnography or the macro-sociological analyses done by anthropologists since the Community's inception. This is all the more surprising because of the long and substantial roots of anthropological analysis and discourse in European society (summarized in Cole 1977), and the problematic nature of anthropological research and writing in many important areas of European social science (e.g., in the relationship between nation and state in Europe, see Grillo 1980b). In his introduction to that volume, the editor identified some of the issues which influence many of the cultural constructions of the EC found at all levels of European society, i.e., the connections between ethnicity, cultural identity, nation, and state:

> All the same, if organizations such as the EEC model themselves after existing nation-states, and seek integration – an ethnicization of polity – through the construction of common identities and cultures, they are likely to be faced with problems similar to those encountered by their predecessors. There is no reason to suppose they would be any more successful in solving them (Grillo 1980a: 26).

Integration in the EC has become much more than Grillo suggested it might in that, in many ways, it has succeeded in politicizing ethnic and national groups, who have recognized the possibilities for gaining more political power through the organs of economic integration. But the question remains: To what extent do the framers of EC integration model their supranation on the nation-state, and in which ways has the actuality of the EC transcended some of these notions?

The model of the nation-state is so pervasive in European political culture, and so persuasive when one attempts to conjure up a model for a supranational EC, that many Europeans can only see the EC in terms of their nation, their state, or both. The English and their political party leaders are clearly wrestling with the issues of national sovereignty, precisely because they do not wish to relinquish the powers that symbolize sovereignty which are vested in Parliament; the Scots, Welsh, and Northern Irish are increasingly viewing the EC in terms of their nations and are divorcing the issues of integration from that of state sovereignty. After all, their nations are ruled by an English-dominated Parliament in an English-dominated state. This illustrates why the issues of national sovereignty are crucial ones in debates about the future of the EC, and they are reflected in a number of chapters in this book (notably those by Jaffe, McDonogh, and Wilson).

The 1992 project is both the present and the future of the EC as a set of institutions and as a process of international integration. The relative avoidance of the EC as a research focus for sociocultural anthropology is understandable, especially if one sees the field as solely dependent on local ethnographic studies for both its data and theory. But modern anthropology is interested in much more than cultural preservation. Anthropologists have unique perspectives on nations and cultures as seen from below, at the local levels of village, town, farm, and housing estate. These perspectives are also both images in the construction of more inclusive regional and national portraits of social and cultural life (see, e.g., Davis, 1977, for such a view of the cultures of the Mediterranean) as well as important influences in the development of European-wide, if not world-wide, perspectives on the systemic nature of cultural development (see, e.g., Wolf 1982).

An anthropology of the EC, in 1993 and beyond, cannot be rooted or fixed in place and time, nor can it be static or structural-functional ethnographic slices of life, to which a researcher will return in another field research project. An anthropology of the EC must include the historical understanding of European society and culture from, at the very least, the Second World War. As such, it will contribute to a growing interest in anthropology and history (see, e.g., Burke 1987; Davis 1981; Sahlins 1985; Schneider and Schneider 1976; Sider 1986) which investigates both European culture and its effects on the world's cultures. It will also add to the anthropological literature on the organs and dynamics of the nation-state in Europe, a body of work which up to now tended to look at the impact of the state on peripheral regions, local elites, and patronage networks (Grillo 1980a). An anthropology of the EC is also the contemporary analysis of European societies in flux; as such it should pay speculative attention to the Europe that will be. The authors of this volume have focused their essays away from the micro-ethnography of village or neighborhood in order to address the larger issues of cultural and national identity, the symbolic boundaries and material borders which separate and unite, and their relationships with the facts and fancies of the EC. The EC, in the form of its institutions, its decision making processes, its member states' diplomacy, and its changing ideologies of what integration means, and to whom, provide some of the many competing contexts for this anthropological interest, from the top down, so to speak, and one of the most exciting political arenas in the world today. But it is perhaps to the processes of economic integration, which, after all, is what the IM 1992 project and EMU are all about, that an anthropological focus should first turn.

Completing the Internal Market

The Treaty of Rome which established the EEC made clear that in order to unite the member economies all existing economic barriers had to be removed. The six original members (Belgium, the Federal Republic of Germany, France, Italy, Luxembourg, and the Netherlands) wanted a common market in which goods, people, services, and capital could move without hindrance. It has taken over thirty years for the EC to come close to this goal. The timetable adopted in 1985 intended that the IM would be completed and the EC constitute a "Europe without frontiers" by 31 December 1992 (European Communities – Commission 1987). Although this will not be achieved by that date, the EC and the member states have used the goal of completing the market to open up the process; since 1990 economic and monetary union have been seen by most of the EC decision makers as an end result of this integration.

The single market, economic union and monetary union are complementary. Just as completion of the single market is a precondition for economic and monetary union, so the single market can only be fully realized when economic and monetary union is in place (European Communities – Commission 1991b: 4).

The need for a true common market in Europe was clear by the early 1980s. Low productivity, slow economic growth, rising unemployment, debilitating agricultural policies, and tough competition from Japan and the United States demonstrated to European leaders the necessity to close all the gaps among the member states. Removing barriers to the movement of capital, people, goods, and services, they reasoned, would create an economy of scale that should improve productivity, attract foreign investment, lower prices, and create the largest and most powerful consumer society in the world, a single market of over 340 million consumers. And it is these EC projections on the economic advantages to a barrier-free customs union which have become increasingly persuasive to many people in the EC, from politicians and bankers to factory workers and farmers.

The European Commission thus compiled a list of almost 300 measures (later reduced to 282) that needed to be acted upon for the common market to become a reality. These measures, when passed by the EC Council of Ministers, are binding on all member states. As of 1992 over 70% of these directives have been passed by the EC; some member states, notably Italy, France, Greece, and Portugal, have been slow to turn them into national law (Owen and Dynes 1992:27). Most of these measures require the elimination of legislative barriers between countries. The EC White Paper, which allowed ample time for members to enact the necessary legislation, called for the removal of physical, technical, and fiscal barriers. Physical barriers to people and goods involve taxes, the police, tourism, agriculture, and health checks. Technical barriers affect the standards and regulations that nations set for their imports and exports. There is also to be a common market for services, requiring the harmonization of education and professional training, financial services, transportation, information technology, and broadcasting. Fiscal barriers need to come down in order to integrate many of the direct and indirect taxes Europeans are assessed in their member states, the difference between states often being astounding (European Communities – Commission 1987). These efforts reflect a changing institutional framework within the EC as well as changes in the relationships between member states and the EC (Calingaert 1988).

The road to 1992 has not been a smooth one. Member governments must publicly relinquish a modicum of sovereignty in order for the EC to have the power to accomplish economic integration. But to many people in the member states, not least some politicians, the loss of any sovereignty is the loss of it all. Thus, the issue of national sovereignty is becoming central to the developing political culture of the EC (leading to such diverse dilemmas as the growing numbers of "Euro-sceptics" in the UK's Tory Party, and the Danish referendum results which were partly due to Danish fears of losing their sovereignty to a German-dominated EC). Because of these political issues many groups within and between states oppose some EC proposals and favor others. Many states and their nations are also worried about the effects of free market competition on their uncompetitive industries and regions, and the EC itself has pointed out the pressures that integration will put on the social conditions of those regions already lagging behind the EC's more developed regions.

At this stage it is difficult to assess who will gain and who will lose in the IM. But perceptions of one's role (or, for that matter, of one's company, city, region, or political party) in a new economic Europe are instrumental to one's actions in attempting to adapt to what is an impending reality. The explosion of literature on EC 1992, largely written for business people and academics in order to get them up to speed, seem to conclude that the race will go to the swiftest. In other words, the best prepared to operate in a changed world economy will fare best. Not surprisingly, much of the criticism of 1992 has attacked the lack of planning regarding those people without political and economic power, who do not have the resources or ability to plan ahead. The potential victimization of workers, for example, who are sure to be affected by relocating employers, redundancies due to market competition, an influx of "other" European labor, and changes in prices for consumer goods, but who are powerless to relocate themselves or too poor to prepare for emergencies, has led to an EC-wide movement to adopt a Social Charter. Interestingly, at the recent Maastricht summit, only the UK refused to adopt common measures on social policy, which it saw as a step toward unwanted interference in its national employer and labor relations. Many of the UK's citizens, principally in the peripheralized North of England and Scotland, are afraid that the common market may make UK industry far less competitive, and that their wages will drop or their jobs disappear. Such perceptions have not changed the Tory government's views on a "Social Europe," nor did they seem to be influential in the Labour Party's general election defeat in 1992. But workers throughout the UK – indeed, throughout the EC – are wondering what this New Europe will mean to the material conditions of their lives. One thing is clear. The political leaders who have already committed their countries to an IM are joining with such groups as business leaders, bankers, and farmers in a massive and extremely expensive effort to sell the values of the EC, and the IM, to the general public. In the politicians' case, at least for those politicians whose governments and parties have been "pro-Europe" since their countries joined, their political futures may depend on both the results of the processes of EC integration in their constituencies, and their constituents' perceptions of the EC and its impact. In fact, a war of images about the EC has been increasingly waged in the communication media of the member states.

This media blitz – it is impossible to pick up any major newspaper in any of the capitals of the EC12 and avoid reading about "the EC, the government, the nation, and you" – reflects both the importance of the events taking place and the need for individuals and groups to recognize their material interests in the process. For example, many books that serve as academic overviews or business primers on the potentials of a common market which are published in the UK havesections entitled something like "What's in it for Britain?" (an actual chapter title from Pelkmans and Winters 1988).

One of these handbooks sets out what its authors see as "twelve benefits of the single market . . . on the way *we* live and work in Europe" (Owen and Dynes 1992:24, emphasis added, to point out the problematic use of the first person pronoun – the entire book is geared for Britons). Among the benefits they see are easier travel for people, because internal frontier controls will be gone; easier travel for goods, with no more delays for trucks and lorries at borders, which cost the EC an estimated £17 billion a year; a boom in business, due to a free and fair access market for all companies in the EC; EC-wide job recognition for all professionals and workers; the removal of restrictions on cross-national financial services, so that investors and consumers of all varieties can take advantage of the market for capital; consumer protection, which will be strengthened through common EC standards for foodstuffs and manufactured goods; and the harmonization of state indirect taxes, which should bring many prices down (Owen and Dynes 1992:24-26). Whether this is an accurate projection or not only time will tell, but this list does reflect the intended outcome of the EC's 1992 project, including the economic benefits which are supposed to accrue to workers, consumers, and capitalists. As in most of the rhetoric on the IM, it does not incorporate aspects of social and political integration which, as we have seen, are also vital parts of the total movement towards economic and monetary union, and, perhaps eventually, political union.

This artificial bifurcation of the EC's 1992 project into the processes of "economics" and "all others" is not necessarily the way Europeans experience them. To many, the EC and its integrationist forces are perceived as a sociocultural package, i.e., they are experiencing these changes in their totality, in every aspect of their day-to-day lives. The EC is affecting their food, clothes, wages, education, television, and newspapers. It is making them redefine their histories and cultural traditions, re-evaluate the importance and futures of their cities and regions, and re-explore their attitudes towards race, ethnicity, and nationality. They are recognizing that there will be many problems at national levels which will affect them in their factories, on their farms, and in their homes. Borders without frontiers will not be borders without symbolic boundaries or cultural barriers, but they may make the movement in drugs, terrorism, crime, and illegal residents easier. Free markets may mean international ownership of what are considered to be national treasures or national traditions. Reactions to Germans buying Danish property, or to Japanese building golf courses in the Highlands, or to any other business ventures which are seen by local communities as threats by "other" nations or cultures, may run to the xenophobic or racist, as have many rightist backlashes to "immigrant" or "foreign" workers in Spain, France, and Germany. At what point will the communities of the Mediterranean or of the peripheral regions of the British Isles be fed up with the influx of their fellow Europeans who are attempting to escape the plasticities of a Euro-Disney by exploring their "common" European culture?

Regardless of the ways in which the citizens of the New Europe will experience these changes, all have been made to question the sociocultural foundations of their lives, and, in doing so, have redefined the symbolic boundaries which separate those who are "the same" from those who are "the other" in Europe's cities, regions, nations, and states. The EC, in its superficial attempts at creating official "Euro-culture" through the adoption of such symbols as a European flag, passport, and anthem, may hope to create a definition of "we Europeans" vs. "those others." This does not seem to be a likely outcome of these processes of cultural change, especially because most of the countries of Europe which are not at present in the EC are intending to apply for membership. On the contrary, symbolic constructions of the EC, in 1993 and beyond, will be largely created by and will reside with those who live and work in its local communities.

The chapters in this volume explore the EC's 1992 project as both a symbol of and the processes towards the cultural integration (i.e. political, economic, and social integration) of the EC. But the single market has also become a lightning rod for the conflict of ideas about the New Europe of a future EC, a conflict among groups of people in and across all the member states who are attempting to make their interpretations of the meanings of their past and future in the EC dominant ones. Many of these symbolic inventions and traditions are being used to privilege both old and new definitions of local and regional culture, ethnic identities, and nationhood (see chapters by Gullick, Jaffe, Varenne). The boundaries which individuals and groups construct to sustain themselves are being transformed in the face of the polarities of centralization and decentralization, subsidiarity and supranation-building (see chapters by Parman, Smith, Wilson). To many Europeans both the EC and its internal market are creating political, economic, and cultural domains which must be contested, because the very future of their definitions of culture and community are being threatened by a New Europe (see chapters by McDonogh, Costa, Jurjus, and Shutes).

Cultural Relations and the EC

Many Europeans perceive that the EC is not fully working, as both an institution and an idea. This is not to say that the EC is seen by its citizens to be either unsuccessful in achieving its stated goals or wrong in its stated purposes (although these perceptions are filtered through member governments and the national medias, which often represent the EC in markedly different and sometimes contradictory ways). But many people are unsure of what these purposes and goals are, and what they should mean to them. With the possible exception of Europe's farmers, who up to now have benefited from the guaranteed prices and markets of the EC's Common Agricultural Policy (CAP) but who are angry about much of recent agreement on CAP reform (May 1992), many EC citizens see the EC as an intrusive and meddlesome institution which interferes with too much of their day-to-day lives. Integration means more than the streamlining of an inefficient economy. It also represents a harmonization and standardization of products and images to such a degree that many Europeans, rightly, fear a homogenization of European Cultures into some as yet unknown "Euro-culture." Perceived threats to the British pints of milk and beer, French cheeses, and the Spanish bullfight may seem a bit trivial to outsiders, but to the people who see these as less a symbol and more a definition of culture, Euro-standards are an unwanted aspect of EC membership. In the part of Ireland I have lived in and researched for fifteen years, many farmers and their families are "pro-Europe" because of the economic benefits the EC has brought them (Wilson 1988, 1990), but most people of the villages and towns are confused about what the EC means to them.

I suggest, as do a number of contributors to this volume, that many peoples throughout Europe share this ambivalence. Most Europeans identify themselves as members of a nation, e.g., of France or of Euskadi, and they are aware that they are Europeans by birth and culture. But many are not so sure of their identity as "EC Europeans." Some, for a host of reasons, do not care. Others recognize that citizenship – a new symbol of the post-Maastricht EC – of a supranational EC presents them with new rights and responsibilities and new opportunities and constraints. They understand, in ways it has taken anthropologists a long time to discover, that the EC's evolution as an ecosociopolitical system has created a new culture, in which both "natives" and "outsiders" can debate the mode or substance of this new cultural identity. This is not a very different experience from the many cultural worlds which anthropologists have been studying since the origins of the discipline, albeit that the EC is one of the largest and most populous modern social systems which has constructed itself before their eyes. Anthropologists are witnessing the EC's evolution in areas where the EC is effecting great cultural changes; these areas are also the least explored by the EC itself, namely the communities which define Europe's cities, regions, ethnic groups, and nations. The EC, and social scientists who share the EC's macro-models of political, governmental, and economic integration, are ignoring the ways in which the EC has an impact on local culture, including the ways in which the EC is perceived and represented. They do so at their own risk. Those who believe that the EC will construct itself from the top down, on the model of Italy in the last century (Hobsbawm 1992:4), by establishing the extent and limits to its sovereignty and *then* devising the means of reconstructing local, regional, and national cultures by injecting a new layer or level of "Euro-identity," should remind themselves of similar attempts in the USSR and Yugoslavia.

The residents of this reconstructing New Europe often see the EC and its intrusion into their lives in terms of tradition and change. Anthropology has much to offer contemporary European and EC scholarship precisely because the study of cultural traditions, including their roles in resistance to and the transformations of social change, has largely defined the discipline over the last seventy years. Although it has "become fashionable to deconstruct" traditions in social science today (Appadurai et al. 1991:18), in large part by dissecting their cultural and historical invention (Hobsbawm and Ranger 1983), the exploration of the ways local communities and their traditions adapted to past changes, or are presently seen to have adapted in the culturally defined past, are both clues to present constructions of cultural identity and a means of understanding much of that community's historical and contemporary cultural relations. As a number of scholars working on notions of gender, genre, and power in South Asian traditions have succinctly concluded:

> Tradition is about "pastness." (Halbwachs 1980 [1950] and not just about the past. It is not a positive discourse but a reflective and reflexive one. In it, and through it, societies explore the limits of their histories, and replay the points of tension in these histories. It is a metadiscourse, which allows the past to cease to be a "scarce resource" (Appadurai 1981) and allows it to become . . . a renewable resource. Tradition is another zone of contestation . . . about temporal boundaries themselves (Appadurai et al. 1991: 22).

I suggest that the anthropological analysis of traditions in European communities, which are changing due to real or perceived input from the EC, is one of several possible avenues towards the recognition and understanding of the ways Europeans reconstruct their contemporary identities in their attempts to resist, internalize, and/or transcend the EC as a set of new cultural relations. Traditions are not just zones of temporal contestation but are multiple areas and levels of spatial and cultural contestation which, in the New Europe, are being exacerbated through the processes of EC-building as well as state and empire dissolution in the Balkans and among the former Soviet nations.

The renewed presence of the EC in the lives of its citizens is not just a matter of a new cultural context within which traditions adapt and new cultural forms develop. Much of this new cultural identity of "EC European" is framed within the context of economic and political competition. Not only is the EC as an idea a new aspect of culture for its residents, but the EC is also a new arena, wherein groups of people battle for scarce resources. Farmers want the CAP left untouched, but dairy farmers and cereal growers have different agendas at the EC bargaining table, as do the farmers of the Mediterranean nations vs. those of the North (see Shutes and Jurjus in this volume). Cities compete with each other for vital EC structural funds, and do so across national borders, often bypassing their national governments in the process (see Smith in this volume). Regions such as Northern Ireland open up lobbying offices in Brussels both to establish their identity on the EC scene, and to maintain or increase the levels of EC monetary support. Groups of regions join together because of common economic goals, and because their national governments cannot argue their cases as forcefully as they would like because of the constraints of national political agendas For example, the industrial regions of the EC have been lobbying for an increase in funds allocated to industrial regions in the next five year EC budget. This group of forty-five industrial regions, which includes Catalonia, Tuscany, Nord Pas de Calais, North Jutland, and North Rhine-Westphalia, wish to ensure that each gets as big a slice of the pie as possible, even if that means less funding for other regions of the EC, or other areas of their own countries.

The EC is also an arena of political power, within which regions, nations, states, and the EC contest sovereignty and hegemony (state wrangling over the development of the EC is as old as the EC itself, see Bull's analysis in this volume). The nation-state in the EC is being redefined because the state's legitimate use of force in a territory with clearly defined borders, which is symbolized by notions of national sovereignty, is being contested from above and below. Regions, which often define themselves as composed of separate nations, are eschewing past forms of ethnonationalisms in order to wrest more power and independence from the state; many are using the EC as a forum to redefine their national and international identities. This not only threatens the state's sovereignty, it strengthens the EC's role as arbiter of international and inter-regional integration, further calling into question the degree to which joining the EC has transformed or reduced national and/or governmental sovereignty. One of the key cultural relations which the EC is redefining at state levels, and in many ways is supplanting, is that of sovereignty. Since the expansion of the EC and its moves toward EMU, all member governments and their constituent parties have had to debate the impact of the EC on their national control over the resources which each state has taken to be their exclusive domain.

Socialist parties' debates about the nature of supranationalism and internationalism (Featherstone 1988) are symptomatic of the ways all political parties of the EC – from national front to communist – have been forced to deal with the recontextualization of their political systems. Still other critics point out that the recent Maastricht agreements pave the way for the possibilities of governmental decentralization in those member states with highly centralized polities (Kearney 1992). This could be due to the Maastricht notion of EC subsidiarity, i.e., the EC should not deal with any aspect of integration which can be better handled at a lower governmental level. Although the ways in which this principle of subsidiarity will function are unclear, in part because the identification and definition of the issues to be dealt with at lower levels will remain with national and EC leaders, subsidiarity nonetheless gives new life to regional and urban claims to more power for local government, and transcends state control of the right to deal with all matters within its jurisdiction as it sees fit. In fact, the four guiding principles of the Maastricht agreements (threatened but not overruled by the results of the Danish referendum in June, 1992) – "subsidiarity, pooled sovereignty, social cohesion, and a federation of regions" (Kearney 1992:5) – together suggest a transformation of the EC and its relationships to member states which is so great as to make the states' original reasons for creating or joining the EC all but obsolete. The evolution of the EC has changed the contexts of sovereignty for all, suggesting that the leaders of today's Europe need to redefine the objectives of the EC, in order to catch up with an EC already overtaken by events. The conditions which gave rise to the "Europe of Jean Monnet" no longer exist:

> Europe cannot be defined by its geographical borders. Europe is a political culture where the idea of liberal democracy has become integrated with the practice of *soziale Marktwirtschaft* (social market economy). A concept of citizenship including civil, political and social rights has developed as a common pattern in the patchwork of nation states, one we now are trying to stitch together (Holm 1992: 10).

The conditions which gave rise to the local and national versions of "nationalism" (as reviewed by Varenne in this volume and in Hobsbawm 1992) have also been transformed, although people continue to believe in the many "fictions of Europe" which privilege a common "European culture" (Pieterse 1991:3-5). These cultural constructions, which inform the actions of many of those who lead the EC, are aspects of an imagined Europe (in much the same way nations are imagined communities, Anderson 1991); such views of Europe are perceived by some to be misguided views of a historical and cultural facade. This imagined Europe:

> is wrong as regards the origins of European culture; it is wrong in so representing European culture that European regional cultures and subcultures are overlooked; it is wrong in representing elite culture as culture *tout court* and in denying popular culture; it is wrong in defining European culture in terms of the past ("inherited civilisation") and in totally ignoring Europe's contemporary multicultural realities (Pieterse 1991: 4).

The EC is thus also a focus for European ideas about the meanings of European culture. And it is these contested constructions of cultural identity which anthropologists should explore in order to give definitions to the past, present, and future of Europe and the EC.

Contested Domains

Regions are often believed by their residents to be composed of a "nation," a group often defined through a common or shared ethnicity or culture (e.g., Euskadi, Catalonia, Scotland, and Corsica). Many have revitalized their hopes and plans for devolution or independence from their dominant "nation-state." A number of these regions support plans to reshape the EC in order to better privilege the roles of "national" regions in the international scene, i.e., by bypassing state institutions in order to create an EC "Europe of the Regions" (see Jaffe in this volume and Hume 1988). Such plans may make violent revolution against the state anachronistic. Other regions are inventing forms of common regional culture in order to weaken the hold of a state seen by them to be retarding their development. Thus the Lombardy movement is attempting to reconstruct northern Italy's relationships with Italy's center, southern Italy, and Sicily. Still other regions cross national borders, and their elites have organized their interests to take advantage of all possible state and EC supports for their, perhaps newly defined, regional economies and cultures. Since 1963 the "supranational region" of Regio-Basiliensis, comprised of an area of the Upper Rhine framed by

French, German, and Swiss cities, has constructed itself in order to exploit the changing economies and polities of a New Europe (O'Dowd and Corrigan 1992).

These new definitions of region – which owe something, perhaps a great deal, to the reconfiguration of EC and state relations – also owe much to the contest for scarce resources and power, and do much to support the conclusions of research in regional political economy which has been conducted in Europe over the last thirty years (see, e.g., Cole and Wolf 1974; Schneider and Schneider 1976; Schneider et al. 1972). A number of these conclusions have been overtaken by events as well. Catalonia's regional political culture is increasingly modelling itself on those of European multicultural states like Switzerland (although there are difficulties for many non-Catalan minorities in the region, as McDonogh reviews in this volume, much like non-Swiss in Switzerland) while at the same time emphasizing the distinctiveness of its nationhood from that of Spain. Catalonian political elites fully expect to use the new democratic and devolved Spain and the New Europe to achieve some form of independence, or "separatism Euro-style," i.e., over the supranational bargaining table (Hooper 1992:27). This situation is a far cry from the rather pessimistic views of Catalan culture under Franco's regime (Hansen 1977).

The people of Europe are contesting cultural relations at every level of sociocultural integration, below and above the region and the state. Cities no longer solely rely on their national governments to lobby for them in Brussels, and join with other cities to reconfigure such important but increasingly stereotyped relationships as rural and urban and North and South (as Smith reviews in this volume). Local government councils, like Irish county councils, debate the merits of appointing an EC development officer, to both pressure their central governments for their EC funds and to represent them in Europe. Islands have joined together to explore EC strategies based on their common needs and experiences (see Jaffe in this volume). And individuals and groups who speak for the widest range of European managers and workers, farmers and fishermen, old and young, men and women, see the EC as an arena within which one must wage battles over capital, power, and identity. Neither bankers nor government leaders can escape the travails of cultural dissonance and stereotyping (as Gullick shows in this volume). Irish women are at present debating the gains to women and feminism which have resulted from EC membership, and many hope to use the EC to attain their long-neglected rights to choose in terms of abortion and divorce.

In short, there is not one organization or individual in the EC12 whose cultural ground rules have not changed due to the EC. And as definitions of culture, region, and nation become increasingly problematic as a result, Europeans have begun to debate their notions of cultural identity almost as much as anthropologists have.

Boundaries and Identity

The anthropology of European societies has increasingly turned to the exploration of the symbolic nature of cultural boundaries (see, e.g., Cohen 1982, 1986). Such views of boundaries are also views of cultural identities, because they are part of a community's determination of "us" vs. "them" (Grillo 1980a). Identities, as we have seen, are contextualized in a number of ways by groups hoping to exploit the EC's resources and power base. But such instrumental views of cultural identity are incomplete; definitions of membership and otherness involve complex values and beliefs regarding one's past and present. Most groups who define their membership culturally, i.e., based on such factors as common history, language, dress, residence, and way of life, do not do so primarily because of the power and wealth that might be theirs. Ethnicity and nationhood can become economic and political in many ways, which will help define group boundaries, but those boundaries are based on much more. The symbolic nature of these boundaries, the self-defined limits to a community's culture, continue to be a focus of anthropological discourse, whether those boundaries are between communities of immigrants defined in part by race, or those between dominant nations of the EC, as expressed by politicians, or those which establish the distinctiveness of both a region and the social bounds of the EC itself (see the analyses of McDonogh and Parman in this volume). It should not be surprising if most EC citizens recognize their own membership in a number of culturally defined groups – most people in the world do – and do not feel that these overlapping identities are incompatible. A Basque from the countryside who lives in Paris and works for the central government has a number of identities with which she identifies and is labelled. But the critical moments when one or more identities take precedence over the others are crucial ones for the understanding of individual and group motivations. The timing and location of these events is not the choice of the social scientist. Ethnographic research provides one important but underused method in recognizing and understanding the cultural relations which help define the limits to identity in the New Europe.

Liminal moments such as these seem commonplace at international borders between states. Border cultures can be held together through ethnic ties, but much of the commerce between communities on either side of the borders has been limited by state laws. The completion of the IM should encourage more cultural integration by removing the barriers to people and services, but border cultures often revolve around much more than the state allows. For example, the future of cross-border smuggling is in question in the New Europe (what will be smuggled other than drugs, weapons, and people?) whereas increased international consumerism may have a number of unpredicted results (see Costa and Wilson in this volume). An anthropology of international borders would seem to be another fruitful area of EC research, as the EC itself has recognized through its INTERREG scheme; the EC will expand over the next generation in ways which are now unpredictable (Austria, Finland, Sweden, and Switzerland are among the countries seeking admission) but which may take it from the Atlantic to the Urals. The scholarship of this expansion must heed the definitions of culture and nation of the peoples who are incorporated. As the people of Northern Ireland, the Basque country, and the former Yugoslavia can attest, these definitions can become a matter of life and death.

An anthropology of the EC in 1993 and beyond can take many paths. Some of the most productive and relevant, for researchers, decision-makers of the public and private sectors, and EC citizens alike, may be through the application of ethnographic methods and anthropological theories to the totality of the EC as a set of cultural relations. Borrowing from Verdery, who views "'nation' as an element of the relations between state and subject, understood as a *cultural* relation" (emphasis in original, 1992:8), I would go further and argue that the EC is also an element of the relations between the state and its residents and citizens. It has reconstructed Europe as a social system so as to allow regions and states to act as elements in the relations between citizens and residents and the supranation. All of these elements are understood by Europeans in the New Europe to be *cultural* relations.

The Prodigal Returns?
Anthropology in the New Europe of the EC

In 1977 John Cole's review of the anthropology of Europe suggested that the overall field of anglophone sociocultural anthropology had come only "part-way home." In his view, an emphasis in the anthropological literature on the concepts of tradition and modernization, and a reluctance of anthropologists to conduct field research in the mundane, predictable, and comfortable cultures of a "home" Europe, far away from the preferred exoticism of field work hardships and adventure, had for too long stultified the development of an anthropology of Europe. One way in which anthropology could regain its relevance, he concluded, was through the realization that whatever traditional or fashionable aspect of society is studied by anthropologists, that it is a "product of social forces." "In this perspective the integration of community into regional and national processes is as decisive for community and region as local ecological and social relations" (Cole 1977:374). He also argued that regions should be seen as part of the wider world political economy.

Leaving aside the question of the aptness of his metaphor, I would like to use it to second the call Cole made for a relevant anthropology of Europe. The EC is one more context within which anthropologists can work to the same goals as our colleagues in the other social sciences, including the analysis of those modern social forces which shape culture and community from the village to the Berlaymont. But an anthropology of the EC does not take the voyager all the way home. It is but one part of the larger anthropology of Europe and the modern world, which is alive, well, and multi-faceted in both Europe and North America (the combined membership of the Society for the Anthropology of Europe and the European Association of Social Anthropologists nears two thousand; for a review of some of the directions this growing interest is taking, see Ulin 1991). And the best of this anthropology applies interpretive and materialist models to the ethnographic understanding of cultural transformations (see, e.g., Cohen 1987; Harding 1984; Herzfeld 1985, 1987; Holmes 1989; Kertzer 1980; Rogers 1991; and the ethnographies written by a number of this volume's contributors).

Nonetheless, the dearth of ethnographically informed studies of the EC in context, or of speculative writing on the EC as elements of the cultural relations of Europeans, suggest that the EC and its social forces are uninteresting to anthropologists. If this is so, how can we anthropologists suggest that our discipline is relevant to the lives of the people we live with and study? If, as I have argued here, the EC is becoming an essential element in the day-to-day lives of Europeans, then an anthropology of Europe is in crisis if it cannot meet the theoretical, methodological, and intellectual demands of a social system of the scale of the EC. The ethnographically informed essays of this volume, which are intended to cross the bounds of the local level in order to be both comparative and speculative, are a first attempt to avert such a crisis, and to begin to set a research agenda for future anthropological investigations. Perhaps this volume represents another "experimental moment" in our field, in which anthropology continues both to resist the forces of cultural homogenization dominant in

Western scholarship and to reflect self-critically on our ways of understanding and writing about ourselves and culture (Marcus and Fischer 1986: vii,1). This volume, it is hoped, stands as both an experiment in and a critique of the anthropology of Europe. It also intends to present views of the diversity of cultural change which the EC has meant, and may yet mean, to Europeans. Perhaps these essays will influence a number of people outside of our field to reflect critically on *their* New Europe.

Finally, a word about what this book is not. These chapters are only indicative of the ways anthropologists can bring their insights to bear on the multiplicity of cultural relations which make up the EC. As such, the contributors did not set out to portray aspects of change in all of the member states. To do so would privilege a notion of nation-state of which many of us are critical . However, it became clear through the process of writing and editing, how few anglophone anthropologists are working on EC related issues. Part of the answer to this lies in the continuing fascination of anthropologists with the peripheralized and more inaccessible regions of Europe, part lies with the lack of employment opportunities for those Europeanist anthropologists who stray from more traditionally defined disciplinary interests. Both this introduction and the volume itself suggest a number of areas in the anthropology of the EC which are either now the focus of ethnographic research or should be in the near future. These include research in: EC decision making and EC institutions (to my knowledge at least three anthropologists – Marc Abélès, Douglas Holmes, and Maryon McDonald – are involved in such work); international borders; the changing roles of cities; the politics of the social charter; women's rights; immigration; race; regional devolution and independence; agrarian systems and family farms; and the representations of European culture and identity, from the "fictions" of an "imagined" EC to a "Euro-culture" of fact and fancy. The EC is both flawed and forceful, and it is not going away. Like the people of Europe, anthropologists can either make their war or their peace with it, but they cannot ignore it.

Notes

This essay is based, in part, on research funded by the National Endowment for the Humanities, the Wenner-Gren Foundation for Anthropological Research, and the British Council. I am indebted to Elizabeth Tonkin and the Department of Social Anthropology, as well as Ronald Buchanan, Brian Walker and the Institute of Irish Studies, for their collegiality. I acknowledge with thanks the critical readings of drafts of this chapter by Hastings Donnan and M. Estellie Smith.

References

Anderson, Benedict. 1991. *Imagined Communities*. 2nd edition. London: Verso.
Appadurai, Arjun. 1981. "The Past as a Scarce Resource." *Man* (n.s.) 16: 201-219.
Appadurai, Arjun, Frank J. Korom, and Margaret A. Mills. 1991. "Introduction," in A. Appadurai et al., eds., *Gender, Genre, and Power in South Asian Expressive Traditions*. Pp. 3-29. Philadelphia: University of Pennsylvania Press.
Burke, Peter. 1987. *The Historical Anthropology of Early Modern Italy*. Cambridge: Cambridge University Press.
Calingaert, Michael. 1988. *The 1992 Challenge from Europe*. Washington: National Planning Association.
Cohen, Anthony P., ed. 1982. *Belonging: Identity and Social Organization in British Rural Cultures*. Manchester: Manchester University Press.
____. ed. 1986. *Symbolising Boundaries: Identity and Diversity in British Cultures*. Manchester: Manchester University Press.
____. 1987. *Whalsay*. Manchester: Manchester University Press.
Cole, John W. 1977. "Anthropology Comes Part-Way Home: Community Studies in Europe." *Annual Review of Anthropology* 6: 349-378.
Cole, John W., and Eric R. Wolf. 1974. *The Hidden Frontier: Ecology and Ethnicity in an Alpine Valley*. New York: Academic Press.
Davis, John. 1977. *People of the Mediterranean: An Essay in Comparative Social Anthropology*. London: Routledge.
Davis, Nathalie. 1981. "Anthropology and History in the 1980s: The Possibilities of the Past." *Journal of Interdisciplinary History* 12: 267-276.
European Communities – Commission. 1987. *The European Community: 1992 and Beyond*. Luxembourg: Office for Official Publications of the European Communities.
____. 1991a. *Opening up the Internal Market*. Luxembourg: Office for Official Publications of the European Communities.
____. 1991b. *A Citizen's Europe*. Luxembourg: Office for Official Publications of the European Communities.
Featherstone, Kevin. 1988. *Socialist Parties and European Integration*. Manchester: Manchester University Press.
Giordano, Christian. 1987. "The 'Wine War' Between France and Italy: Ethno-anthropological Aspects of the European Community." *Sociologia Ruralis* 27: 56-66.
Grillo, R. D. 1980a. "Introduction," in R. D. Grillo, ed., *"Nation" and "State" in Europe: Anthropological Perspectives*. Pp. 1-30. London: Academic Press.
____. 1980b. *"Nation" and "State" in Europe: Anthropological Perspectives*. London: Academic Press.

Halbwach, Maurice. 1980 [1950]. *The Collective Memory.* Tr. by F. J. Ditter, Jr. and V. Y. Ditter. New York: Harper and Row.

Hansen, Edward C. 1977. *Rural Catalonia Under the Franco Regime: The Fate of Regional Culture.* Cambridge: Cambridge University Press.

Harding, Susan Friend. 1984. *Remaking Ibieca: Rural Life in Aragon under Franco.* Chapel Hill: University of North Carolina Press.

Herzfeld, Michael. 1985. *The Poetics of Manhood.* Princeton: Princeton University Press.

_____. 1987. *Anthropology Through the Looking Glass: Critical Ethnography on the Margins of Europe.* Cambridge: Cambridge University Press.

Hobsbawm, Eric. 1992. "Ethnicity and Nationalism in Europe Today." *Anthropology Today* 8 (1): 3-8.

Hobsbawm, Eric and Terence Ranger. 1983. *The Invention of Tradition.* Cambridge: Cambridge University Press.

Holm, Erik. 1992. "The end of the beginning." *The European* 28-31 May: 10.

Holmes, Douglas R. 1989. *Cultural Disenchantments: Worker Peasantries in Northeast Italy.* Princeton: Princeton University Press.

Hooper, John. 1992. "Enough Money to Yearn." *The Guardian* 22 May: 27.

Hume, John. 1988. "Europe of the Regions," in R. Kearney, ed., *Across the Frontiers.* Dublin: Wolfhound Press.

Kearney, Richard, ed. 1988. *Across the Frontiers: Ireland in the 1990s.* Dublin: Wolfhound Press.

Kertzer, David. 1980. *Comrades and Christians.* Cambridge: Cambridge University Press.

LiPuma, Edward, and Sarah Keene Meltzoff. 1989. "Toward a Theory of Culture and Class: An Iberian Example." *American Ethnologist* 16 (2): 313-334.

Marcus, George E., and Michael M. J. Fischer. 1986. *Anthropology as Cultural Critique.* Chicago: The University of Chicago Press.

O'Dowd, Liam, and James Corrigan. 1992. National Sovereignty and Cross-Border Cooperation. Unpublished paper. Sociological Association of Ireland Annual Conference, Cork, 8 - 10 May.

Owen, Richard, and Michael Dynes. 1992. *The Times Guide to the Single European Market.* London: Times Books.

Pelkmans, Jacques, and Alan Winters. 1987. *Europe's Domestic Market.* London: The Royal Institute of International Affairs.

Pieterse, Jan Nederveen. 1991. "Fictions of Europe." *Race and Class* 32 (3): 3-10.

Rogers, Susan Carol. 1991. *Shaping Modern Times in Rural France.* Princeton: Princeton University Press.

Sahlins, Marshall. 1985. *Islands of History.* Chicago: University of Chicago Press.

Schneider, Jane, and Peter Schneider. 1976. *Culture and Political Economy in Western Sicily.* New York: Academic Press.

Schneider, Jane, Peter Schneider, and Edward Hansen. 1972. "Modernization and Development: The Role of Regional Elites and Noncorporate Groups in the European Mediterranean." *Comparative Studies in Society and History* 14: 328-350.

Shutes, Mark. 1991. "Kerry Farmers and the European Community: Capital Transitions in a Rural Irish Parish." *Irish Journal of Sociology* 1: 1-17.

Sider, Gerald. 1986. *Culture and Class in Anthropology and History: A Newfoundland Illustration.* Cambridge: Cambridge University Press.

Ulin, Robert C. 1991. "The current tide in American Europeanist anthropology." *Anthropology Today* 7 (6): 8-12.

Verdery, Katherine. 1992. "Comment: Hobsbawm in the East." *Anthropology Today* 8 (1): 8-10.

Wilson, Thomas M. 1988. "Culture and Class Among the 'Large' Farmers of Eastern Ireland." *American Ethnologist* 15: 678-693.

_____. 1989. "Large Farms, Local Politics, and the International Arena: The Irish Tax Dispute of 1979." *Human Organization* 48 (1): 60-70.

_____. 1990. "Ethnography and Political Science: Agricultural Politics in Eire." *Politics* 10(1): 9-16.

Wolf, Eric R. 1982. *Europe and the People Without History.* Berkeley: University of California Press.

2

Widening Versus Deepening the European Community: The Political Dynamics of 1992 in Historical Perspective

Martin J. Bull

This chapter outlines the history of the European Community (EC) from a political and institutional perspective. The objective is not simply to describe the main events and institutions in the development of the EC but to locate them within the context of a continuous struggle over competing concepts of "European unity." The struggle between these concepts has, more than anything else, shaped the development of the EC, and it is only through a consideration of them in historical context that one can understand fully the meaning and implications of what has popularly become known as "1992," i.e., the completion of the EC's internal market (IM). Such an approach also provides both a background to the rest of this book, the main focus of which is the responses of different peoples to European integration, in the specific context of 1992, and a pointer to the importance of social anthropological studies of culture change in the New Europe of the EC.

Origins and Formative Conceptions

Although the modern idea of European unity can be traced to the 1920s (and, in particular, to Aristide Briand's motion, advanced at the League of

Nations in September 1929, for a federal bond between European states), the first realistic steps towards its practical achievement occurred in the period after the Second World War. The devastating effects of the war turned what had previously been an essentially idealistic vision of European unity (and one restricted to a minority of people) into, for many, a political and economic necessity. A number of factors were involved.[1] Firstly, with Europe having suffered from two world conflicts in less than half a century, the concepts of "nationalism" and the "nation-state" had become discredited. Indeed, for some countries the nation-state was deemed to have failed in its primary task of providing law and order and protecting the citizens living within its boundaries. A new order was needed, therefore, which would undermine nationalism or, at the least, provide some form of protection for European citizens from the potential excesses of the nation-state.

Secondly, Europe was no longer the Europe of old, where Vienna and Berlin had been as central as Paris and London, but was now split between East and West. Europe's main problem of containing Germany was replaced by the problem of containing the Soviet Union and the satellite states of Eastern Europe, all in the context of a balance between the two new superpowers, the USA and the USSR. Simultaneously, the command economies became increasingly intertwined with the Soviet economy, and economic links with west European countries declined. Thus, in political, economic and strategic terms, the pressure for European unity was, in fact, pressure for a *west* European unity which was more manageable.

Thirdly, there was a general trend in the immediate post-war period towards the setting up of international organizations to resolve problems of a cross-national nature in almost all areas of government. The United Nations and its network of specialized agencies (including organizations such as UNESCO, the International Monetary Fund [IMF] and the Food and Agriculture Organisation [FAO]), was the prime example of this trend. The universalism represented by these organizations, however, was rapidly undermined by the escalation of the Cold War and the subsequent prospect of a communist-bloc veto over common action. The result was an emphasis on regional-based organizations of an eastern or western type (e.g., COMECON, ASEAN, NATO, and, later, the EEC) to promote areas of common action in areas where such common action was a realistic possibility.

These three factors combined to give a fresh impetus of pragmatism to what had previously been primarily idealistic calls for European unity. But if the basic consensus for some sort of west European organization was consequently wide-ranging, there remained considerable disagreement over what sort of unity it might embody. Broadly speaking, there were two groupings which surfaced in this disagreement, and the distinction between them was to color and shape the development of European integration thereafter. The objective of the first grouping (the "federalists") was a United States of Europe modelled ultimately on the United States itself. Supranational (or "federal") institutions were to be set up in a new constitutional settlement, to which would be transferred powers from the various nation-states on an irreversible basis. The supranational interest – as opposed to national interests – would provide the working basis for the system, and a gradual transfer of allegiance and loyalty would occur amongst the citizenry of Europe. The second grouping (the "intergovernmentalists") viewed European unity in a much less radical manner. Common institutions should be set up but only in order to facilitate greater levels of coordination and cooperation amongst different nations. Those nations were to remain independent and autonomous, with the national interest providing the guiding principle on which the new intergovernmental institutions would operate. This meant that any changes would not be irreversible, but could be modified according to the (changing) needs of national interests.

The federalist view of Europe's development was most enthusiastically espoused by a hard core of countries which were amongst those which had either suffered most in human and economic terms from the Second World War (France, Belgium, Italy and Luxembourg), or had seen nationalism carried to its most extreme conclusion (Germany, Italy). These countries likened Europe's two twentieth century wars to the American Civil War which had ended in Union. Also within this hard core were three smaller states (Belgium, Luxembourg and the Netherlands) which had traditionally close economic ties, and saw distinct economic and political advantages from transcending their own, relatively weak, nation-states. Moreover, in the case of all six of these countries, the institutional structures of the nation-state were relatively recently established and loyalty to those structures was consequently a nascent one.

As victor and chief ally of the United States, the role of the United Kingdom was fundamental to the institutional development of Europe. Winston Churchill had first written about the concept of a "United States of Europe" in 1930 and, during the war had appealed for the post-war creation of a Council of Europe. He returned to this theme in his famous 1946 Zurich speech. Churchill's vision, however, was primarily intergovernmental. It was also ambiguous about the UK's role in it; in the Zurich speech he described the UK as a "friend and sponsor of the new Europe." Churchill's speech led, by way of the Hague Congress of Europe, to the signing, in 1948, of the Brussels Treaty which provided for the establishment of machinery for "economic, social and cultural collaboration" between the United Kingdom, France and the Benelux states. But while France and Belgium championed a supranational approach, the

UK insisted on an intergovernmental approach. The result was a compromise. The Council of Europe, established on 5 May 1949 with ten member states (Denmark, Ireland, Italy, Norway and Sweden joined with the original Brussels Treaty five), consisted of both a consultative parliamentary assembly and an intergovernmental ministerial committee. Yet, although the Parliamentary Assembly and the Human Rights mechanisms commanded considerable moral authority it was the Committee of Ministers which, through unanimous decision-making, exercised the Council's weak powers.[2] Similar UK resistance to the establishment of some sort of customs union resulted in the creation of a purely intergovernmental institution, the Organisation for European Economic Cooperation (OEEC, later to become the OECD) in April 1948. In short, due in no small part to the influence wielded by the UK, the organizations founded in the 1940s represented the triumph of intergovernmentalism over the more idealistic federalism, something which appeared to be consolidated by the failure to establish a European Defence Community in 1952.

The victory of intergovernmentalism, however, did not close the debate. Federalism had proved to be unacceptable to some countries essentially because it proposed a political blueprint, an end-product, from which economic, social and cultural integration (and hence the erosion of the nation-state) would begin. Some federalists saw, therefore, that their aims might best be served by reversing the whole process. This meant starting with the economy, from which *political* integration would subsequently occur. Common European policies could be started in certain economic and social sectors (not the whole economy) and, as national economies became increasingly interdependent, political institutions to manage policy at this new level of aggregation would become necessary. The theory behind this compromise between intergovernmentalism and federalism came to be known as "functionalism" or "neo-functionalism."[3] The emergence of genuine political union would flow naturally from the integration of the different economies of western Europe. The first move in this more pragmatic direction was the setting up, in 1952, of the European Coal and Steel Community (ECSC). The ECSC was the brainchild of a French technocrat, Jean Monnet, and two politicians, Robert Schuman (the French Prime Minister) and Konrad Adenauer (the West German Chancellor). The common concern these men shared was how to tie the French and German economies together in such a way as to make another war unimaginable. The UK was invited to participate, but declined, thus leaving the hardcore federalists to establish their preferred organization. The consequence was that purely supranational institutions were set up which had authority over all matters concerning European steel and coal production in the six member states. They could make decisions with which a particular member might disagree but that member could do little to change them. The ECSC's High Authority enjoyed unrivalled executive powers. The momentum created by the success of the ECSC led to negotiations amongst the same six members which resulted in the creation of the European Atomic Energy Authority (Euratom), and the European Economic Community (EEC) or Common Market in 1957.[4] The objective of the EEC, as stated in the Treaty of Rome, was "to establish the foundation of an ever-closer union among the people of Europe". This was to be through "progressively approximating the economic policies of Member States to promote throughout the Community a harmonious development of economic activities." The EEC, then, was primarily an *economic* community, but which nonetheless retained implicitly the – undefined – goal of political union.

In one sense, the creation of the EEC was a vindication of functionalist theories and an encouragement for the federalists, but its institutional configuration also reflected the familiar tension existing between the federalists and intergovernmentalists. Where the ECSC High Authority specifically enjoyed sole executive power, the EEC Treaty introduced a new, essentially intergovernmental institution, the Council of Ministers. The result was a curious mix of the two principles of federalism and intergovernmentalism.[5]

The Institutional Framework of the European Community

The Treaty of Rome established four major institutions which provided the basic institutional framework of the Community.[6]

The Commission

The European Commission is the supranational element of the Community. Its membership consists of civil servants (over 16,000 of the total EC administrative staff of 23,500 are located in the Commission) headed by a College of Commissioners (17), appointed by the national governments for a four year period (soon to be extended to five). Each Commissioner is responsible for particular policy areas (the Commission is divided into 23 Directorates General in a similar fashion to the division of responsibilities between ministries in national governments). The most important position is that of the President of the Commission who is its principal representative and whose task it is to provide direction and coordination to its work. Although appointed by national governments, the Commissioners are not supposed to act as national nominees. On appointment they give a "solemn undertaking" that they will serve the interests of the Community and will "neither seek nor take instructions from any government or any other body." The Commission has several tasks. Firstly, it proposes and initiates legislation which is subsequently acted on by the Council of Ministers (which, with a few exceptions, cannot initiate and draft legislation by itself). The Commission, then, was designed to be the motor of integration. Secondly, it is responsible for the management, supervision and implementation of Community policies. Thirdly, it is the Community's external representative and negotiator, acting as a key point of contact for international organizations, non-member states and also determining and conducting the Community's external trade relations. Finally, the Commission is responsible for ensuring that the Treaties and Community legislation are respected by member states. The Commission is expected to perform these tasks without consideration for sectional and national interests – to be, in short, the conscience of the Community.

The Council of Ministers

The Council of Ministers is the intergovernmental element of the Community. It does not have a permanent membership but consists of the ministers from the different member-states for the specific policy area under consideration. The General Council, consisting of the Foreign Ministers, has the widest responsibilities. More sectoral matters are dealt with in the "Technical Councils" which are made up of the Ministers of Agriculture, the Environment etc. The national governments decide by whom they wish to be represented so that the level of seniority present from the different member states is not always uniform. A large amount of the work inside the Council is undertaken not be ministers but by the Committee of Permanent Representatives (COREPER). This comprises civil servants of ambassadorial rank who examine Commission proposals and liaise between national officials, the Commission and other COREPER officials. The Presidency of the Council of Ministers rotates between the states on a six monthly basis. It is the task of the Presidency to organize meetings, launch initiatives, ensure policy continuity and represent the Council in dealing with outside bodies. The primary function of the Council of Ministers is to make policy on the basis of the proposals of the European Commission and in consultation with the European Parliament and the Economic and Social Committee (an advisory body comprising representatives of employers, workers and other professional and consumer bodies). Since the Council ultimately decides policy it is, in effect, the Community's legislature, but its legislative capacity is restricted by the fact that, by the Treaties, it cannot initiate legislation. Decision-making in the Council can be through three possible methods according to the subjects under consideration: a unanimous vote, an absolute majority or a qualified majority (whereby each state has a number of votes according to its size and a two-thirds or three-quarters majority is required). Under the Treaties, majority voting was to be extended automatically in 1966 to specified areas, although unanimity would still be required for decisions regarded as fundamental to the future development of the Community. Such an extension was regarded as essential if genuine integration were to occur.

The European Parliament

From the outline of the first two institutions it is apparent that the Parliament's role, as envisaged in the Treaties, was not that of a normal legislature. It is the representative element of the Community, but even this was limited by the fact that MEPs were – until 1979 – nominated from the membership of the national parliaments. It is now directly elected, but on the basis of different national electoral arrangements. The various national parties have formed a number of different political groups through which partisan political activity is mainly channelled (e.g., Socialist Group, Group of European People's Party, Liberal Democrat and Reformist Group, European Democratic Group, Group of the Greens). Much of the Parliament's work is carried out by committees as in national parliaments. The Parliament has a primarily consultative role in the legislative process. It reviews the Commission's proposals and its opinion (which it gives in the form of an amended version of the proposals) is then forwarded to the Council. This opinion is non-binding but (since a ruling in 1980) the Council cannot act until the Parliament's opinion has been expressed. The Parliament also has the task of controlling and supervising the activities of the Commission, and ultimately has the power of censure of the Commission through dismissal of the body on a two-thirds majority (a power which has never been used). The Parliament's legislative and budgetary powers were increased in the 1970s and 1980s, and these increased its effectiveness, but the Parliament's status remains predominantly consultative.

The Court of Justice

Finally, the European Court of Justice (which should not be confused with the European Court of Human Rights) is the judicial element of the

Community. It comprises thirteen judges, each of whom is appointed for a six year term of office which may be renewed. By the Treaties judges are to be appointed "by common accord of the Governments of the Member States." In practice, each Member State is permitted one nomination that is automatically accepted leaving only the thirteenth judge to be appointed by mutual accord. Six advocates-general assist the Court in the carrying out of its duties. The Court's main tasks are to interpret and enforce the application of Community law (ensuring the application is consistent and uniform), to rule on the compatibility of national laws with those of the Community and to make judgements on the activities of the other European institutions, annulling their decisions if deemed to be incompatible with the Treaties. The Court cannot itself initiate actions, but must wait for cases to be referred to it.

What is apparent from this brief outline of the Treaty of Rome's institutional framework is that it represents a compromise between two competing conceptions of European unity. The institutional framework was distinctive from national political systems in the sense that it contained elements of both federalism and intergovernmentalism. This meant that, notwithstanding functionalist theory, the EC could develop in either direction. Consequently, the institutions of the EC became a battleground between the competing conceptions, and the EC became fundamentally shaped by the nature of the tensions existing between them. From this perspective the development of the EC can be seen in two broad phases.

1958 – Early 1980s: Intergovernmentalism Prevails

Article Three of the Treaty of Rome laid down the objective of the establishment of a common market within twelve years, which involved removing all internal trade barriers, establishing a common external tariff and the abolition of all obstacles to the free movement of goods, services and enterprise. Article Three also included provision for the development of common policies in various areas from agriculture to transport. In the first twenty five years, these objectives were not comprehensively met, but considerable progress towards achieving them was made. Internal tariffs were removed and a common external tariff adopted. A Common European Monetary system was established with an Exchange Rate Mechanism and a European Currency Unit (Ecu) to limit fluctuations in the exchange rates of national currencies. Common policies were developed in a wide range of sectors; and the structural funds, the European Regional Development Fund (ERDF), the European Social Fund (ESF) and the European Investment Bank (EIB) were put into operation. Yet, there remained much to do for the creation of a single market and economic union. Moreover, the achievements that had been made in the economic sphere were not matched by concomitant developments in the political sphere. Indeed, while it is true that the European Parliament was given new budgetary powers in 1975 and became directly elected in 1979, real progress in the political sphere was hampered by three important developments.

The first was in fact a lack of development: the failure to move towards a definitive system of qualified majority voting, although such a transition had been envisaged in the Treaties. In 1965 the European Commission put forward a series of proposals to the Council of Ministers which linked increases in farm prices to an increase in the independent budget of the Commission and an increase in the budgetary powers of the European Parliament. With one year remaining before majority voting was due to be introduced, the package would have amounted to a strengthening of the supranational and representative elements of the Community at the cost of the intergovernmental element. The French government objected to these proposals and refused to attend meetings of the Council of Ministers for seven months (the so-called "empty chair" strategy), and de Gaulle embarked on a crusade against the ambitions of the "technocratic" Commission. The crisis was resolved by the Luxembourg compromise which, in the ambiguity of its wording, effectively allowed any member-state to veto policies in the name of its national interest.[7] Majority voting, then, the key to supranationalism, was put in abeyance, and there was a shift in power away from the supranational Commission towards the inter-governmental Council.

The second development was the expansion of the EC in 1972 through the accession of the UK, Ireland and Denmark. While, from one perspective, this was a major achievement, at the same time it reinforced the intergovernmental trend of the Community, because this was primarily the vision of European unity of these countries. Indeed, the debate over the expansion of the EC would later reinforce the arguments of intergovernmentalism by tying the concept to expansionism. A terminologically new division was to arise between those who favoured élargissement ("widening") and those who favoured approfondissement ("deepening"). The "wideners" argued that it was not possible to expand the Community at the same time as "deepening" it (in the sense of taking it further down the road to economic and political union). In their view, therefore, a choice between the two had to be made.

The third development was the creation, in 1974, of a new institution, the European Council, at the suggestion of the French President Giscard d'Estaing.[8] Membership of the Council consists of the heads of governments of the member-states and the President of the Commission, assisted by the Ministers for Foreign Affairs and a member of the

Commission. It met three times a year (recently reduced to two), either in Brussels or in the country hosting the Presidency for that period. Because of its lack – until the 1980s – of any legal or constitutional standing (it was established by a rather vague communique issued by the Heads of Government), the Council has had a wide degree of autonomy in deciding what it should and should not do. The original idea was that it should discuss and plan the long-term development of the Community, but it has also, at times, involved itself in detailed policy issues. Nugent (1991: 205) identifies three major functions which the Council has come to perform: first, as a forum, at the highest political level, for deciding on medium and long-term goals; second, as a policy initiator and dispenser of policy guidelines; third, as a decision-maker on a wide range of issues including matters where it acts as a form of court of appeal for problems unresolved by the Council of Ministers. The significant point to note here is that in the 1970s this institution – which embodies intergovernmentalism *par excellence* – effectively absorbed much of the political power of the Commission and Council over the direction the Community should take, and gave a privileged position to national interests in the institutional framework, thereby strengthening the representation of those interests. This was accompanied by other institutional developments – such as a shift in policy initiation from the Commission to the Council and the failure of the Parliament to show much effectiveness – which confirmed the general trend of the Community towards intergovernmentalism.

In short, the period from the founding of the Community until the early 1980s revealed the weaknesses of the assumptions of functionalist theory. Insufficient developments were made on the economic front, and what progress had been made appeared to have little effect on the political front. There appeared to be a growing distinction between technical and economic matters which were dealt with by the supranational organs and political matters which were dealt with primarily by the intergovernmental organs. The integration process, in short, seemed to have petered out. It was revived, however, in the early 1980s by a federalist offensive on both the economic and political fronts.

1980s – Early 1990s: Towards Economic and Political Union

In the 1980s the federalists showed that it was possible to achieve both *élargissement* and *approfondissement*. This most recent period has seen the accession of Greece (1981), Spain and Portugal (1986) at the same time as marking major moves towards the creation of an internal market and economic and political union. The federalists used the European Parliament to promote the "deepening" initiative through drafting a treaty calling for a federal European union, and then placing pressure on the European Council to act on it. In 1984, the European Council set up a committee to consider the proposal which called for an intergovernmental conference to be set up to draft a new treaty of European union. Britain, Denmark and Greece objected to this, but this did not stop the conference being held in 1985, the nine other member states hinting that they might go ahead and create a "two-tier" Europe as had effectively happened in 1957. The conference passed the Single European Act (SEA) which was eventually ratified in 1987, after approval in each of the member states.[9] This was one of the most significant acts in the history of the EC and marked a shift in the federalist-intergovernmentalist struggle to the advantage of the former. Amending the founding treaties, the SEA calls for action along a number of closely interrelated dimensions to make further progress towards economic and political union. These have come to be identified as the "1992 program."[10]

The Economic Dimension

The SEA calls for the establishment of an internal market without frontiers which provides the free movement of goods, persons, services and capital by 31 December 1992. This will involve the removal of three types of obstacles identified by the Commission. First, no tariffs will be allowed to be raised on goods passing across borders. Second, member-states will not be allowed to block the import of goods on the grounds of "national technical standards." For most goods there will be a common European minimum standard (which has involved the identification of 342 areas to be standardized by the end of 1992) or the principle of the mutual recognition of national standards will apply. Third, so-called physical barriers will be removed. These include frontiers and frontier checks, restrictions on financial services and capital movements, restrictions on foreign business and the operation of public procurement, and mutually recognized job qualifications. Those member-states found to be obstructing the introduction of common standards can be taken to the European Court.[11]

The Political Dimension

The program involves a major advance toward political union through political and institutional changes. First, qualified majority voting has been adopted in most of the cases where unanimity was previously required, and is also applicable for most 1992 issues. The intergovernmentalist tendency, however, managed to obtain the upholding of the unanimity principle in relation to fiscal policy and the vexed areas of the free movement of people and immigration. Second, there is an increase in the powers of the European Parliament in legislative matters, the formulation of the budget and in relation to external policy. Third, there is an enlargement of the Community's competences to cover new areas such as technology, the environment, research and development, and currency matters.

The Social Dimension

Obviously, some elements of the internal market – and particularly the proposal relating to the free movement of labour – have a social dimension to them. Other articles of the SEA, however, refer specifically to social matters. Article 118 calls for harmonization, at the highest level, of work, health and safety regulations, and gives the Commission the responsibility for "social dialogue" between workers and employers. This has involved the drafting of a European "Social Charter" dealing with issues relating to labour, women, immigrants, and the unemployed.

The Regional Dimension

Article 130 of the SEA refers to the idea of "harmonious development." This involves not only removing barriers to free competition but commits member states to reducing the disparities between regions through the use of structural funds. The EC is no longer to be seen as twelve nation-states competing for structural funds but as one unit with a multitude of regions at different levels of development which must be harmonized.

The External Dimension

The SEA declares that an essential means by which Europe can develop its own identity in relation to the outside world is through closer cooperation on matters of security (with the implication that defence might follow), while not conflicting with the competence of NATO. There are also moves to protect and develop a European culture which is distinct from other cultures of the world, including the American one.

The passage of the SEA gave a major boost to the integration process on all fronts, particularly because a major part of the Act (the economic dimension) was given a strict deadline to meet. Indeed, the moves toward the creation of the IM gave a fresh impetus (as many had hoped) towards Economic and Monetary Union (to which the SEA had referred as an aspiration). In April 1989 a report signed by the President of the European Commission, Jacques Delors, and the Governors of the central banks of the twelve member states called for a three stage move to full economic and monetary union. This report itself was later overtaken by decisions made at the Maastricht Summit held in December 1991 which is a further milestone in the Community's history.[12]

The Treaty signed at the Maastricht summit effectively replaces key objectives in the Treaty of Rome and has finally given the prospect of economic union the air of irreversibility and made political union a distinct possibility. Indeed, the Treaty establishes a "European Union" which "shall be founded on the European Communities, supplemented by the policies and cooperation established by this Treaty." The Treaty "marks a new stage in the process of creating an ever closer Union among the peoples of Europe, where decisions are taken as closely as possible to the citizens" (*Financial Times* 1991b).[13] Common EC citizenship is established which confers the right to vote in local and Euro-elections. Several major decisions agreed at Maastricht map out the EC's course until the end of the century.[14] Firstly, a definite commitment has been made to an economic and monetary union with a single currency by 1999 by those countries that reach the qualification threshold, with Britain being granted the right to opt out. The qualification threshold consists of a number of economic criteria which are necessary for the economies to converge successfully. The "critical mass" of countries needed to form a currency union has been set at a majority of the member states of the Community. A new "Cohesion Fund" has been established to help the poorer EC countries (Greece, Ireland, Portugal, and Spain) catch up, which will supplement the existing funds aimed at reducing the disparities between the various regions of the EC.

Secondly, there will be an extension of Community competence, particularly in two areas. The first regards a common foreign and security policy (with implementing moves taken by majority vote) "which might in time lead to a common defence" but in collaboration with NATO. Responsibility for the European Union's decisions and actions that have defence implications are to be delegated to the Western European Union (WEU), whose membership is to be expanded to include Greece, and the WEU's future will be reviewed in 1998. The second area regards a more extensive social program, although without the participation of the UK. Indeed, because of the UK's refusal to sign up to the social element of the Treaty, the eleven others, in deciding to go ahead, have effectively opted-out and created a separate European Social Community which nonetheless uses EC machinery to carry out its decisions. Action will be taken, by qualified majority, to "support and complement" governments' activities in the following fields: workers' health and safety and working conditions generally; the consultation of workers' equality between men and women with regard to labor market opportunities and treatment at work; the integration of persons excluded from the labor market. Unanimity among the eleven will be required for action in the following fields: social security and social protection; protection of workers where their employment contract is terminated; representation and collective defence of the interests of workers and employers; conditions of employment for third-country nationals legally present in Community territory; and financial contributions for employment promotion.

Thirdly there are several institutional developments. The European Parliament will have new powers to amend and veto certain Council acts, to scrutinize Community finances and to set up committees of inquiry to investigate alleged contraventions or maladministration in implementation of Community law. The European Commission's term of office is extended (from 1 January 1995) from four to five years, its President is to be appointed by governments "after consulting the European Parliament" and once appointed the entire Commission will be subject to a vote of confidence from the Parliament. Finally, a new Committee of the Regions is established which will comprise representatives of regional and local authorities and which will have an advisory role.

In short, the impetus towards further integration created by the passing of the SEA in the mid-1980s has been sustained. It has become increasingly clear that whether or not the IM is fully operative by 1 January 1993 is no longer a critical issue.[15] The real issue is whether sufficient momentum towards economic harmonization has been generated to prompt further moves towards economic and political union, and the last year, and specifically the Maastricht summit, has suggested that this is, in fact, the case. "1992" retains its popular catch-appeal, but, by the further drives to integration it has created, it has confirmed its nature as a process (or "progressive establishment") rather than a finite event. That a new momentum has been created is finally confirmed by the increased polarization of positions between the "wideners'" and the "deepeners," with the British finding themselves increasingly isolated and forced to react to the "deepening" initiatives of others. The plaudits of European Union and its advantages have become the most vocal, and they are now in the driving seat.[16] Yet, it would be wrong to assume that the road to European Union will be inevitable, trouble-free or without its dangers. The conclusion to this chapter will evaluate the prospects for European Union from the perspective of these obstacles and dangers.

The Paradoxes and Problems of European Unity

This chapter has laid emphasis on the politics of European integration as a means to understanding its history. Two evident paradoxes emerge from this perspective. Firstly, the very issue – European *unity* – on which there has been a broad consensus has also been the cause of *division* amongst West European countries principally because of the question of how far and how fast to go. Secondly, if, as argued earlier, one of the underlying causes of the emergence of the EC was the discrediting of the nation-state, the development of the EC has in itself led to a reassertion of the importance of the nation-state in that the integration process has obliged member states to take up a position, if only a negotiating stance, on every policy area and issue subject to that process.[17] Neither of these paradoxes seems likely to disappear in the near future. Indeed, they can be seen at work at the heart of the SEA and the 1992 program (which, as already noted, is a familiar mixture of the intergovernmental and federal) and of the negotiations at the Maastricht summit. They will, in all likelihood, continue to be at the heart of the process by which the EC hopes to move towards economic and political union, particularly because of the presence of three major problems which must be resolved on the road to that goal.

The first major problem concerns the change in nature of the old Europe since the revolutions in eastern Europe and the future expansion of the Community. Significantly, the events in eastern Europe of 1989 had the effect of temporarily calling into question the 1992 program and polarizing the debate between the "wideners" and the "deepeners." As argued at the beginning of this chapter, the idea of European unity had been a product of the shift in focus of world politics from the containment of Germany to the containment of the Soviet Union. The collapse of the Warsaw Pact and the emergence of the issue of German unification changed the focus back again to the question of German domination in a united Europe. The "wideners" (Britain, Denmark, Greece) began to suggest that political and economic union was now a thing of the past and that the EC should maintain, if not revert to, a loose intergovernmental structure, which would allow the accession of other countries. It would be wrong, they argued, for the EC to remain an exclusive club, turning its back on the newly emerging east European neighbours. The "deepeners," on the other hand, argued that with the end of the Cold War a fully-integrated EC should become the cornerstone of the new European order and that integrating a united Germany into the EC would deter any prospect of future German expansionist ambitions. Special trading privileges should be set up, meanwhile, to help guide the east European countries in their transition from communist rule. It followed that the 1992 program should proceed with ever more speed.

After four to five months the latter view prevailed, but the issue of expansion is far from being resolved. Indeed, the pressure of potential entrants to the EC is becoming irresistible. Turkey, Austria, Cyprus, Malta and Sweden have all applied to join. Applications from Norway, Finland and Switzerland are in the course of preparation. Poland, Czechoslovakia and Hungary are all clamouring for a timetable for membership. Finally, the Baltic States wish to join and Ukraine late in 1991 (during a preliminary visit by an EC Commissioner) announced its intention of applying to join the EC within two years. In short, the old status of the EC as a *western* community is now under threat and in the New Europe that is emerging the national governments of the member states are confused and in disagreement about the priorities which should govern the future development of the EC. As William Wallace has noted, too many of the key actors, including the European Commission, are "stuck fast in the orthodoxies of a west European integration appropriate to the world before 1989" (Wallace 1991; see also Palmer 1992). How the EC responds to the issue of expansion will be critical to the unfolding of the other two problems.

The second problem is that there is a potential contradiction in the pursuit of the goals of the creation of an internal market on the one hand and of regional harmonization on the other, just as economic union will not be possible in the absence of the convergence of national economies. Unless the structural funds and the new cohesion fund are used effectively, there is a danger that an unregulated market will, in the long term, exacerbate the present North-South divide and the now pertinent East-West divide in Europe. An expansion of the EC would not only exacerbate this problem but could bring it to a head.

The third problem is the potential for the "democratic deficit," from which the Community already suffers, becoming acute if institutional and political reforms continue to lag behind the creation of a single market and moves towards economic and monetary union. The SEA and the Treaty drafted at Maastricht involve a gradual loss of sovereignty to Brussels. Jacques Delors, the President of the European Commission, has estimated that within a decade 80 percent of all economic and social decision-making will be made at the EC level. Yet, despite the presence of a directly-elected Parliament, the line of accountability between the European peoples and the supranational level remains indirect. The executive – the European Commission – is not accountable to the legislature, but consists of members appointed by, and accountable to, the national governments. The danger, then, is that unless a democratization (in the sense of increased accountability and control) of European institutions occurs, any shift of powers will be to the benefit of the bureaucrats and technocrats in Brussels. The principle, reaffirmed and for the first time officially defined at

Maastricht, of "subsidiarity" (by which decision-making for each policy area is allocated to the lowest level of government appropriate) is insufficient by itself to act as a safeguard against this danger.[18] As David Marquand has recently written:

> On present form we shall have an economy that cries out for federal management, but no federal political institutions; a European bank but no European government; a loss of accountability on the national level with no compensating gain on the supranational one. Instead of going to the European Parliament, the power which national parliaments are bound to lose will flow to the interlocking technocracies of the Commission, the Committee of Permanent Representatives, and the huge transnational firms which it is part of the 1992 project's purpose to foster (Marquand 1991).

Further expansion of the Community is likely to exacerbate this problem. Achieving institutional reforms has proved difficult enough with twelve members. The introduction of new members before democratization is complete could paralyze moves in that direction, if only because of the problems of agreeing on the details of any major reforms.

Collectively, these problems expose a final paradox in the history of European integration, one that might be termed "the free market versus the superstate": at the same time as the dominance of the nation-state is reduced, the spectre of a new over-regulating and unaccountable super-state surfaces. This point is crucial because, ultimately, the success of the 1992 program and ultimate union will depend upon the acceptance of it by the European peoples, and this will, to a large extent, be determined by the degree to which their expectations of 1992 are met. If their expectations are not met, and if alienation and hostility set in, the prospect of a legitimacy crisis can not be precluded.[19]

It is for this reason that the themes addressed in this book are of critical (and until now understated) importance. The dramatic developments which have taken place in the EC since the mid-1980s have opened up a vast new area for research, and one which requires an interdisciplinary approach and the participation of all disciplines in the social sciences and humanities. In the past, perhaps, too much emphasis has been placed on a "top-down" approach to analyzing and evaluating European integration (and this is particularly noticeable in political science). Monitoring and understanding the cultural changes taking place at the local level in, for example, common perceptions of national identity, behavioral changes regarding work and social life, and the perceived role and function of the EC, are areas which traditionally have received much less attention. Their importance now is such that they can no longer be overlooked. They are areas, moreover, in which sociocultural anthropology can, and should, make its contribution.

Notes

The research and writing of this chapter, as well as its presentation in draft form at the conference on "The Anthropology of EC Integration in 1992" in New York in October 1991, was made possible through the generous financial assistance of the Center for Urban, Labor and Metropolitan Affairs (CULMA), Wayne State University, Detroit; the University of Salford International Conference Fund; the Department of Politics and Contemporary History, University of Salford; and the Council of European Studies. I should also like to thank Martin Westlake for his insightful comments and suggestions on an earlier draft of the chapter. Responsibility for the arguments contained in the text remains mine alone.

1. For more detailed accounts of the formative period see Lipgens 1982; Spinelli 1957; and Robertson 1973: ch.1.

2. The Council of Europe, it should be stressed, is not a European Community institution, as will become apparent in the text that follows.

3. Both ideas were chiefly championed by American theorists. They are, in fact, different ideas, although the results are meant to be similar. The first, associated originally with David Mitrany (1966), is based on the premise that the greater the degree of cooperation amongst nation-states the more the latter begin to lose the capability of independent action. The second, associated with Leon Lindberg (1963) and Ernst Haas (1968), is based on the premise that as integration develops so will political pressure for further integration because the nature of lobbying in pluralist society will shift towards the European level.

4. A merger treaty only later (in 1967) grouped the ECSC, the EEC and Euratom into the European Communities (EC), with one Commission and a Council of Ministers. This explains references in the text to the Treaties.

5. Ironically, this intergovernmental level was introduced by the smaller member states who had earlier seen political advantage in transcending the nation state, and who feared economic and political domination by the larger member states (see Kuesters 1989).

6. There is a considerable body of literature on the institutions of the EC. For useful introductions see Lodge 1983, Nugent 1991, Lintner and Mazey 1991.

7. "Where in the case of decisions which may be taken by majority vote . . . very important interests of one or more partners are at stake, the Members of the Council will endeavour, within a reasonable time, to reach solutions which can be adopted by all the Members of the Council" (quoted in Lintner and Mazey 1991: 19). The empty chair crisis has been commonly viewed as a culmination of the personal rivalry between de Gaulle and the President of the EC Commission, Walter Hallstein, but it was also another example of the clash between federalism and intergovernmentalism.

8. The creation and naming of this institution has created considerable confusion for many between the Council of Europe (which is not a Community institution) the Council of Ministers and the European Council. The habit of shortening the European Council to 'the Council' has tended to enhance the confusion.

9. Space does not permit an analysis of the national debates on ratification of the

SEA. The range and depth of analysis varied from country to country. While in Britain, for example, the government limited parliamentary time to discuss and approve the SEA Ireland had to amend (through a referendum) its constitution in order to be able to absorb the SEA.

10. Interestingly, the Single European Act has become popularly associated with the idea of "1992," but 1992, in fact, refers, formally speaking, to *one* part of the Act, that dealing with the economic dimension. Many politicians, journalists, academics and the public at large use the catchphrase '1992' mistakenly as referring to all the other dimensions (on this and other problems with the concept see Westlake 1991). There is a burgeoning literature on 1992 and the other dimensions of the SEA. See, for example, Cutler et al. 1989; Graham and Teague 1990; Haufbauer 1990; Crouch and Marquand 1990; Wistrich 1991; and Hurwitz and Lequesne 1991. *The Economist* and the *Financial Times* provide extensive coverage of unfolding 1992 issues as well as specialist surveys (see, for example, *Financial Times* 1991a); and the EC itself is a rich source of guides to the issues (e.g., European Communities – Commission 1991).

11. It should be noted that the SEA, while establishing clear steps for the completion of the Internal Market (IM), did not do so for Economic and Monetary Union (EMU). The section of the Act dealing with this consisted largely of aspirations. However, many hoped that moves towards the IM would create an impetus towards EMU and this is, in fact, what happened.

12. There are various reasons why the three stages of the Delors Report were not to become the blueprint for economic and union, one of which was external: the events in eastern Europe which temporarily brought the integration issue into question.

13. Of note is that the phrase "ever closer union" appeared in the first draft of the Treaty as "Union with a federal goal." This was changed to appease the British for whom the words represented too clear a commitment to a form of political union.

14. The following does not aim to be comprehensive but to highlight the key decisions reached. Quotations from the Treaty are taken from the detailed coverage of the Treaty in the *Financial Times* 1991b.

15. The prospects, on paper at least, look good. Of the 342 areas to be standardized, less than 70 remain to be adopted, and about a third of these are already before the Parliament. However, the degree and speed of implementation of these decisions remains uncertain, and some of the most difficult decisions, where unanimity is required, remain to be taken.

16. The advantages of, specifically, the IM have been well-documented. A major two-year study has estimated that implementation of the SEA will save European industry about $250 billion (which is the equivalent of about five per cent of the EC's gross domestic product) through the removal of the costs of operating twelve national markets, at the same time as promoting economic growth, competition, productivity and consumer choice (Cecchini 1988).

17. In some countries, particularly, the UK, the effect has been even stronger in the sense that the nation-state has often been presented by political elites as constituting a means of "protecting" the nation against the potentially adversarial effects of EC decisions. On these paradoxes see, for example, Pryce and Wessels 1989 and Hoffman 1982.

18. The Maastricht Treaty states that in the areas which do not fall within its exclusive jurisdiction, the Community shall take action in accordance with the principle of subsidiarity. Subsidiarity is defined in article 3b where it is stated that "the Community shall take action . . . only if and insofar as the objectives of the proposed action cannot be sufficiently achieved by the Member States and can therefore, by reason of the scale or effects of the proposed action, be better achieved by the Community" (Quoted in *Financial Times* 1991b).

19. For a good summary of the issues involved see Westlake 1989.

References

Cecchini, Paolo. 1988. *The European Challenge 1992: The Benefits of a Single Market*. Aldershot: Gower.

Crouch, Colin, and David Marquand, eds. 1990. *The Politics of 1992: Beyond the Single European Market*. Oxford: Blackwell, Political Quarterly Publishing.

Cutler, Tony, et al. 1989. *1992 - The Struggle for Europe*. Oxford: Berg.

European Communities – Commission. 1991. *The European Community: 1992 and Beyond*. Luxembourg: Office for Official Publications of the European Communities.

Graham, John, and Paul Teague. 1990. *1992 - The Big Market. The Future of the European Community*. London: Lawrence and Wishart.

Financial Times. 1991a. "Survey: 1992: The European Market." 18 December: 1–6.

_____. 1991b. 12 December: 2-7.

Haas, Ernst. 1968. *The Uniting of Europe*. Stanford: Stanford University Press.

Hafbauer, Gary Clyde, ed. 1990. *Europe 1992. An American Perspective*. Washington D.C.: The Brookings Institution.

Hoffman, Stanley. 1982. "Reflections on the Nation-State in Western Europe Today." *Journal of Common Market Studies*. 21 (1/2): 28-38.

Hurwitz, Leon, and Christian Lequesne, eds. 1991. *The State of the European Community: Policies, Institutions and Debates in the Transition Years*. Harlow: Longman.

Kuesters, Hans Jurgen. 1989. "The Treaties of Rome (1955-57)," in Roy Pryce, ed., *The Dynamics of European Union*. London: Routledge.

Lindberg, Leon. 1963. *The Political Dynamics of European Economic Integration*. Stanford: Stanford University Press.

Lintner, Valerio, and Sonia Mazey. 1991. *The European Community: Economic and Political Aspects*. London: McGraw Hill.

Lipgens, Walter. 1982. *A History of European Integration, Volume 1, 1945-47*. Oxford: Oxford University Press.

Lodge, Juliet, ed. 1983. *Institutions and Policies of the European Community*. London: Pinter.

Marquand, David. 1991. "Fudge Manufacturers of Maastricht." *The Guardian* 3 December.

Mitrany, David. 1966. *A Working Peace System*. Chicago: Quadrangle Books.

Nugent, Neill. 1991. *The Government and Politics of the European Community*. London: Macmillan.

Palmer, John. 1992. "The Growing Pains of Union." *The Guardian*, 12 May.

Pryce, Roy, ed. 1989. *The Dynamics of European Union*. London: Routledge.

Pryce, Roy, and Wolfgang Wessels. 1989. "The Search for an Ever Closer Union: a Framework for Analysis," in Roy Pryce, ed., *The Dynamics of European Union*. London: Routledge.

Robertson, A. H. 1973. *European Institutions. Co-operation, Integration, Unification*. London: Stevens and Sons.

Spinelli, Altiero. 1957. "The Growth of the European Movement since World War II," in C. G. Haines, ed., *European Integration*. Bologna: Johns Hopkins Press.

Wallace, William. 1991. "Queuing Up for a Euro-Crisis." *The Guardian*. 9 December.

Westlake, Martin. 1989. *Cultural, Social, Economic and Political Identities after 1992*. Florence: European University Institute.

____. 1991. "1992 and '1992': Potential Paradoxes in the Date and Concept." Unpublished manuscript, author's file.

Wistrich, Ernest. 1991. *After 1992. The United States of Europe*. London: Routledge.

3

The Incidental City: Urban Entities in the EC of the 1990s [1]

M. Estellie Smith

As the European Community (EC) continues to take shape, attention has centered on the national polities, and the trans-national as well as infra-national regions that go to make up the supranational EC. These entities are also the foci for the work of the Commission Directorates of the EC governmental structure. The thesis of this chapter is that urban issues, relative to those of, on the one hand, rural/regional locales and, on the other hand, the national polities, have been relegated to second place.[2] This is surprising since, firstly, other critical sectors have Government Directorates that have an explicit concern with such areas (for example, agriculture [DG VI] and fisheries [DG XIV]), and, secondly, cities are increasingly the focus of pressing problems for the EC as a whole.[3] The puzzle deepens when one realizes that issues grounded in four of the six newly announced Structural Policy Objectives[4] seem especially problematic when viewed in the urban domain.

Paradoxically, one reason for urban neglect appears to be the very profusion of directorates that, in one way or another, *are* concerned with issues germane to cities. Lacking an EC Directorate that concentrates on urban concerns, it is argued here that a significant portion of urban plans and schemes are denied an integrative focus that produces an economy of effort as well as the synergy of a holistic approach (the importance of such a Directorate should not be minimized; for example, there is a possibility that, within a year or so, a new DG for Regions will be established). Further, directorate dispersal of responsibility and accountable personnel mystifies routes through what become (or, at least, appear to "outsiders" to be) ever more complex and frustrating bureaucratic channels. Finally, this diffusion of Directorate involvement lends itself to the evolution of informal systems for getting assistance, leading to inequity in the distribution of such resources as projects supported, information, and influence on future EC directions.[5]

That urban decision-makers (whether in the public or private sector) are expected to initiate action is also the result of the explicit formulation of the principle of subsidiarity which argues that, "a policy should be executed at the lowest level of government and only when that is determined ineffective and inefficient and when other compensation mechanisms fail," are the regulatory and implementation aspects of a policy to be assigned to a higher governmental level – and then only to the next most immediate structural level (Molle 1990:27).[6] Thus, in theory, once policy has been articulated, specific urban issues related to such policy and necessary to address (e.g., urban pollution) are expected to be addressed in a bottom-up rather than top-down fashion – from city to EC, not vice versa.

While this chapter will emphasize the extent to which this "benign neglect" by EC personnel has both allowed and required urban leaders to (1) experiment creatively, (2) be more flexible in searching out opportunities, to "stretch the limits of possibilities," and (3) seek to develop local initiatives as well as attempt to establish extended networks with other urban entities. It cannot be overlooked, however, that the full potential of the time, money, and energy that has been and continues to be invested is lost as, in locale after locale, replicative attempts are made to "reinvent the wheel" – only to discover that it is square.

Let me hasten to say that I am not arguing that cities have been ignored. Funds have been forthcoming to assist locales with urgent problems (e.g., housing for immigrants; slum clearance; improvement of port facilities; assistance in planning industrial parks, convention centers, tourism programs, and setting up job training programs). However, despite the assistance given, problems persist and, I think, for two important reasons. First, such assistance has been provided on a locale-by-locale basis and, too often, falls into the category of a bandaid solution, the superficial "quick fix" that fails to address the underlying regional/national problem that attracted attention initially. Secondly, and more critical, in the majority of cases, *regions* are, indeed, the primary object of concern; urban issues tend to be recognized only as they affect the well-being of larger administrative divisions or areas, or as they might be deemed capable of underwriting regional development plans.

Even before its recent revitalization in the time of the Single European Act, EC policy has long been geared to address urban issues from a macro-level perspective and in the context of what are deemed the more critical regional malaises.[7] The consequences of this policy, though sometimes obscure, have been significant. For example, it can be hypothesized that the Common Agricultural Policy (CAP), often charged as being "merely a ploy" to keep rural farmers politically satisfied, is at least partially the result of an early attempt to address urban rather than rural issues per se. Several decades ago, concerned that the capacity of cities to absorb newcomers was dangerously strained and, at that time – seeing internal rural-to-urban relocation as the major source of such arrivals – the decision was made by a number of countries to provide incentives to rural populations and the small town personnel who serviced them to stay where they were.[8] Though the urban emigrant flow altered in character, the CAP took on a life of its own. Now, cities are facing the additional challenge caused by external migration – from the Caribbean, North Africa, East Europe and elsewhere – but the CAP continues to divert urgently needed funds to the rural rather than urban component of regions and national polities.

Urban Strategies

Though this chapter stresses the development of urban networks – usually in many directions and at all levels simultaneously[9] – rivalry also occurs and can exist between those who, in other contexts, are actual or potential partners. Most cities take the expected route of puffing up their attractive points; but some attempt to develop strength through weakness, e.g., attracting structural funds by concentrating on one component of city life currently in crisis in order to gain funds that in point of fact are, at least in part, intended to underwrite some more locally favored component.

In such competitive contexts, one can also make a virtue of vice, a tactic employed by Milan when it competed with Cambridge and Copenhagen to be selected as the site for the EC Environmental agency (a potentially lucrative drawing card for related industry and business). City leaders emphasized that – in addition to its five universities, 150 research centers, and 300,000 square meter Technocenter – their own experience and struggle with industrial pollution made it the most appropriate of the three locales (*The European* 1990c: 7).[10]

Italian cities, however, seem to prefer a collegial style, favoring the association and league approach. Leaders in Milan, Florence, and Venice, to name just three, have actively moved in this direction. Milan has been an important voice in the Lombard League whose candidates, in the April 1992 national elections, took 30% of the northern Italian vote and ousted most local candidates of the ruling Christian Democrats. Venice has played a central role in, to name just two such organizations, the formation of the Northeast League and the Pentagonal (now, with Poland, the Hexagonal) initiative. The latter seeks links with the non-EC countries of Austria, Hungary, (former) Yugoslavia, Czechoslovakia, and Poland.[11] Italy's Foreign Minister, Gianni de Michelis (a fervent Venetian and President of the Northeast League) sees organizations like the Hexagonal initiative and the Northeast Association as strategies by which, in a revived Middle and Eastern European economy, Venice will be the primate city of a community within the Community[12] – and offset the domination of this region by an eastward-looking united Germany (*The European* 1990b:7).

The Hexagonal initiative has already established various working committees to research specific projects linking the six countries, e.g., coordinating new and improved transportation and high tech telecommunication networks; cooperating on problems of toxic waste; establishing eco-parks and nature reserves; exploring renewable energy resources (a concern of Austria's especially since it has no nuclear power plants); and jointly sponsoring an annual trade fair specifically geared to attract small and medium sized firms.

Another strategy is not so much to compete with as to work independently of national sister cities. Barcelona's city leaders have been most inventive in establishing ties with EC urban centers located outside of Spain – but, as well, in placing a heavy development emphasis on attracting international investment. Currently, the Japanese contribute about one-third of foreign investment in Spain and most of that is centered in Barcelona (e.g., Nissan is putting a plant there). As a result of this and other activities, Barcelona has obtained three billion dollars to modernize its infrastructure (e.g., waterfront and dock development, the upgrading of roads and its telecommunication system).

Cities in the former East German *Länder* have also adopted a variety of strategies. For example, although there is a traditional rivalry among the three Saxony cities of Leipzig, Dresden and Chemnitz,[13] they are cooperating to form a regional triangle in which differences provide complementary strengths. In an area already the main eastern focus for national investment, the three cities are aiming to recapture their pre-war eminence by expanding airports and upgrading an already extensive system of autobahn and rail links. Dresden is focusing on updating its service sector; Leipzig stresses its 800 year old trade fair tradition and is building a DM 1 billion trade center to re-establish its role as a marketing center; and Chemnitz is concentrating on updating industrial production facilities (*The Economist* 1991b: 53).

At the other end of the spectrum, the *Länd* of Mecklenburg-West Pomerania has traditionally been one of the most industrially under-developed areas of Germany. Today, it has the highest unemployment levels in the country[14] and, with the collapse of trade with its main customer, the USSR, the expectation is that the worst is yet to come. It is estimated that, in 1992, 90% of the jobs in agriculture (which employs 20% of the population) will disappear (*The Economist* 1991c: 63), adding not only to regional problems but – if these displaced rural workers move to the cities as is expected – further exacerbating urban difficulties. The very lack of industrialization is being emphasized by the state's Premier, Alfred Gomolka, who is urging development of "gentle" tourism – "eco-parks" and luxury resorts for "the discerning traveller." However, urban leaders, sceptical of the extent that such strategies will bring significant benefit to their locales, are, instead, seeking to rebuild trade connections with northern European cities (e.g., Bremen, Hamburg, Lübeck, Rotterdam, and Bergen) using the language of the historic linkages that existed among the free-trading cities of the Hanseatic League. Though some might dismiss this as anachronistic and impossibly romantic,[15] one German businessman cautioned me, "You must not underestimate the extent to which we Europeans have long memories – and, besides, we like our dealings to have a sense of dignity and long-term commitment." Further, the practical-minded *The Economist* (1991c: 63-4) has noted that:

> The prestige-bearing *Hansestadt* prefix (carried by Bremen, Hamburg and Lübeck in the west, and now by Rostock, Wismar and Stralsund in the east) is more than mere symbolism. Money and advice [are already flowing] from one *Hansestadt* to another.

Mecklenburg has been a significant recipient of federal aid and the effects are visible in, e.g., a public-sector building boom. The private sector has also been successful and (according to *The Economist)* a former Bremen banker now active in Mecklenburg has been surprised at the amount being invested – though it is clear that part of the attraction of certain locales are such magnets as the financing of joint ventures through German and EC structural funds.

The Eurocities Movement[16]

The Eurocities Association is both typical of the thrust toward urban networking and atypical because its organization and processual strength shows a steady progression. Initiated in 1985 by Dr. Bram Peper, at that time Mayor of Rotterdam,[17] Eurocities began as an informal association of the political representatives of six core cities (Rotterdam, Barcelona, Birmingham, Milan, Lyon, Frankfurt) to facilitate the flow of information and to work cooperatively on common problems. The organization now makes regular assessments of its members, assigns and coordinates research projects that bring political, economic and university centers together, and includes both EC and non-EC associate members.

As one of the world's largest ports, an international gateway to Europe, and with its status as a free port[18] Rotterdam was particularly sensitive to the new dynamics of European trade. This and broader considerations, led Dr. Peper to move to establish an urban network to facilitate the flow of information and more concrete forms of cooperation.[19] The 1991 Eurocities meeting (Birmingham), played host to some two hundred representatives from thirty-eight cities, within and beyond the Community[20] (and representing a total of more than twenty-eight million urban residents). Agenda topics covered such diverse issues as urban traffic patterns, environmental issues (especially urban air pollution), the quality of urban life (e.g., the need for optimum levels of green space such as parks and play areas for children) and ways to address common urban dilemmas within an EC framework. Special working groups have been created, with specific cities accepting responsibility for overseeing research on one or another opportunity windows or problem areas, e.g., communications, social welfare, culture, transport, environmental control. It was also decided to establish a Brussels secretariat to serve as a permanent center for coordinating the annual meeting and, more to the point, to be the Association's voice for addressing the EC, and actively promoting an integrated and aggressive urban component within the EC structure. Noting that the work of the association has already been rewarded by EC funding for a series of pilot projects (e.g., the choice of Birmingham as a site for testing innovative forms of computerized traffic control systems), Dr. Peper emphasized that: "There is need for formal and informal contacts if we are to promote a Europe of cities. If cities don't work, the EC won't work" (MacLeod 1991: 25).

One observer at the 1991 Conference commented that the Eurocities Association shows that:

Europe's larger cities have reason to think that they deserve a better deal from Brussels. EC economic and social policy is tilted deliberately toward helping farming communities, which means that 70 percent of European funds benefit only 8 percent of the people (MacLeod 1991:25).

Urban leaders find the association's potential for coordination and cooperation offers an important fulcrum for moving the EC away from this rural/regional emphasis and towards addressing what are seen as ubiquitous and intensifying urban problems. For example, the mayor of Lyon, Michel Noir, discussed the joint problems of budgetary allocations and urban pollution, noting, for example, that one-fourth of his city's budget was being spent to improve the environment and when he finished

> he was immediately approached by Grzegorz Palka, mayor of Lodz [Poland], which like many cities of the former Communist bloc has a severe pollution problem. Mr. Palka pointed out that his city was "too poor to solve problems created by heavy industry." He urged that the Eurocities movement focus on providing money and scientific expertise to help clean up cities like his. . . . Under another plan, 14 West European cities will get together to offer advice to Moscow's city council on how to organize city management along more democratic lines. The English city of Bradford has offered to help Pilsen, Czechoslovakia, with advice on manufacturing buses in a market economy (MacLeod 1991:25).

As the Lord Mayor of Birmingham (William Turner) put it to me (4 November 1991):

> You know, we've all been knocking at the same door at the different times; it would be better if we all knocked at the same time. Our [European] MPs are proving very helpful [and] . . . very effective. For example, thanks to their work, the city of Birmingham obtained the largest single grant ever given an individual city – £42,000,000 to build a convention center. We couldn't have received it without them and want to see the Parliament play a bigger role in the EC.

Then, perhaps summing up the sense of the meeting and those attending, he concluded:

> Cities are doing a better and better job of pulling themselves up by their bootstraps. Not the big capitals, so much . . . but the large provincial cities.[21] We're places with people who have ideas – and good ones – about where we want to go.

Conclusions

Part of the problem addressed here stems from the fact that the EC is still reflexively tied to the states from which it has emerged. And each state deals with cities in substantively different ways. For example: in France, the government deals with cities as subsidiaries of regions – with both of the latter treated as ancillary components of a centrist, *dirigiste* State.[22] Italy's government has abrogated its responsibilities to the cities, at once leaving the urbs to make do with local improvisation but, paradoxically, putting the national government in bondage to the elite (and not so elite!) of the cities. The UK (most particularly under Margaret Thatcher) has had a confrontational relation with local government, addressing urban problems through special, national agencies (e.g., the London Docklands Development Corporation).[23] And the German approach has been to rely on cites to work out their problems within the *Länder* structure, thereby allowing powerful, cartel-like industrial and financial interests to play an important role in managing all three layers of government.[24] Overall, then, different national attitudes towards urban issues are reflected in the absence of an EC position on the place and future of urban entities in the Community. This lack of consensus among the national polities is further reflected in the shape of decisions as to which (and how) a directorate will handle an urban-related issue.[25]

EC member states hold in common, however, the tendency to handle urban problems by disguising, for a variety of reasons, the extent to which their populations have urbanized, e.g., building new towns (really accretions to or extensions of major metropolitan centers on whose fringes they exist). These obscure the extent to which the urban implosion – now drawing more on external than internal migration – is fuelling both the growth and the problems of the megalopolitan centers.[26]

Not the least of the reasons why policies and programs designed and/underwritten by national governments to address urban problems are proving inadequate is that national budgets are inadequate for the magnitude of the problem.[27] So, increasingly, citizens are looking to the EC for solutions. There is hope on the horizon; the EC has just completed a comprehensive five year projection of Europe 2000 and directorate personnel are studying it. *If* they have addressed urban issues by asking new questions in new ways, and *if* all concerned are prepared to weave together the macro- and the micro-level approach, they may begin to find appropriate solutions.

And it is here that anthropologically-grounded research can make the greatest contribution to EC research. On the one hand, anthropologists can offer the fine-grained picture (cf., "thick description") that illustrates the extent to which cities are impressively unique, capable of imprinting their hinterlands with their own specific characteristics while simultaneously subject to the opportunities and constraints defined by these same hinterlands. On the other hand, we also emphasize the linkages – the networks and the systemic characteristics of the networks – in which such linkages are embedded, tying the microlevel foci into a broader, macrolevel sociocultural context which local scenes both reflect and resist. In the process of limning out cross-cultural comparisons and contrasts we are able to expose robust commonalities among cities as well as between cities and regions or states, and, finally, cities within a world-system.

State leaders, having created a super-state, must now deal with dynamics that threaten to make them redundant before their "new European house" is ready for occupancy. Indeed, perhaps the "devolutionary" processes currently at work in a significant number of Europe's nation-states are, at least in part, grounded in the growing perception that the millennium will arrive (literally and figuratively) and "Europeans" will find themselves living in Cockaigne – with the cornucopia of plenty gushing forth from Brussels (or Strasbourg, or Luxembourg, wherever!).[28] It would be wise to note that, when we look at what happens as national polities are transformed/dissolved – from the earliest states to the most recent – that it has been the city that has served as locus and focus for the expansion of one or another "new world order." This is where the state, even the super-state, begins – and, in the past, has begun to end. To relegate the city to second place, to treat it as incidental and fail to address in timely fashion its weaknesses and its strengths would be a fatal flaw in the planning for the millennium to come.

Notes

1. This paper was originally presented in the session organized and chaired by T. M. Wilson, "The anthropology of European Community integration in 1992," annual meeting of the American Anthropological Association, Chicago, 1991.

2. It is not only within the EC or the states which comprise it that this is so. EC scholars seem to hold cities in equal disdain (though it must be noted that those who study European cities have not been much more concerned with studying them within the context of the EC – Paul Cheshire's work (1990) being an uncommon and noteworthy exception). As a case in point: At neither of the

two biennial conferences of the European Community Studies Association (sponsored by the Center for European Community Studies, George Mason University, Fairfax, Virginia – see bibliography) have cities or the city appeared (the first conference had 80 papers on the agenda; the second had 112).

3. I will not get into the tired question of "What is a city – as opposed to a town and as distinct from a metropolis?" I will point out, however, that size does not seem to me to be the critical criterion. For example, Lugano is, I think, a genuine city, despite that it has a population of only c. 30,000 – hardly a decent sized "small town." However, with its 50 banks and 75 finance companies, this city serves as the European financial center for a network of continental and international connections (Burtenshaw et al. 1991: 7).

4. There are actually only five in number: 1. Promoting the development and structural adjustment of regions whose development is lagging behind; 2. Conversion of declining industrial regions; 3. Combating long-term unemployment; 4. Integration of young people into working life; 5a. Adjustment of production, processing and marketing structure in agriculture and forestry; 5b Development of rural areas (European Communities – Commission 1991:14).

5. It is also making Brussels the center of intense lobbying activities – and, if the EC Parliament gains a stronger voice in governing affairs, they too will be subjected to the usual forms of wheedling, pressuring and assorted arts of "persuasion."

6. The ambiguities and potential minefields in this vague statement of principle are too numerous and obvious to explore here. As *The Economist* noted, however (1989a:42), the term "subsidiarity" is familiar to Vatican-watchers. Since its adoption at the Second Vatican Council in 1962-65, the idea has been controversial. Conservative Roman Catholics think the principle is fine so long as it is not seen as a way to take power from the center; on the contrary, they reckon subsidiarity should enhance the Vatican's power since it will be free to concentrate on broad issues while more "trivial" matters are handled at a lower level. The same holds, I suggest, for most EC personnel.

7. For examples of some of the work done on cities during the period 1950-1985 see: Giner and Archer (1978); Harloe and Lebas (1981); Stave (1981); Burtenshaw et al. (1981). For a representative overview of European urban issues (emphasizing the French perspective) in the immediate post-World War II era, see Friedmann (1952). For more recent research, see, e.g., Dogan and Kasarda (1988) and Lane (1989) *passim*. For a more popular but highly readable and sensitive view of five European cities in the late 1970s, see Ardagh (1979).

8. The specter of the third-world urbanization and the consequences of rural depopulation was and still is perceived by not a few European leaders as a very real scenario within their own countries, resulting in a lack of national self sufficiency and overburdened city structures.

9. Indeed, in observing aggregate behavior of those in some cities, "strategy" seems too systemic a word to apply to an apparently chaotic, "shotgun approach" to improving urban opportunities; one inevitably is reminded of the Hollywood cowboy hero who "'rode off in all directions at once."

10. It also argues that the UK had already been awarded the plum of the European Bank for Reconstruction and Development and, by the informal but very real rules (the *Realpolitik* of the EC) some other member will expect to get the next agency allocated.

11. *The Economist* (1991a:55) noted, however, that, even as states were falling apart, states were coming together in a veritable snowstorm of associations: The Alpen-Adria, set up in 1978, includes Slovenia and Croatia (members since the beginning), five of Austria's *Länder* or provinces, three of Hungary's western regions, four northern regions of Italy, and the German Land of Bavaria. The organization aims at regional cooperation in the promotion of, e.g., tourism, energy, environment, transport, and sports. In May, 1990 under the leadership of Austria the Donauländer was established; its aim is to "upgrade the Danube as a cargo route" with the aim of reviving historic trade and cultural links among regions from Bavaria to Moldavia. "Every six months there is to be a special exhibition aimed at attracting at least 500,00 people to a particular region in the hope of stimulating tourism and conserving of monuments. Bavaria and Austria have pledged to help clean up their Danubian associates' polluted environments."

The Visegrad was established in February, 1991, named after a locale near Budapest where the leaders of Czechoslovakia, Hungary and Poland met to form an association to coordinate their efforts to join the EC, cooperate on economics and security, and have a stronger power base with which to deal with the USSR (in whatever form it emerges). Finally, in July of 1991, Turkey, Bulgaria, Romania and the USSR approved a draft of an association for Black Sea Economic cooperation.

12. He is also explicit about both organizations serving as a counterbalance to German movement towards the east, stressing, e.g., that, "Prague is nearer to Venice than Bonn or Bari" (*The European* 1990b:7).

13. "One works in Chemnitz, trades in Leipzig, but lives in Dresden."

14. Bismark is said to have said that if he heard the world was about to end he would go to Mecklenburg because things there are 100 years behind the times.

15. The approach is also legitimated by the studies that relate current to historic patterns. For example, Hall (1988:112) notes that: "City size and distribution also in part reflect the existence of powerful historic forces, which have operated over many centuries despite profound changes in economic organization; thus a line of major cities still follows the historic *Hellweg*, the great east-west Central European trade route of medieval times, while the concentration of cities in Flanders and the Netherlands recalls their trading role in the early modern period."

16. I am indebted to the following individuals who, harried by busy schedules, paused to give most graciously of their time: Michael Price, Sandwell; Dr. Bram Peper, Mayor of Rotterdam; Prof. Leo Van den Berg, Erasmus University; William Turner, Lord Mayor of Birmingham; Jackie Adams, External Relations, The European and International Affairs Task Force, Birmingham. As is obvious, I also draw extensively on the data provided in the

brief but excellent report on the conference by MacLeod (1991) in *The Christian Science Monitor*. Interestingly, no other major paper thought the conference important enough to cover (cf. *the Guardian*, the *Times* of London, the *Times* of New York – nor even *The European*, a newspaper which claimed to concentrate on news of the EC) an indication of how little attention the positive activities of cities seem to attract in the media or elsewhere.

17. Predictably, there is a French complement to Eurocities, Eurometropole, organized from and situated in Bordeaux with the aim of establishing linkages between various Chambers of Commerce and different universities all over Europe. I say "complementary" because, unlike Eurocities which stresses the connection between the research potential of university centers and the needs of urban governing officials, Eurometropole's aim seems to be to concentrate the potential synergy between university research centers and the business sector.

18. In free ports, goods are permitted to move in and out of the port without duty; a similar exemption permits raw materials to be brought in, processed and reshipped. In Rotterdam's case, this has permitted it to become one of the world's largest ports, with 60% of its tonnage in crude oil, and the site of five giant oil refineries. Further, Rotterdam was a uniquely apt place for the genesis of Eurocities. The city's budget comes not from property or income taxes but, rather, it receives almost all its income from the central government. The independent city authority has developed its own docklands through a private-public partnership and not, as W. Hutton (1990: 13) recently put it, "via central government agency by-passing local government. . . . The end result . . . is a development more respectful of local economic needs than [the London Docklands project] and whose transport infra-structure has preceded the private development rather than after it."

19. The Eurocities association was not, however, the only product of Dr. Peper's forward-looking vision. There now exists a network of universities and cities, linked together to provide direction and substantive data on a variety of issues. The network is entitled Euricur and its lead office is at Erasmus University (Rotterdam, Dr. Leo Van den Berg, Director). First, the center suggests certain topics of regional concern; then, other universities and cities are contacted as to whether they, too, see one or another topic as important in their region and are interested in participating in a general conference on the topic; a conference is then organized around the topic of choice; finally, the proceedings are commercially published as well as circulated to the various members of Euricur and the Eurocities network. Thus, the first such Proceedings dealt with *Cities: Engines behind economic recovery* and was held in 1986. Political representatives, university-based individuals and business community members from twelve European cities were invited to come and discuss the topic. The topic for the next meeting (December 1992) will deal with regional airports, and will address such problems as the problematic trade-off between the need for regional cities to offer transportation accessibility as balanced against environmental concerns.

20. Quoting Eneko Landabrau Illaramendi, EC Director-General for Regional Policy, in attendance at the meeting, MacLeod notes (1991: 25) that, "so far five

cities of Eastern Europe – Prague; Gdansk, Krakow and Lodz in Poland; and Iasi, Romania – [have already] decided to become associate members." The city councils of St. Petersburg and Moscow also sent representatives and it is expected that they will also seek associate status.

21. Of the EC capitals, only Athens and Madrid belong to Eurocities.

22. It should be noted however, that the French technique is to establish a central agency which then serves as the contact point for local level personnel. Thus, for example, one of former Prime Minister Cresson's first acts during her brief tenure was to establish a new "superministry" of finance, economics, trade, industry and telecommunications to carry out a more aggressive industrial policy. This was a deliberate imitation of Japan's powerful Ministry for International Trade and Industry (MITI) – though this latter organization technically maintains a separate finance ministry. The new superministry is designed to stimulate and coordinate industrial policy within/among departments and regions. Its first head was Pierre Bérégovoy who also continued as Finance Minster (but replaced Cresson as Prime Minister, following her dismissal in Spring, 1992).

23. See a discussion of urban problems, particularly Britain's, by Rudolf Klein (1991).

24. The small countries of the Community – e.g., Denmark, Luxembourg, Greece – also have particular relations and in some cases are dominated by the capital. Thus, e.g., Greece saw its capital region shift from having 18% of the population (1950) to having 57%. A 1990 poll showed that c. 53% of Athens, nearly 4 million people, would live elsewhere if there were viable alternatives, given the traffic problems that not only lead to economic waste but account for much of the urban pollution and attendant health problems (Burtenshaw et al. 1991:121).

25. This variability is exacerbated by the characteristic of some of the EC directorates having a predominance of key staff from one or another particular country.

26. For discussion of this from a different perspective see Hall 1988.

27. In far too many cases, the apparent inadequacy of resources is really because of what is charitably described as "slippage in allocation."

28. This view is reinforced by the increasing ubiquity of signs adorned with the EC's blue and gold flag, highly visible symbols of the extent to which EC funding is responsible for highways, housing, bridges, sewers, forests and fields – and even, as in Oviedo (Asturias, Spain), garbage dumps.

References

Ardagh, John. 1979. *A Tale of Five Cities: Life in Europe Today*. New York: Harper and Row.

Burtenshaw, D., M. Bateman, G. J. Ashworth. 1991. *The European City: A Western Perspective*. New York: John Wiley & Sons.

Cheshire, Paul. 1990. "Explaining the recent performance of the European Community's major urban regions." *Urban Studies* 27: 311-333.

Dogan, Mattei and John D. Kasarda, eds. 1988. *The Metropolis Era: A World of Giant Cities.* Vol. 1. Newbury Park, CA: Sage Publications.

The Economist. 1989. "Twelve-letter words." 1 April: 42.

____. 1991a. "Hello, neighbors." 13 July: 55.

____. 1991b. "The star of the east." 14 September: 53-4.

____. 1991c. "Escape from the end of the world." 26 October: 63-4

The European. 1990a. "Close briefing for solicitors." 3 August: 2.

____. 1990b. "Central European nations forge cooperation in new initiative." 3 August: 7

____. 1990c. "Dirty Milan seeks green role." 14 September: 7

European Communities – Commission. 1991. *The European Community: 1992 and Beyond.* Luxembourg: Office for Official Publications of the European Communities.

European Community Studies Association. 1991. *The Challenge of a New European Architecture: Implications for the European Community's Internal and External Agenda.* Abstracts. Fairfax, VA: Center for European Community Studies.

Friedmann, Georges, ed. 1952. *Villes et campagnes: Civilisation urbaine et civilisation rurale en France.* Paris: Bibliothèque Génèrale de l'Ecole Pratique des Hautes Etudes.

Giner, Salvador, and Margaret Scotford Archer, eds. 1978. *Contemporary Europe: Social Structures and Cultural Patterns.* Boston: Routledge & Kegan Paul.

Hall, Peter. 1988. "Urban growth and decline in Western Europe," in M. Dogan and J. D. Kasarda, eds., *The Metropolis Era: A World of Giant Cities* (Vol.1). Pp. 111-127. Newbury Park CA: Sage.

Harloe, Michael, and Elizabeth Lebas, eds. 1981. *City, Class and Capital: New Developments in the Political Economy of Cities and Regions.* New York: Holmes & Meier.

Hutton, W. 1990. "Creeping paranoia threatens economy." *The Guardian* 13 June: 13.

Klein, Rudolf. 1991. "City Blights." *Times Literary Supplement* 1 November: 23.

Lane, Christel. 1989. *Management and Labor in Europe: The Industrial Enterprise in Germany, Britain and France.* Aldershot UK: Edward Elgar.

MacLeod, Alexander. 1991. "European cities band together to gain clout in Community." *The Christian Science Monitor* 25 October: 4.

Molle, Willem. 1990. *The Economics of European Integration (Theory, Practice, Policy).* Brookfield VT: Dartmouth Publishing Co.

Stave, Bruce M. 1981. *Modern Industrial Cities: History, Policy, and Survival.* Beverly Hills CA: Sage.

4

Corsican Identity and a Europe of Peoples and Regions

Alexandra Jaffe

On 1 January 1993, all trade frontiers in Europe are scheduled to drop. When Europeans refer to this moment as "1992," they are talking about much more than the economic reality of an integrated market. The deadline of 1992 has become a symbol for social and cultural change, a potent new myth of identity which is tantalizing and troubling at the same time. For all the members of the European Community (EC), the idea of Europe after 1992 raises significant questions about the future of national identity and about the nature of future economic and cultural relationships. This is particularly true for "minority," "peripheral," and economically disadvantaged regions like Corsica, where 1992 is anticipated as a turning point, a moment in which the contours of power that shape their lives may be redefined. "Europe," as the EC is often referred to, offers the possibility of breaking away from a single, often conflictual relationship with a particular state, and provides a framework for the development of new, regional alliances.

In Corsica, the idea of Europe has been a powerful catalyst for a reflection on the nature and potential outcome of future cultural, economic and political relationships. Newspaper headlines like "Should We Be Afraid of 93? European Deadline: Calamity or Opportunity?" (*Corse-Matin* 24 May 1991) show that it is at once a source of hope and fear. The following excerpts (from an academic colloquium, a Corsican nationalist publication, and a magazine article, respectively) are typical

of the conflicting reactions to the prospect of a "European" future
evident in Corsican discourse about 1992:

What will islands be, face to face with Europe? What will Europe be in
relation to islands? . . . for islands, Europe is a threat, a danger. . . . the
requirement to change our behavior, our politics and strategy . . . [it]causes
fear, [but it also] represents an enormous potential . . . an immediate,
financial opportunity [1] (Biggi 1989: 16-17).

Europe remains a mosaic in its population. . . . so, what will be the role of
Corsica in the Mediterranean, and in this Europe? Who will be its allies?
Will the European new deal change the rules of the game? . . . Is the
perspective of the unified European market a menace for regions as fragile as
the mediterranean islands (Franceschi 1991: 1)?

Will the already excessive situation of dependence intensify? . . . What means
should we use to avoid becoming a vast "bronzodrome?". . . worry remains
the most widespread sentiment [about Europe] on the island (Serra 1991: 23).

These excerpts highlight several key Corsican concerns related to
increasing political and economic integration in Europe. First of all,
there is a heightened consciousness of economic fragility. Secondly,
there is the sense of uncertainty about the nature and implications of a
new European order. This uncertainty stems, in part, from Corsicans'
inability to predict the way in which an integrated Europe will define
interests, coalitions and the distribution of power for either national or
regional players. This has translated into an explosion of academic and
political meetings and colloquia in the last two years taking up the topic
of Corsica's identity and role in relation to other islands, peoples,
underdeveloped regions and cultural minorities, especially those in the
Mediterranean. There has also been a marked increase in the discussion
of cultural and economic links to Italy, links which have been seldom
mentioned in the last two decades.

The EC is not only a source of economic and political uncertainty, but
also, a source of cultural uncertainty. First of all, while the EC's regional
and social policies have validated cultural differences (Armstrong 1989;
Lodge 1989c), it is not yet clear what the long-term consequences of the
assertion of those differences will be. Secondly, the consideration of
various levels of identity, from "islandness" to "Europeanness" has led
Corsicans to evaluate themselves as a community, and to assess the
strengths and weaknesses of Corsican culture in the perspective of 1992.
This has led to some uncomfortable reflections on Corsicans' ability to
reach consensus and take collective action.

There are two main poles of reference in Corsican discourse about 1992: the Europe of Peoples versus the Europe of Nations. A survey of articles, both popular and academic, finds the following clusters of related images and values: A Europe of Nations (or States, Merchants, or Multinationals) and "Vertical Relations" is contrasted with a Europe of Peoples (or Small Nations, Regions, Citizens, Communities, or Cultures) and "Horizontal Relations." The idea of a Europe of Nations stands for a Europe in which fundamental power relations are unlikely to change. The Europe of Peoples and Regions, on the other hand, represents a cultural and moral order which transcends and challenges the law of the marketplace and of State-centered politics.

These two main poles of reference in Corsican discourse about 1992 represent fundamental tensions in European philosophy about the nature of the community. The "Europe of Peoples and Regions" and the "Europe of Nations" are competing models of political organization, social responsibility and economic development. One unresolved tension is played out in the contradictory role of the Council of Ministers, in which EC interests versus state sovereignty must be negotiated (Lodge 1989a: 49). Another has to do with the conflict between the principle of a Free Market economy and the principles of social justice articulated in the Treaty of Rome, which, as a European Commission document states, "subordinates the economy to that cause . . . repudiates unbridled growth, ruthless towards the economically weak, subject only to its own logic and indifferent to the concerns of the individual" (de Kerchove d'Exaerde 1990: 19). This chapter focuses primarily on the cultural dimension, looking at the "Europe of Peoples" and the "Europe of States" as opposing concepts of identity and power which shape Corsican perspectives on their future in Europe.

A Europe of Peoples

The notion of the interdependency of all communities at all levels is embedded in the idea of the Europe of Peoples, and is a primary source of optimism. In his 1992 address to the European Parliament, Jacques Delors emphasized this principle by evoking the birth of new democracies in Eastern Europe and the underdevelopment and threat of conflict on Europe's southern Mediterranean flank. "These problems," he stated, "are our problems too, given their influence on security and migratory pressure" (Delors 1992: 5).

For Corsica, the idea of interdependency allows a reformulation of "center-periphery" relations with France. Seen only in relation to

France, Corsica is far removed from the political center of the continent, Paris. Viewed in the context of the entire European territory, however, it is far from peripheral. In several recent Corsican analyses, Corsica is represented as a critical, mediating cultural and geographical node in lines of communication between the North (read, continental Europe) and the South (North Africa, Greece, Turkey) (Balbi 1989; Accolta Naziunale Corsa 1991). The idea was graphically represented in the proceedings of one of three nationalist conferences in the summer of 1991 devoted to the role of Corsica in the Mediterranean and in Europe: a map covering Europe and North Africa was printed upside down, emphasizing, as the caption said, the "vastness of the desert," and by extension, minimizing the European continental land mass and its occupants and placing the Mediterranean and its islands, in the center (Franceschi 1991: 3).

The political implications of this geographical reframing of center-periphery relations are clear. European political integration is a sacrifice of national autonomy in the context of global power relations which make Europe vulnerable and can be seen as "a response to the growing inadequacy of the Western European Nation State" (Smith 1981: 23). De Kerchove d'Exaerde points out that

> States are increasingly interdependent . . . [and consequently] policies thus have to be framed . . . at a European level. . . . the way the Community is going is clear: we are witnessing a strengthening of its authority and power brought about by the force of events. (1990: 25).[2]

This perspective is significant for members of "marginal" regions like Corsica, because the EC has gone much farther than most of its member states in recognizing the cultural and economic specificity of minority regions and islands, and in committing resources to their development. The economic commitment goes back to one of the guiding principles of the 1957 Treaty of Rome, which was to reduce disparities in the standard of living between the industrial North and the relatively underdeveloped Southern European regions. The cultural commitment was formalized in the 1981 Charter of Regional Languages and Cultures, a non-binding document that gave equal weight to the promotion of economic and cultural vitality. These principles have been accompanied by money: regional development funds have been available since 1975, and, since the signing of the Single European Act (SEA) in 1986, Objective One of the Community's Structural Development Funds has been to allow underdeveloped regions like

Corsica to "catch up" economically. After 1992, the money allocated to this objective should be doubled from 19% to 38% of the total EC budget (European Communities – Commission 1990: 7).

In addition to economic incentives, the EC has also provided a political framework for the development of regional coalitions and lobbies. Corsica has become involved in several of these groups, including one of the oldest and most important – the sixty-member Conference of Peripheral, Maritime Regions and its subgroup, the "Island Commission." Now in its eleventh year, this group lobbies the European Commission, which has executive and managerial responsibility for European Regional Development Funds. Since 1986, there has also been a coalition called the "Island Intergroup" within the European Parliament which was formed and is headed by one of two Corsican European Deputies.

In an interdependent Europe, the power of these lobbies is the threat their members pose to European unity. This was recognized long before the SEA (McCrone 1969: 198) and emphasized by Delors in his 1992 address. Thus part of the promise of 1992 is that the Europe of Peoples will be recognized as an EC-wide concern, and will be given priority (Stagnara 1991: 38). For Corsica, Europe is a new "imagined community" (Anderson 1982) which may mediate between the island and France, which has, up to this point, signed but implemented few of the policies of the Charters on regionalism mentioned above. Bindi expresses this hope in a recent essay on Corsican political culture, writing, "Ought not Europe be a more responsible France, one with a greater sense of obligation to correct [Corsican] underdevelopment?" (1991: 50).

In the last year, Corsicans have begun to test this community. Several groups have bypassed Paris, and taken their concerns directly to Brussels for adjudication or financial support. In one case, a union of Corsican village communes went to Brussels in June of 1991 to promote (apparently successfully) a project for the development of a high-technology center for the study and implementation of oxygen therapy for high-altitude athletes. During the same month, a delegate from the Union of Corsican fishermen went directly to the European Commission and obtained an exception to post-1992 policy which will allow the island to maintain the current twelve mile protected fishing zone around the island until the year 2002.

The process of European integration has also led Corsicans to compare and contrast their political autonomy with other European regions, and there have been several studies, as well as numerous articles in the press, describing the statutes of Sardinia, Sicily, the Provincial Autonomous Parliaments of Spain, the Portuguese Azores and so on. Most of these regional governments enjoy a greater degree of economic and political self-determination than does Corsica. Some regions' autonomy, as in the Catalonian case, can be clearly linked with their strong economic base. But in the case of other regions which are as economically dependent as Corsica, their greater autonomy is clearly a function of national, state political philosophy. Thus there is the hope that in the process of harmonization of the social and political arena in the European Community, regional economic and cultural autonomy will be given increasingly greater weight, and that France will be led to bend to majority by granting greater autonomy to Corsica (Simeoni 1991; Olivesi 1991).

New Cultural Partnerships After 1992: Hopes and Uncertainties

The anticipation of new political alliances in a Europe of Peoples has led Corsicans to consider the possibilities for cooperation and competition in the domains of both economics and culture. The closest and most obvious cultural and geographical partnership for Corsica is Italy. The idea of Europe, as I have suggested, has reawakened Corsicans to a long-dormant cultural connection. In several publications, Europe is represented as placing Corsica back in its "natural" cultural and geographical environment. Corsica belonged to Genoa up until 1767, when it was ceded to France in partial repayment of a debt. Italy remained, however, the cultural and linguistic reference for at least another 100 years; Corsican elites (like Napoleon's family) read and wrote in Italian and sent their sons to Italy to be educated. I should add that the vernacular, Corsican, was no further removed from an elite register of Italian than the languages of other regions of Italy and remains, today, as distant from French as Italian is. Over the last century, the status of Italy in Corsican eyes was diminished by both the influx of Italian migrant laborers and the Italian occupation during World War Two. Despite the proximity of Corsica to Sardinia (11 kilometers) and to the coast of the Italian continent, there has been very little cultural or economic exchange between the two islands during the last fifty years.

But the last few years have seen the conjuncture of the prospect of a New Europe and a rapid increase in the numbers of Italian tourists visiting the island. These tourists tend to be fairly well off, and in comparison to the other major category of tourists on Corsica, the Germans, they are perceived as good spenders with whom it is easy to communicate. They have done a great deal to dispel the anti-Italian bias, and there has been a general increase in interest in Italian language and culture. The language issue is significant, and the endorsement of Italian represents a turning point in Corsican cultural activism. Until recently, any promotion of Italian was seen as an elitist attempt to undermine both the status of Corsican and the resources allocated to its teaching. Only in the last two years have well-known cultural activists come out in favor of Italian as a complementary, rather than a competitive, subject.

Links with Italy have also begun to be cultivated by the Chambers of Commerce and professional organizations. In May of 1991, the Craftsman's guild of Bastia, the major city of Northern Corsica, established a partnership with Livorno which was inaugurated in June by the participation of Corsican and Italian artisans in a colloquium. Another significant relationship with Sardinia was established in May of 1991 by the Corsican Regional Chamber of Tourism (CRTC), which launched a cooperative program with its Sardinian counterpart in order to define what the president of the Corsican Chamber called "the common card they have to play in the promotion of tourism" (*Corse-Matin* 23 May 1991).

The idea of cultural and linguistic complementarity has also begun to shape the policy of the regional radio station, RCFM. This past summer, it began to broadcast reports from an Italian correspondent every weekday morning. The correspondent called in live from an Italian city, where he reported on current cultural events in Italian. In return, RCFM sent tapes about Corsican events, in Corsican, to Italy. The idea was to encourage Corsicans and Tuscans to take the four hour boat ride in order to attend each other's cultural events. To reinforce the point, the station conducted a weekly contest, during which one clue per day was broadcast about the identity of a famous Italian historical figure. The prize was a weekend in Florence. All of these measures were a way, the station director told me, to remind Corsica of the "other continent" as a point of cultural reference. In the long run, the director said he hoped to contribute to the development of economic relations between Corsica and Italy, and was planning to broadcast a series of roundtables bringing together Corsican and Italian businessmen and politicians to explore issues of commercial exchange in the integrated market.

Another cultural partnership was inaugurated in the summer of 1991 when Ajaccio, the major southern city, and the Sardinian island of La Maddalena formally celebrated their new relationship as "twin cities." During the course of the Sardinian delegation's visit to Ajaccio, there was extensive press and radio coverage in which the twinning was represented as a return to a state of cultural continuity. Corsicans were reminded that La Maddalena was Corsican up until 1767. The press reports read that "contacts with the delegation proved that they had not forgotten their origins," and it was reported with pleasure that "it was in *lingua nustrale* ("our native language," in Corsican) that the conversations took place" (*Corse-Matin* 3 August 1991).

However, this growing rapprochement with Italy has also generated a certain unease. Its very closeness poses an economic threat. It was, for example, fear of superior Italian fishing fleets that threatened Corsican fishermen, and led them to seek a ten-year extension of the twelve-mile protected fishing radius from the EC. In June of 1991, Corsican fishermen conducted a public debate on "The menace of '92 for Corsican Fishing," and spoke of the urgency of upgrading an ageing fleet to the standard of foreign boats before their ten years of protected fishing came to an end (Giudici 1991). And despite the accent on unity and cooperation during the first meetings between Corsican craftsmen and their Italian counterparts, one of the facts that was brought to light was that there are over 113,000 Tuscans in the Livorno Guild and only 4000 in Corsica's entire Northern region. This imbalance, a Corsican participant hastened to add, "does not preclude willing (read balanced and fair) exchanges" (*Corse-Matin* 1 June 1991). Nevertheless, the threat had been mentioned. Similarly, during a conference in the summer of 1991 organized by the *Unione di U Populu Corsu* (or UPC, the oldest autonomist party), the General Secretary invoked political solidarity and spoke of plans for future cooperation between his party and the Sardinian autonomists invited to the conference. He said that this would insure that their future economic relations were complementary rather than competitive. In both these cases, the ceremonial votes of confidence belie very real concerns: the Italian regions neighboring Corsica, especially Tuscany, are much stronger and more productive than Corsica, which risks becoming a captive market of Italy in the same way as it is now a captive market of continental France. In addition to competition in the marketplace, there is also competition for resources within the EC. Corsicans are not unaware that this struggle for funding has the potential to test the limits of solidarity amongst alliances of the most in need.

Change at the Center

These lingering, as yet unconfirmed doubts about the quality of future alliances with Italy and with other islands and peripheral regions are overshadowed by some profound uncertainties about the extent to which a Europe without frontiers will change the character of current, state-centered power relationships. In the proceedings of one nationalist conference on Europe in the summer of 1992, Pini wrote

We must not forget that the last thing that the Nation-States, and France in particular, want to do is disturb or alter established state structures whatever they might be, despite their declarations of intention (1991: 2).

Another nationalist party document put it this way:

European construction may enable us to escape from the rigid context of the Nation-State, and to develop new relationships with our mediterranean neighbors. But it is even more likely that unification will confirm, at an European echelon, already established positions and choices which will inevitably favor those who are the strongest economically (Accolta Naziunale Corsa 1991: 87).

This view of the vested interests of European states in maintaining the status quo, coupled with the principle of a free and unified market raises the question of how long, and to what degree, exceptions to European unity and uniformity of policy (ranging from the economic support of the Structural Funds, to the protection of local markets, as in the case of the Corsican fishermen) can be made in the interest of regions like Corsica without undermining fundamental components of EC building. Recent claims for autonomy by economically prosperous regions like Lombardy and Baden-Wurtemburg underscore their reluctance to underwrite the economic development of Southern Europe.

These concerns led the President of the Corsican Regional Assembly to formally petition France "not to use European harmonization as an excuse to eliminate advantages already granted to the island"[3] (*Corse-Matin* 6 July 1991). These advantages include the application of the reduced Value Added Tax rate to goods such as building materials which are not classified elsewhere as "basic necessities." Economic harmonization implies that equivalent categories of goods should be taxed within the same percentage band ("reduced" or "standard") in every country (Bos and Nelson 1988). From this perspective, a policy of economic harmonization poses a threat to Corsica so long as the cost of transportation to island regions is not taken into consideration. As the Corsican Social and Economic Council put it, "when it comes to islands, the notion of a free internal market is based on a geographical fiction" (Conseil Economique et Social 1991: 4). Appealing to France, however, was a double bind. As the regional newsmagazine put it, "the [French] policy of territorial continuity has two sides; while it brings Corsica closer to the French continent, it distances the island from the rest of the European continent" (Frigara 1991: 11).

A similar perspective emerged in the course of Corsican nationalist debate over the chances for autonomy in the European context during the summer of 1991. Before 1991, most nationalist discourse about other European autonomous regions was geared towards discrediting French policy and providing examples of the ultimate triumph of cultural identity and militant nationalist strategy. For example, language policy in Catalonia or the Basque country was often presented as an inspirational model for Corsicans, despite significant differences between these regions' and Corsica's economic and demographic vitality. In the 1991 meeting of the UPC, however, there was a distinct shift in the emphasis of Corsican nationalists' interpretations of other autonomous regions' success. Although Catalonia and the Azores were invited to the UPC conference on Europe as representatives of successful models of regional autonomy, the question and answer period that followed their presentations ultimately emphasized the degree to which their gains had depended on the cooperation of Spain and Portugal. In other words, it was the political relationship with the "parent" state, rather than any inherent cultural or political features of the nationalist program which was identified as the most significant point of contrast. In one of his responses to a question, Simeoni, the leader of the UPC and a European MP, said that despite their hopes about what Europe will mean for small regions, they should remember that Europe is not going to force member states to grant regional autonomy. He also remarked that the Island Commission had little power. The overall message was that Corsica, at least in the near term, must work through its relationship with France, while continuing to act in concert with other regions within the EC in order to try to lead member states to respect regional and insular identities.

The Dilemma of Difference

In addition to foregrounding the continued dependence of peripheral regions on their states, references to the state in both the nationalist meeting and the Value Added Tax situation illustrate the way in which difference – whether economic or cultural – poses a dilemma for a region like Corsica. The EC complicates the political articulation of difference because it legitimates issues of economic and cultural specificity at the same time as it maintains the goal of "harmonization." As Constant (1990) points out, this opens the possibility that changes in current state regional policy may or may not benefit less-developed regions.

For Corsica, the assertion of difference in France was the source of ambivalence and uncertainty, both in a pragmatic and a philosophical sense. From the pragmatic perspective, Corsicans did benefit from France's policy of "territorial continuity," and enjoyed some other tax advantages based on their geographical difference. But they were also acutely aware that France believed that the current set of benefits already represented the "threshold of national solidarity" with the island.[4] The assertion of cultural difference in the French context is even more problematic. As Culioli (1990: 255) writes, it is

> experienced in contradictory ways by Corsicans. Are they different from the French? A majority will respond – We are French! So, you are the same as the French? Oh no, not at all; we're Corsican and proud of it.

But what does it mean to be Corsican in the European context? As we have seen, access to political power outside the state is through regional lobbies and coalitions which assert their collective difference. The strength of this collective difference rests on the internal sameness of the group. Like the Shetland islanders who voted against devolution of power from England to Scotland (Cohen 1987: 89-91), Corsicans may not wish to give up claims to specificity among French departments, European regions or any other forum of collective membership. In their relations with France, Corsicans have often resisted attributions of commonality that lump the island with other regions they perceive as culturally more peripheral than they are. During the 1989 strike, for example, a Corsican journalist responded to the implication that the situation resembled New Caledonia by saying that "This image of Corsica as the exotic dancing girls of France is simply unacceptable" (Santarelli 1989: 15). France's DOMs/TOMs (Départements/Territoires Outre-Mer) are frequently used as an image of exotic otherness against which Corsicans measure their inclusion in French society.

Thus the widening of cultural and political horizons and the development of new partnerships with other regions encouraged by European integration can also produce what Bindi (1991: 50) calls a "reflex of refusal" when it comes to establishing relations with other regions, since the island "is, and above all wishes to be so different." Corsicans may also be reluctant to assert commonality with other peripheral regions because of their lack of full confidence that Europe will really be one of Regions and Peoples, in which common problems would call for common solutions. As Vandamme (1981: 53) remarks, "What has . . . not been proved is that [European] regional policy will be a truly 'community policy' and not an indirect means of reinforcing or supporting the regional policies of member states." For example, Armstrong (1989: 181) notes that many member States have used European Regional Funds to subsidize their own regional spending plans, rather than as an additive set of monies. Lodge (1989c: 314) also points out that up to the present, the EC has been an inefficient mechanism for the coordination of regional policy and the correction of discrepancies in regional policies between states. And the question still lingers about the limits of European solidarity with its underdeveloped regions. These doubts raise the suspicion that underdeveloped regions' strongest card – the fact that they are an anomaly and a problem – is also a point of weakness, since they represent a threat to the idea of unity.

The dilemma of difference for Corsicans is both a practical and a philosophical issue, in which politics and culture are woven together. The prospect of 1992 has made the issue of cultural difference politically and economically salient, and has led to a renewed and critical reflection by Corsicans on the nature of their own culture.

Culture and Development

In the "White Paper" of the Corsican Regional Assembly, under the above topic heading, it is noted that:

> The set of Corsican cultural characteristics . . . favor the development of the emergence of a post-industrial society and economy . . .[but] in the cultural domain, for example, the tight network of social relations which characterizes insular cultures . . . can be an impediment to innovation. . . . An optimistic discourse on Corsica, land of sun and "grey matter" contrasts sharply with a fatalistic vision of an island destined to fail (Préfecture de la Région de Corse 1990:11).

This set of social relations they refer to is based on kinship, and the prospect of Europe has led to a reflection on the particular nature of Corsican kinship as a model for society, and as a mode of comportment within the new European context.

Kinship

For many Corsicans, kinship as a model of society embodies what the president of the University of Corsica, Jacques Balbi, calls a "pre-industrial mentality." He believes this is well suited to a post-industrial, technological age. This analysis is based on the emphasis, in the Corsican family, on egalitarian rather than hierarchical relations, which is frequently cited by Corsican nationalists such as Franceschi and Geronimi (1991: 26) as evidence of the fundamentally democratic nature of Corsican culture. Balbi contends that the Corsican combination of strong, egalitarian family ties and a fierce individualism make Corsicans poor candidates for an industrial economy, which requires hierarchical economic and social relationships. He notes that "anglo-saxon" models of human relations are being questioned worldwide, citing as evidence the trend, in management philosophy, towards greater employee participation and empowerment. This makes him optimistic that Corsica and other Southern European cultures would be well-adapted to a post-modern economic age, in which he believed successful economic relations will be characterized by equality and interdependence (Balbi 1991). Nonetheless, Balbi concedes that within an externally-imposed bureaucracy, strong ties of kinship on Corsica perpetuate "le piston" – nepotism and patronage. As Biggi (1989: 14) writes, "it is very difficult to have strictly professional, economically-efficient relations in a society in which most people are bound by kinship." In this sense, kinship can be seen as a conservative force, one which stands, as the White Paper suggests, in the way of political or economic innovation.

It is also true that the individualism and independence that most Corsicans cite as significant cultural traits have a double edge. On the one hand, they insure cultural continuity in the face of outside aggression. Franceschi and Geronimi (1991: 24) claim that "Our family system nourishes the hate of authority – especially when it is imported – it refuses to grant legitimacy to any central authoritative state structure." In an interview I had with the UPC leader Simeoni, he cited Corsican concepts and practices of justice as a living example of this rejection of external authority and values. He reminded me of Corsican reactions to a 1985 incident in which Corsican nationalist commandos broke into a prison in Ajaccio and killed two prisoners being detained for suspected murder of a nationalist. In the press, and in private conversation, almost no Corsican reactions, even from anti-nationalist camps, expressed concern that (French) principles of justice had been perverted. Rather, they commented on how scandalous it was that security was so lax as to have allowed the event to happen.

As the anthropologist J. Gil points out, however, egalitarian segmentation, in which conflict and power is balanced in a continuous cycle of reciprocity and public display of independence, is only one of the current organizing principles of Corsican culture. The other is the clan. The principle of egalitarian segmentary opposition politically activates individual identity at progressively more inclusive levels (family, village, canton, island) (Gil 1984: 58). The clan, on the other hand, represents a primarily political allegiance, forged by clientelistic relations.[5] The clan has a family dimension – two families have shared political control over the island for over one hundred years, and political loyalty is exacted on the basis of family relations. But it short-circuits the political expression of social unity beyond the family level (and even within families) since competition for resources creates cleavages in every social unit.

Clanism, writes Gil, "systematizes fraud, corruption and violence . . . which are not problems in an otherwise healthy system but [a set of] accepted, valued, *customary* behaviors which govern the operation of the entire political and social machine" (1984: 168-9). There are some obvious negative implications of these customary behaviors insofar as Corsica's ability to negotiate a satisfactory status within the EC context is concerned. So long as political action on Corsica is a sectarian battle for resources, both political consensus and collective action are extremely difficult to achieve. The Corsican Regional Assembly, for example, has been unable to formulate and agree on a Development Plan in the two-year time frame set by the French government, despite the fact that drawing up such a plan is one of the primary ways in which the Assembly could exert influence and set priorities rather than have them imposed by outside forces (Olivesi 1990; Pestorel 1990).

The influence of the clan in obtaining and distributing government resources also raises another issue. In interviews I conducted, and in the press, Corsicans spoke about the obstacle of "an assisted mentality." One editorialist put it bluntly, saying that she did not believe that a people who had grown used to always looking for a handout, for someone else to solve their problems, would be able to take charge of their economic future, and really confront the Europe of 1992 competitively (Poli 1991). If we are to make it, she said, we must change. It is clear to some Corsicans that their long history of relations of dependence – on Italy and then on France – which is the source of their current economic fragility is also the source of features of their culture.

Land

Corsicans have always resisted foreign encroachment on property. All Corsicans represent themselves as having a passionate, visceral attachment to the land (Codaccione 1989: 34). Gil writes about the passionate link between self and place, the "lack of a radical distinction between the physical and the human universe" in the village, which is the symbolic center of Corsicans "non-rational attachment to their island" (1984: 16-17). Their unwillingness to sell property, even to another Corsican, even when they have not lived on the island for years and may not intend to return, is infamous. This attachment to property can be seen as a powerful cultural obstacle to the threat of real estate speculation by foreigners. Corsicans express their fear of becoming a "bronzodrome," and talk about avoiding "balearization," the touristic fate of the Spanish islands like Majorca. However, as the UPC leader Simeoni said in an interview, Corsican resistance to outside encroachment is almost always manifested at the individual rather than at the collective level. This, he said, was not enough. The island needed to elaborate policies that will limit, and manage the extent and the nature of foreign speculation Corsicans so wish to avoid. This kind of collective action was crippled, he said, by Corsican political process, which is so often governed by competing local interests that it can hardly turn a unified face towards the outside world (Simeoni 1991). And, referring back to the "White Paper" on Culture and Development, there are also those "fatalistic" Corsicans who do not have faith in the ability of the individual to remain faithful to the cultural principle of keeping Corsican land in Corsican hands faced with the temptation of high prices that are likely to be offered by other, richer Europeans.

Both the power of the clan and Corsican attachment to land are implicated in the long-standing debate among Corsicans about the right to vote of Corsicans of the diaspora – that is, of property owners who are not permanent residents of the island. This debate was reopened this year by a law passed by the French National Assembly concerning Corsica (Loi Joxe) which called for a reformulation of Corsican electoral lists. On the side of the Corsicans of the diaspora is the sentiment of cultural attachment expressed in the saying "One never leaves Corsica, one is just temporarily absent." Many Corsicans, however, identified the votes of the diaspora with a pattern of loyalty to a clan based on relationships of family, patronage and tradition, as well as with widespread fraud in elections. Blind loyalties and fraud were contrasted with democratic principles of disinterested and responsible voters. In other words, there was a strong sentiment that sentiments of cultural attachment, and the model of political responsibility of the traditional political class were handicaps in a new, European context (Jaffe 1992). So in one sense, the clan represents the alienation of Corsicans from the political process. But rejecting it – like rejecting the logic of expatriate voters – is also a rejection of the central cultural values of kinship and land which were cited over and over again as inalienable rights by those Corsicans who supported the vote of the diaspora.

So Corsicans are not only wondering if Europe will offer them the chance to exercise greater control over their destiny, but they are also questioning their ability to seize the opportunity if it is offered. In the nationalist fold, for example, there is a strong desire to believe that nationalism, rather than the clan, is the true expression of the value of kinship in Corsican society. In an article on Corsican political culture written for a the proceedings of a nationalist conferences on Europe, the authors were forced to conclude that neither the disappearance of the clan nor independence from France will "automatically bring about the [free and egalitarian] Corsican society we dream of" (Franceschi and Geronimi 1991: 26).[6] In other words, although they would like to cast the influence of the clan as a "perversion" of Corsican values imposed or encouraged by France, they are far from sure that their society has not undergone a sea change.

Another source of Corsicans' cultural uncertainty has to do with their capacity to adapt to a new economic reality. In one newspaper article about a successful Corsican business, it was remarked, "Land of pastoralism, Corsica does not have a culture of business" (*Corse-Matin* 20 February 1991). "In the Corsican mentality, there has been no passage from a mercantile to a capitalist concept of money," writes Ravis-Giordani in his monograph on Corsican pastoralism (1983: 21). This perspective was echoed in many conversations I had with Corsicans, who said that they were simply not culturally adapted to commercial activity and that these kinds of exchanges were incompatible with their traditional models of human relations. They represented themselves as unable to find a happy medium in regard to their pricing of tourist goods and services: I was often told that "Corsicans either give it away, or they charge you too much." The cultural gloss on these inconsistent poles of behavior is that the first coincides with the traditional host-guest relationship, in which the host is obliged to give, and gains status from doing so (Caisson 1974; Gil 1984). Overcharging is interpreted as an act of defiance, a wish to dissociate oneself from an economic transaction in which the person who sells is dependent on the patronage of the buyer. This can be likened to public displays of indifference to the power of others to induce envy (Gil 1984). These comportments, however, are predicated on local, egalitarian social relationships and balances of power. They are not adapted to the outsider who is neither a guest nor an enemy.

Conclusions

One significant cultural consequence of a long history of dependent and antagonistic relations with France and other powers is that the peaks of Corsican solidarity have always been in response to an outside threat. This is, of course, a common phenomenon in minority cultures, and a fundamental principle of segmentary opposition. But these moments of solidarity are marked as unusual on Corsica, even by Corsicans themselves. They contrast sharply with everyday behavior and relations. Thus as Corsicans look back on their history, they have many examples of strong, unitary *reactions*, but no cultural fund of internally-driven cooperation except the fourteen year democratic rule of Pascal Paoli in the 18th century. Many of those Corsicans I interviewed expressed doubts about their collective ability to make the cultural adaptations that would enable them to act in concert to build a new model of society in the new environment of an integrating Europe that might offer them the possibility to do so.

The ambivalence of the meaning of Europe for Corsicans is due, in part, to the island's geographic, economic and political marginality; to the cultural and social consequences of the experience of dependency; and to other aspects of their cultural character. But this ambivalence is also the symptom of a more general phenomenon, a crisis of identity that applies to all members of the EC approaching 1993. This is because, as with the Corsicans, Europeans have the sense that there is much to be gained or lost in the redefinition of old categories of identity and relationships of power. The Corsican questions – of what defines them as a culture, as a people, and as a region – will reverberate at all levels across Europe as the two models of the Europe of States and the Europe of Peoples confront each other with growing intensity.

Notes

My research in Corsica was partially funded by a National Endowment for the Humanities Travel to Collections Grant, and a Bryant College Summer Stipend. Archival research was conducted in the library of the University of Corsica, the library of the Corsican Studies Center, and the video archives of FR3, the regional television station. I am grateful to all those who made these resources available. In addition to searching the popular and academic press on the subject of Europe (covering the last two years), I also conducted interviews with politicians, scholars, and other figures in Corsican public life who have been directly involved with issues of European integration.

1. All translations of quotations from the French are my own.

2. This analysis was shared by Max Simeoni, Corsican autonomist and member of the Green party delegation to the European Parliament. He noted that it was clear that in the regulation of monetary policy, and in the European response to the War in the Gulf, that France was quite clearly not free to make an independent decision.

3. This fear does not seem unfounded. In June of 1991, the French Economic Minister, Charasse, made a fairly ambiguous statement that "We are not taking apart the edifice of Corsican advantages. We are content not to perpetuate [these advantages]" (*Corse-Matin* 7 June 1991).

4. This was a phrase used by the Finance minister during the course of a three-month general strike in 1989 (Jaffe 1991: 101).

5. As Gil (1984: 69) and many others have noted, the power of these political families emerged in the context of the growth of the role of the French State in education and employment after the late 1800s. They served as mediators between the centralized French state and a dependent, underdeveloped, largely agro-pastoral community, funnelling and distributing government money on the island and serving as a relay for the placement of Corsicans in government posts on the French continent and in the colonies.

6. The fact that there were three separate nationalist conferences/meetings about the role of Corsica in Europe after 1992 is a symptom of the difficulty of cohesion among nationalist ranks, in which there is a broad spectrum of philosophies regarding ends (the degree of autonomy Corsica should seek) and means (such as the use of violence, or collaboration with other "progressive" political parties).

References

Accolta Naziunale Corsa. 1991. *Pruposti pulitichi (Propositions pour une projet politique)*. Ajaccio: Editions Cyrnos et Méditerranée.

Anderson, Benedict. 1983. *Imagined Communities: Reflections on the Origin and Spread of Nationalism*. London: Verso.

Armstrong, Harvey. 1989. "Community Regional Policy," in Juliet Lodge, ed., *The European Community and the Challenge of the Future*. Pp. 167-185. New York: St. Martin's Press.

Balbi, Jacques Henri. 1989 "Identite Culturelle. Actes du colloque sur le développement économique et l'identité culturelle des îles de l'Europe." *Cahiers de l'IDIM* 1:115-119.

_____. 1991. Interview with author. 15 July, Corté.

Biggi, Michel. 1989. "Présentations des îles invitées et de la problématique du colloque. Actes du colloque sur le développement économique et l'identité culturelle des îles de l'Europe." *Cahiers de l'IDIM* 1:12-19.

Bindi, Ange-Laurent. 1991. *Inventer la Corse*. Paris: L'Harmattan.

Bos, Marko and Hans Nelson. 1988. "Indirect Taxation and the Internal Market." *Journal of Common Market Studies* 27(7):27-44.

Caisson, Max 1974 "L'hospitalité comme relation d'ambivalence." *Etudes Corses* 2: 115-127.

Codaccione-Meistersheim, Anne. 1989. "Images d'îleité. Actes du colloque sur le développement économique et l'identité culturelle des îles de l'Europe." *Cahiers de l'IDIM* 1:30-36.

Cohen, Anthony. 1987. *Whalsay: Symbol, Segment and Boundary in a Shetland Island Community.* Wolfeboro, NH: Manchester University Press.

Conseil Economique et Social. 1991. *Note concernant le régime fiscal particulier de la Corse et la règlementation de la CEE.* Ajaccio: Région de Corse.

Constant, Fred. 1990. "Le fait insulaire et la CEE." *Revue de Science Administrative de la Méditerranée Occidentale* 29/30:9-17.

Corse-Matin. Daily newspaper. Marseille/Ajaccio.

Culioli, Gabriel-Xavier. 1990. *Le Complexe Corse.* Paris: Gallimard.

de Kerchove d'Exaerde, George. 1990. *A Human Face for Europe.* Luxembourg: Office for Official Publications of the European Communities.

Delors, Jacques. 1992. "1992: a Pivotal Year. Address to the European Parliament." *Bulletin of the European Communities Supplement* 1/92 pp. 5-12. Luxembourg: Office for the Official Publications of the European Communities.

European Communities – Commission. 1990. *The Structural Policies of the European Community.* Luxembourg: Office for Official Publications of the European Communities.

Franceschi, Danièle. 1991. "Editorial." *Corsica Infurmazione* 13: 1 - 3.

Franceschi, Danièle, and Vitale Geronimi. 1991. "La Corse entre nationalisme et clanisme--logique ou fatalité?" *Corsica Infurmazione* 13:24-27.

Frigara, Charles. 1991. "Le livre blanc: un document consensuel." *Kyrn* 343: 11.

Gil, José. 1984. *La Corse: entre la liberté et la terreur.* Paris: Editions de la Différence.

Giudici, Claire. 1991. "La pêche après 92: 'pesciu frescu' labellisé." *Corse-Matin* 5 June, p. D.

Jaffe, Alexandra. 1991. "Corsica on Strike: the Power and the Limits of Ethnicity." *Ethnic Groups* 8: 91 - 111.

____. 1992. European Integration and Corsican Nationalist Discourse on Culture and Identity. Paper presented at the Annual Meeting of the American Ethnological Society, March, Memphis, TN.

Lodge, Juliet. 1989a. "EC Policymaking: Institutional Considerations," in J. Lodge, ed., *The European Community and the Challenge of the Future.* Pp. 26-57. New York: St. Martin's Press.

____. 1989b. "The European Parliament – from 'assembly' to co-legislature," in J. Lodge, ed., *The European Community and the Challenge of the Future.* Pp. 58-82. New York: St. Martin's Press.

____. 1989c. "Social Europe: forging a People's Europe," in J.Lodge, ed., *The European Community and the Challenge of the Future*. Pp. 303-318. New York: St. Martin's Press.

McCrone, Gavin. 1969. " Regional Policy in European Communities," in G. R. Denton, ed., *Economic Integration in Europe*. Pp. 194-219. London: Weidenfeld and Nicolson.

Olivesi, Claude. 1990. "Le 'Projet Joxe': vers une recomposition du paysage politique insulaire?." *Revue de Science Administrative de la Méditerranée Occidentale* 29/30:99-120.

____. 1991. Interview with author. July, Corté.

Pestorel, J.P. 1990. "Le bilan du statut particulier de la Corse de 1982." *Revue de Science Administrative de la Méditerranée Occidentale* 29/30:92-98.

Pini, M. 1991. "Marché unique: Iles diverses." *Corsica Infurmazione* 13:4-7.

Poli, Gisèle. 1991. Vive la pollution, le béton et l'exploitation. *Corse-Matin*. 24 March 1991.

Préfecture de la Région de Corse. 1990. *Livre Blanc Préparatoire au Schéma d'Aménagement de la Corse*. Ajaccio: Editions Cyrnos et Méditerranée.

Ravis-Giordani, Georges. 1983. *Bergers Corsses: les communautés villageoises du Niolu*. Paris: Edisud.

Santarelli, Paule. 1989. "Miroir, méchante miroir." *Kyrn* 248: 15-17.

Serra, Mylène. 1991. "A demain l'Europe . . . " *KYRN* 373:22-23.

Simeoni, Max. 1991. Interview with Author. July, Bastia.

Smith, Gordon. 1981. "The Crisis of the West European State," in D. M. Cameron, ed., *Regionalism and Supranationalism*. Montreal: Institute for Research in Public Policy.

Stagnara, Vincent. 1991. *Minorité et Statut: l'exemple de la Corse*. Nucariu: Cismonte è Pumonti Edizione.

Vandamme, Jacques. 1981. "Regionalism in Europe," in D. M. Cameron, ed., *Regionalism and Supranationalism*. Pp 39-55. Montreal: Institute for Research in Public Policy.

5

The Periphery of Pleasure or Pain: Consumer Culture in the EC Mediterranean of 1992

Janeen Arnold Costa

The process of completing the internal market (IM) of the European Community (EC) in 1992 and beyond has been perceived as a potential threat by many people in parts of the EC Mediterranean, particularly in Greece, Spain and Portugal, who joined the EC in the 1980s. Simply put, the forces of free market capitalism, which, by the end of 1992, are anticipated to be relatively unhindered by government protections in the EC of the Twelve, may make large sectors of these three nations even more peripheral than they have been in the past. The EC and the member state governments are doing much to protect the most vulnerable regions in the developing "New Europe," as well as to prepare industries and workers for the inevitable impact of a barrier-free common market. One aspect of the relationship between the North and South of the EC system which will be markedly affected by the frontier-free movement of people, goods and capital, and which has been uncritically treated in the scholarship of the EC's 1992 project relative to many other issues, is the increasing impact of consumer culture on many of the peripheral regions of Greece, Spain and Portugal. The following chapter explores some of the ways the seemingly traditional southern European regions, acting as hosts to tourists and as sources of migratory labor for the EC core, may be affected by the increasingly important role of consumer culture in the definition of local Mediterranean culture. This process, in turn, may strengthen and reinforce the peripheral nature of these regions and states within an EC attempting to integrate.

An anthropological focus on culture is important here. Anthropologists have long thought of the Mediterranean countries as sharing many cultural characteristics. As Pitkin (1963) has suggested, among these are nuclear family structure and orientation; the ideological importance of urban life; an emphasis on maritime trade and commerce; continuous human movements; devaluation of agricultural work and life on the land, as well as of manual labor in general; a lack of local industry; marked status differential according to sex and age, wherein males dominate females, and older siblings are privileged vis-a-vis younger kin; an emphasis on recruitment of personnel along kin lines; personalistic decision-making; a marked differentiation between religious practices of the elite and those in other social strata; and an education system which functions to maintain socially separated classes (see also Arensberg 1963; Blok 1972; Braudel 1972; Goody 1969; Kenny and Kertzer 1983; Pitt-Rivers 1963). Recently, economic reliance on tourism and on migrant remittances to support changing consumption needs and wants has become an important and visible feature of Mediterranean life (for example, see Costa 1988b; Kenny 1972; Rhoades 1978, 1980).

The people of Northern Europe define the southern rim as "other" in many ways. Most notably for the purposes of this chapter, many Northerners see the Mediterranean as a repository of the "quaint" and "exotic" and as a destination renowned for its fun, sun, different culture, and lifestyle. This expectation of "otherness" is further realized through the deliberate efforts of the Mediterranean tourist vendors themselves, cooperating to create an "exotic" experience, and contributing to the perception of cultural peripherality, reminiscent of Turner and Ashe's (1975) "pleasure periphery."

The general similarities among Spain, Greece and Portugal are emphasized in this chapter because of salient cultural convergence. This should not be taken to imply, however, that significant cultural *differences* are lacking as we compare and contrast these countries. Clearly, each nation has distinct areas of culture based on historical background and development. However, for the purposes of this chapter, and because it is these similarities which are most essential to the understanding of the impact of consumer culture within the realm of tourism and migration, I have focused on the cultural similarities rather than on these nation-based differences. It is important to note that some of the discussion which follows may also apply to other parts of the EC Mediterranean as well, particularly southern Italy and southern France.

Nation-states are products of complex forces. State building is not always an easy fit in a cultural sense. National borders and cultural boundaries often do not coincide. Many nations are subordinated to both other nations and the state, and may also be spread across a number of subnational and international borders. Witness, for example, the current civil unrest in Yugoslavia, a clear consequence of attempts to force diverse ethnic/cultural groups into co-existence within the same national borders. In the context of a unifying EC and the formation of a true common market, *national* borders seemingly become less significant, an issue addressed by a number of authors in this volume. Nonetheless, most data on consumer culture are currently collected on a national basis and are presented here in that form.

One of the cultural convergences shared by Greece, Spain and Portugal which may be intensified in the next few years is the rise of mass consumer culture. Membership in the EC has facilitated the movement across national boundaries of individuals who serve as culture change agents (European Communities – Commission 1990; Scappini 1990). As a result, these new EC members are experiencing rapid change in material culture and connected consumption ideologies. These changes will accelerate as the measures involving the unrestricted movement of people and goods come into effect. Overall, the Mediterranean is being increasingly integrated into the consumption repertoire of the rest of Western Europe. This repertoire includes styles of clothing, music, household furnishings, cars, and entertainment goods and services. One of the means by which these changes in consumption behavior are precipitated is through emulation of the specific culture change agents of tourists and circulating migrants. The process is illustrative of the avenues by which international political, economic and social behaviors are transmitted from higher-level systems, such as the EC core, to local-level systems, exemplified here by parts of the Mediterranean periphery.

Mediterranean Peripherality and EC 1992

A number of economic factors contribute to the characterization of the Mediterranean as "periphery." These countries produce "relatively labour intensive products" (Viñals et al. 1990:146). In comparison with the rest of the EC, they have: low wages; lower overall GDPs; relatively greater emphases on tourism and other services; a greater reliance on agriculture; smaller and less efficient, family-based firms; high rates of unemployment and underemployment; and widening trade deficits with increasing emphasis on imports (*Daily Labor Report* 22 June 1990;

Ermisch 1991; Tovias 1990). All of these are classic characteristics associated with underdeveloped regions.

In terms of consumption behavior, the demand for imports has increased rapidly over the last decade, notably for electronics, transport equipment, clothing and textiles, and leather (Viñals et al. 1990). These shifting consumption patterns have been fuelled by the dismantling of protective government tariffs and other trade barriers in the process of accession to the EC. The removal of "remaining protectionism" is a process that will broaden and accelerate with 1992 integration.

The accession to full membership in the EC has generally been labelled as a "shock" to Mediterranean countries undergoing this process during the last decade; the drastic changes – such as democratization, intensification in investment, and increasing tourism – resulting from membership may be further compounded by the EC 1992 project. According to Emerson and Portes (1990: xix), for example, the main question at hand is: can "the relatively weak economies of the new, geographically peripheral Member States withstand the double shock of accession and completion of the Single Market?" (see also Buchan 1990).

The dramatic nature of the changes associated with these events is best understood in the context of a long history of national protectionism. It is the removal of those protectionist barriers which serves as the greatest blow to the peoples who must function in those economies. The protectionism itself has been the product and project of the public sector, which, in each country, is now faced with the need for reorientation, redefinition and re-alignment with the rapidly accelerating private sector. Theorists seem to agree that "it is in this domain that the integration shock will be felt most severely" (Rodrik 1990: 355; see also de Macedo 1990; Katseli 1990; Viñals et al. 1990).

Anthropology and Consumption

Anthropological perspectives contribute to a greater understanding of changes in consumer behavior associated with EC membership and integration. Anthropologists have typically considered material culture – objects, possessions, things – to carry meanings. "It is standard ethnographic practice to assume that all material possessions carry social meanings and to concentrate a main part of cultural analysis upon their use as communicators" (Douglas and Isherwood 1979:59). In the context of changing consumption patterns in the Mediterranean EC, conspicuously displayed material possessions emphasize prestige associated with cultural categories of "foreign" and "modern," counterpoised against Mediterranean identification. Thus, members of the Mediterranean periphery use consumer goods to communicate their affiliation with the EC core.

Some theorists have described societies in which conspicuous consumption is a pervasive cultural value; "consumer culture" is defined as "culture in which the majority of consumers avidly desire (and some noticeable portion pursue, acquire, and display) goods and services that are valued for non-utilitarian reasons such as status-seeking, envy-provocation, and novelty seeking" (Belk 1988a:105). Consumer culture has spread throughout the Mediterranean periphery. Like their fellow Europeans to the North, Spaniards, Greeks and Portuguese increasingly value consumer goods not so much for their utility as for the social statements made by virtue of possessing and displaying the goods (Costa 1988a; Kenny 1972; Rhoades 1978). The desired goods, e.g., household appliances, certain items of clothing, stereos, radios and television sets, are not locally made, however. They come from the EC industrialized core. Capital thus leaves the local area in a process which contributes to the peripheralization of the Mediterranean while on the surface serves to make Mediterranean peoples *look more* like inhabitants of the EC core. The consumption of these products represents Mediterranean desires to be similar to the core, while the very process itself further contributes to Mediterranean peripherality and dissimilarity with the core. As barriers to the movement of goods and people fall in the wake of EC economic integration, it is likely that peripheralization will accelerate.

In Belk's (1988b) analysis, possessions are everywhere considered to be a representation of self. Following William James, who claims "a man's Self is the sum total of all that he CAN call his" (1890:291), Belk indicates "we are the sum of our possessions" (1988b:139). Belk draws on relevant evidence and theory from psychology, anthropology, sociology, and consumer behavior to conclude that the definition of self through possessions:

may be the most basic and powerful fact of consumer behavior. . . . It seems an inescapable fact of modern life that we learn, define, and remind ourselves of who we are by our possessions. . . . we seek to express ourselves through possessions and use material possessions to seek happiness, remind ourselves of experiences, accomplishments, and other people in our lives, and even create a sense of immortality after death (1988b: 160; see also Schultz et al. 1989).

Implicit in this discussion of the spread of consumer culture is comparison of self to others; it is particularly in this context that the roles of the two culture change agents I focus upon – the migrant and the tourist – become salient. One of the primary ways in which the transmission of consumer culture in the Mediterranean EC occurs is through the comparison of self, possessions and constructed self-identity to the behaviors, attitudes and possessed goods of these culture change agents. Emulation of these agents is a central part of changing consumption ideologies involving altered evaluations and perceptions regarding the acquisition and consumption of goods.

While is it likely that, in general, EC 1992 integration will *not* lead to overall cultural homogenization among EC members (Cutler 1990), exceptions to this generalization have been and will be found, specifically in the homogenizing process manifest in the spread of consumer culture. It may be, in fact, that the only "Euro-culture" which will develop in the EC of the future will be a "Euro-consumer culture" of some dimensions. The spread of consumer culture, leading to specific areas of cultural homogeneity, is indicative of "cultural porosity," where "openness and tolerance" exist as two cultures collide, with some elements moving freely between them (Buck-Morss 1987: 223). This "porosity in the boundaries between cultures" (Buck-Morss 1987: 223) is manifest in the diffusion of consumer culture ideology and consumer goods from more central EC countries to the Mediterranean periphery.

Close analysis of the rise and spread of consumer culture in Europe indicates it was accepted and "achieved" by different individuals and social groups throughout Europe at various points in time (see Braudel 1981; Campbell 1987; Costa 1990; McCracken 1988; McKendrick et al. 1982; Mukerji 1983; Williams 1981). With respect to the current consumption situation in Spain, Portugal and Greece in the context of the EC, it is clear that both "acceptability," through adoption of an appropriate consumption ideology, and "achievability," through the availability of adequate productive means to finance consumption expenditures, are critical in the evolution of consumer culture. It is primarily through integration and intimate interaction with the other EC countries that both of these prerequisites – acceptability and achievability – have been obtained. Thus, EC accession has meant both the freer flow of goods for consumption *and* of human labor to finance that consumption (*Daily Labor Report* 22 June 1990; Morais 1988). It is important to realize however, that the spread of consumer culture from the EC core to its periphery maintains the status quo; the emphasis on consumption without adequate local economic development to fund that consumption peripheralizes the Mediterranean even more (Buchan 1990).

In general, it is clear that an emphasis on consumption and new ideas and beliefs surrounding specific material goods is an important social phenomenon which often precipitates sociocultural change (Bar-Haim 1987; Belk 1988a; Belk and Zhou 1986; Bodley 1976; S. Davis 1977; Davis and Mathews 1977). Thus, as people and goods flow more rapidly and easily across national borders in the context of a unified EC, changing consumption patterns in Spain, Greece and Portugal and on-going peripheralization will continue.

Interpersonal Relations

Interpersonal relations are clearly an important factor in the diffusion of new ideas, beliefs, goods and behaviors. Receptivity to new behaviors has been shown to be facilitated when the agent of change – the bearer and exhibitor of these new behaviors – is known well to the potential adoptee. Such acquaintance "serves as a differentiating factor in variability of consumer culture acquisition, to the extent that those with numerous and intimate contacts . . . are more amenable to changes associated with expanded consumption" (Costa 1989: 239). The inhabitants of both rural and urban areas of Spain, Greece and Portugal experience frequent, close interactions with bearers of consumer culture in the form of returning migrants and tourists. While other consumption role models such as media personalities are also very important, and may increase in importance in the future, I focus in this chapter specifically on transmission of consumer culture through two agencies which have represented the most direct and immediate forms of contact between the residents of Mediterranean Europe and the rest of the EC.

A crucial factor in the configuration of consumer culture is the *meaning* possessions acquire in the context of interpersonal relations. As discussed above, consumption objects carry meanings which convey attributes of wealth, age, prestige, gender, education level, and other social statuses in consumer cultures (see especially Belk 1988b). In the context of the spread of consumer culture, this cultural significance of consumer goods is altered, so that the attribution of happiness and prestige to the possessors of goods – the more, the better, *and* the more expensive, the better – becomes a core part of the consumption ideology. McCracken describes the way in which "meaning transfer" occurs from culturally constituted world, to good, to consumer (1988); the process involves attribution and ritual. The qualities attributed to specific goods become the qualities attributed to the possessors, and vice versa, so that object and person share meaning (Baudrillard 1968, 1970; Belk 1982, 1985; Hirschman 1981; Levy 1978; Solomon 1983).

In elaboration of the role of comparison and emulation, Belk and

Zhou (1986) describe several points of reference utilized by mainland Chinese in their comparisons of self to other in the spread of consumer culture; these referents include tourists, other Chinese and Asian cultures, and media lifestyles. In the Mediterranean EC, similar referents are important; the known possessors of favored objects have been largely returning migrants and tourists (see Costa 1988b; Gmelch 1980; Kenny 1972). Tourism is a vital and growing part of the economies of each country, and migration is a systemically integrated part of these Mediterranean countries; returning and/or circulating migrants are a critical point for comparison.

Migrants

Friedl delineated the important role of migrants in the transmission of urban-based ideologies and behaviors to rural communities through a process which she referred to as "lagging emulation" (1964; see also Friedl 1959). Migrating kin become "prestige models" (Friedl 1964: 571) through whom "knowledge about new goods and services" is acquired (Costa 1989: 242). Gmelch (1979, 1980) has described the critical role of returning migrants in the spread of diverse ideologies and non-local goods. Changes in migrants' consumption behaviors generally occur first in the migrant point of destination. When the migrant returns to the local arena, the point of origin, s/he exhibits this new behavior and becomes a role model for those who have never undertaken migration themselves. The migrant also becomes the purveyor of objects produced elsewhere, transmitted directly into the local consumption arena through gifting behavior and/or through the migrants' personal use of the goods. The local arena is altered significantly both in terms of consumption behaviors and ideologies and in productive activities, as the local socioeconomic system reconfigures in response (see, for example, Costa 1988a, 1988c). The alterations serve to maintain the peripheral position of the region. The consumption is of goods produced elsewhere, admired for their carried meaning of "modern," "European," and "non-Mediterranean." The production undertaken to fuel the consumption involves either migration or employment in a local economic sector, which caters to expanding needs for consumer goods and services both on the part of tourists and of local inhabitants exhibiting changed consumption behaviors. In either case, the productive activities reinforce peripherality.

The returning migrant becomes a visible, accessible and admired role model:

The returnee is a living demonstration to young adults in the community that it is possible to go abroad, see a part of the world, obtain a better paying job, save, and return to the homeland, reunited with family and friends and with enough capital to achieve a comfortable standard of living (Gmelch 1980:153).

In such instances, stimuli to production and consumption coincide – youth, those most amenable to culture change, desire the objects and lifestyles they see exhibited by returning migrants. As Kenny indicates, the migrant's "triumphant return and ostentatious generosity incite the youth of the village to emulate his example" (1972; as quoted in Gmelch 1980:153). However, generally lacking the productive means to emulate the migrants, the would-be emulators search for new productive opportunities, often through migrating themselves, but also through new local opportunities in tourism, an economic development which similarly stimulates changes in local consumption behavior.

Several factors must be considered in this process of emulation. Bovenkerk (1974) has shown that the rate of culture change stimulated by migrants increases with the frequency and overall number of contacts between migrants and non-migrants. Over the last generations, Mediterranean EC inhabitants have engaged in a very specific type of migration pattern: they became temporary guestworkers in the central EC countries, a condition under which they returned periodically to their home villages for days or weeks, sometimes months, then re-engaged in the migration pattern. This circulating migratory behavior thus conforms to Bovenkerk's conditions for rapid migrant-induced culture change, as the migrant/non-migrant contacts are both frequent and numerous. It is anticipated that this type of migration pattern may very well expand in the context of EC unification, given lowered barriers to labor movements (although Southern Europeans may face increased competition in the sale of their labor from Central and Eastern Europeans). With respect specifically to Spain, Portugal, Greece, Ireland and southern Italy, for example, it has been concluded

these regions are placed at an even greater disadvantage because of the boost given to trade by the opening of borders. . . . If nothing were done to counter this, the number of unemployed would increase still further in these regions and young people would migrate in even greater numbers to distant industrial cities (European Communities – Commission 1990).

A second important factor to consider in the process of emulation is the specific type of change in consumption patterns. Keyfitz indicates a "standard package" of desired goods can be said to exist on a global basis, "including a home, automobile, and the means to do some travelling; within the house must be electric lighting, a refrigerator, and a television set" (1982:661). Thus, the spread of consumer culture can be said to be rapid, pervasive, and an important factor in acculturation. The changes in consumption behavior in the Mediterranean EC are found in numerous object categories: food, clothing, furnishings, homes, entertainment and transportation. For example, the following consumption aspirations were observed in a rural Greek household:

> The members of an upwardly mobile, status-conscious household . . . own or attempt to acquire the following: a refrigerator; a television set; hot water heater and shower facility; a washing machine; various small appliances such as a clock, blender, hand mixer, can opener; new furnishings for the parlor, complete with store-bought tablecloths, doilies and nicknacks (such furnishings include a dining room set, a couch, one or two cupboards, a sideboard, and extra chairs, as well as lamps, paintings or prints; and rugs); new industrially manufactured Western-style clothing and accessories; expensive store-bought candies, pastries, alcoholic beverages, and delicacies; a camera. Most homes already have radios. Travel to visit relatives in urban areas is increasingly common. . . . residents frequent bars, discotheques and restaurants. . . . the possession of cars is highly desired (Costa 1989: 241).

Berss claims "The 9.5 million inhabitants of Greece want a Western-style standard of living – cars, refrigerators, leisure – but Greece is still a pre-industrial economy" (1984:50), and phrases such as "overheated" demand (D. Smith 1989) and "a flood of consumer goods" (Hurst 1987) are typically used to describe the accelerating changes in consumer culture in the EC Periphery since accession.

An important venue for consumption change is in the home display of objects acquired through migration or migrant remittances. For instance, Rhoades described a typical Spanish returned migrant's home as "lavishly furnished and decorated with virtually everything modern mass consumer markets offer. It is no exaggeration to define the situation as `conspicuous consumption run amok'" (1978; see also Rhoades 1980). Such displays can extend to the structure of the building itself. Aschenbrenner describes similar behavior in rural Greece, where:

> Even people in older houses undertake a variety of improvements such as installing ceilings, replacing deteriorating doors and windows, building additions with kitchens and flush toilets, and paving yards and walkways. Electricity now brought appliances such as refrigerators, kitchen ranges with

ovens, and automatic washers. Most kitchens now have sinks with piped-in water, cupboards and counters (1986: 113).

Gmelch, looking at the effects of return migration on a cross-cultural basis indicated similarly that "it is not uncommon for better-off migrants to build lavish, well-appointed structures. The intent appears to be as much to show off to one's neighbors as to live comfortably" (1980: 149). In the Mediterranean EC, the house and its objects "represent the image the family and individual wish to present to the outside world" (Costa 1988b: 562). This image is enhanced through objects provided by migrating kin; these objects "have a value which derives both from the migration process and from the relative prestige attached to foreign-made items" (Costa 1988b: 565). In the Mediterranean economies, heretofore characterized by a relative lack of local economic development, migration has been an important avenue to upward social mobility. The consumer goods acquired as part of the migration process represent social success and prestige. Through the social process of emulation of admired others, consumer culture is spread.

Tourists

Tourists are a second agent of change important in the spread and adoption of consumer culture. The impact of tourism on local areas has been studied from many perspectives (e.g., Aerni 1972; Belk and Costa n.d.; Canan and Hennessy 1989; Cohen 1978, 1984; de Kadt 1979; Pearce 1982; Rossel 1988; V. Smith 1989; Turner and Ashe 1975; Urry 1990). Regardless of whether they are deemed to be largely beneficial or detrimental to the local community, tourists are facilitators of culture change, particularly through the spread of new ideas, beliefs, attitudes and behaviors about/toward material goods. As with the returning migrant, the tourist moves directly into the local sphere, exemplifying new behaviors and material culture, bequeathing gifts of objects and/or cash to buy objects. The Mediterranean-bound tourist is typically resident in another EC society or the United States, participating in the "consumption" of the touristic experience, the Mediterranean country, its people, its objects and its lifestyles (see, for example, *The Economist* 2 June 1990; Hope 1991; *Institutional Investor* May 1990). It is "precisely those Mediterranean countries that compose the most easily accessible `pleasure periphery' for north European tourists" (Buck-Morss 1987: 201; see also Turner and Ashe 1975). In the context of this touristic experience, two radical changes occur: the commoditization of the host culture (Greenwood 1977), and the transformation of local consumption aspirations. Tourists:

> are walking advertisements for commodity culture. Their very presence promotes Minolta cameras, Levi jeans, Nivea cream, Coca Cola, as agents of what might be called `trademark imperialism.' The images they provide the villagers, reinforced by television advertisements, appear to be compelling the village into `modernity' less by force than by seduction (Buck-Morss 1987: 225).

Like the circulating migrant, the EC-based tourist exemplifies, through behavior and possessed goods, the wealth and power of the core EC countries. In the consumption sphere, this power is ability "to name the objects of desire" (Buck-Morss 1987: 225). Thus, "families now `need' consumer items – cassettes, imported cigarettes, skin cream, blue jeans, cameras, beach equipment – that they never thought of owning and *this is the result of mass tourism*" (Buck-Morss 1987: 224; emphasis added).

Thus, like the migrant, the tourist becomes the role model, the possessor of desired objects, a person to be emulated in terms of consumption behavior. While the Mediterranean EC resident may not wish to become entirely like the tourist, s/he desires the accoutrements of consumer culture. The hegemonic consumer culture of the EC center strongly affects the layers of cultural meaning attached to specific goods; these objects come to represent prestige, social mobility, modernity, and "the good life."

Conclusions

Certain factors appear to be critical in the spread of consumer culture in the EC Mediterranean countries of Greece, Spain and Portugal. First, it is important to view these three countries as similar to one another and as occupying nearly identical positions culturally, politically and economically vis-a-vis the core EC countries. Greece, Spain and Portugal are all recent members of the EC; this fact in itself is suggestive of their peripheral position in the EC world economy, both historically and in current political-economic status. As peripheral regions, these countries are characterized by two important human movements – the circulating flow of labor migrants, and the seasonal, circular visitations of tourists seeking the warm Mediterranean climate and the cultural "quaintness" of Mediterranean villages. It is specifically the frequency and number of contacts between the residents of local areas and these

institutional environment in which he is embedded. . . . it is crucially important to examine more systematically the types of relationships that exist between the farm . . . and various external structures (Long et al. 1986: 3).

I argue that farmers' relationships to their representatives, to the agroindustrial complex, and to the state are responsible for the possibly distinct reactions that will be displayed by olive growers on the one hand and dairy farmers on the other, considered as a consequence of policy changes taken under the 1992 and GATT headings. These reactions will be apparent in the ways farmers decide what their strategies will be and in the changes carried out with respect to the management of labor processes.

Farmers and the Intermediate Structures (I): Olive Growing in Andalusia

Olive growing is a major agrarian activity in Andalusia in the South of Spain and the analysis of the social and political organization of this sector presents an interesting departure from the mainstream of studies on Andalusian rural life, in which either Andalusian community culture is the central point of attention or the realities of changes in rural activity disappear in broadly sketched modernization theories.[2] Almost 400,000 families derive part or all of their income from the production of olives (50% as owners of trees, the rest as laborers).[3] Connected with the production of olives is an important field of agroindustrial activity: mills that process olives, refineries that prepare a large part of the oil for marketing on the Spanish market and abroad, industries that manufacture pressing systems and other equipment used in the mills and the refineries. Furthermore, during this century the Spanish state has intervened in the olive oil sector almost continually (though with varying degrees of intensity). Finally, the production of olives and olive oil in Spain suffer from problems that are crucial to the future of this product. These problems, that have to do with production costs and quality, have been recognized during the 1980s and are debated as we approach the final rounds of decision making on liberalization in 1992. In this section I review the types of farm management among olive growers and the ways they are integrated into the wider socio-economic setting. By connecting both aspects I evaluate the ways in which the pressures emanating from liberalization will influence the work of local olive growers.

The analysis in the next few pages is based on two periods of fieldwork in the Andalusian provinces of Jaén and Córdoba, the key areas of olive growing and production of olive oil in the world. In Jaen research was focused on olive growers living in a village at the foot of the Sierra de Cazorla. I studied the organization of their work, the strategies they followed, and their dealings with the local cooperative olive mill.[4] Farmers were depicted as decision makers, organizing their activities based on their own goals, thereby making use of the chances created by state policies. The second period of fieldwork was no longer centered on the local level, yet research dealt with farmers' organizations, cooperatives, and associations of cooperatives. It took place in the provinces of Cordoba and Jaen. I studied organizations of farmers (mainly olive growers), conducted a survey of olive oil mills, and interviewed state officials in both provinces.[5] The idea researched was that some farmers organize themselves to actively influence state policies in their own favor. In the process they also influence the effect those policies have on agricultural development.

Styles of Farm Management

Since the 1960s olive growing has undergone a number of fundamental changes. State initiated programs introduced fertilizers, tractors, irrigation, plague control, new pruning techniques, and a substantial amount of knowledge that could be used to improve the production of olives. Nowadays a simple trip through the Andalusian countryside during the months of February to June will yield a very confusing picture of what olive growers actually do. Some farmers walk with their shovels from their village homes to their fields, while others use a landrover to get to their fields. Some use irrigation equipment, others do not. Many use tractors to work the land, some do not. Some perform extensive rounds of plague control, others a few, some none. There exists, in short, a great variety of ways to grow olives.[6] Still, the three main styles of farm management in olive growing are based on qualitative production per hectare (optimal), cost minimization (cost-effective), and productive tasks (minimal).[7]

Some olive growers have incorporated most innovations and use these inputs in such a way that yield per hectare is maximized. These *optimal* farmers, who can be found among both small and large-scale growers, distinguish themselves from others by claiming to be better olive growers since they take care that their groves yield many olives of good quality. To reach this goal, they supervise the work done with tractors, they control the ways their trees are pruned and fertilized, they put up irrigation facilities where possible, and they control all the plagues that could damage the crops. Harvest procedures are carried out with care in order not to damage the trees and the olives. Each day the olives are transported to the mills, where they are processed directly and will yield high quality oil. These optimal farmers have the highest costs per hectare, but they are recompensed by very high yields.

Cost-effective farmers manage their farms with the objective of minimizing the cost per hectare. They are not principally concerned with the yields, but they keep a sharp eye on the balance between cost and yield. This is best seen from their dealings with plague control. Instead of fighting all the possibly damaging plagues they only use chemicals against two of the most common plagues and diminish the number of rounds they have their laborers perform. Besides, they try to reduce tractor time by plowing not as deep as optimal farmers do. With respect to the harvest these farmers are only interested in speed: the less time needed, the cheaper it is. Though yields per hectare are significantly lower than those of the optimal farmers, cost-effective farmers seek scale-enlargement as a means of increasing their incomes. Most of them are medium and large-scale growers.

The objectives of *minimal* farmers are the maximization of output and the minimization of costs. These people are mostly small-scale farmers, whose holdings of less than 10 hectares dominate aggregate production to up to 80% (Hoogveld and Jurjus 1990). They follow this minimalist strategy to obtain an optimal income with which to support their families. To achieve this they use fertilizer and, if necessary, they hire tractors to work the land, but they perform other tasks themselves in order to save labor costs and to cut back on the expenditures for plague control. Only when they establish that a certain plague is damaging their crops do they perform a round of spraying pesticides. In their eyes plague control does not contribute to increased production and is not worth its while. Furthermore, many small-scale olive growers are part-time farmers. They concentrate their agricultural activities in the afternoons and in the weekends. Time constraints prevent them from monitoring the development of their holdings on a day-to-day basis, which is necessary for optimal plague control and fertilizing. They are not concerned with the quality of their olives. This is also apparent from the harvest procedure. Because of the limited input of family labor a long harvesting period results. During these weeks or months picked olives remain in the fields for days, packed in plastic sacks. Once in a while the olives are transported to the mill, where they are dumped on a great pile of low quality olives that will yield non-consumable olive oil. Most farmers are not concerned with this, since prices for olive oil in Spain are not based on quality, but on acidity. This implies that differences between high and low quality oil are insufficient incentive to mill managers to penalize farmers who deliver bad olives. Resulting prices for olives are the same for optimal, cost-effective, and minimal farmers.

Intermediate Structures

As reviewed above, the CAP with regard to olive oil is characterized by a price policy, an intervention policy, and the payment of producer aid, to which we must add a number of regulations that supply subsidies to modernizing investments in olive oil mills and programs that back up farmers' attempts to set up cooperative marketing organizations (Hoogveld and Jurjus 1990). Most productive decisions of the farmers are not influenced directly by these instruments. Farmers' choices respond to incentives and constraints created by their cooperatives, their professional organizations, the agribusinesses, and the government. In short, intermediate structures shape CAP regulations into incentives and constraints with which farmers are confronted.

Prices for olive oil, for instance, are not a direct concern for olive growers. Though the majority of the farmers are familiar with the prices the EC sets for olive oil, their major concern is for the prices they can get for their olives. These are not established by the EC but by the mill management. Prices thus also depend on the way the cooperative or private mill is run. In the olive sector, then, the level of the oil mills is important because it aggregates productive activities of many farmers into the supply of an amount of olive oil sold by the cooperative's board (mostly president and manager). It is at this level that CAP regulations make a difference. Official EC policy is to offer far better intervention prices for top quality olive oil than are paid for regular or bad quality. This implies that the mill managers and presidents of the cooperatives are nowadays aware of the possibilities of increasing their results by enhancing the quality of their oil through modernizing the machines and processing procedures in the mills (Hoogveld and Jurjus 1990).

Even producer aid, an income subsidy set and paid by the European Commission to olive growers, is disbursed through specialized producer organizations. Their constitution in Andalusia was dominated by existing professional farmers' groups. As many cooperative presidents were members of these farmers' organizations, many links resulted between the specialized producer organizations on the one hand and the cooperatives and farmers' associations on the other. At this "supra-farmer" level, dominated by the representatives of the Andalusian agrarian elite, a consensus grew during the 1980s with regard to the strategy to follow: modernizing the olive mills to increase the quality of olive oil, while at the same time enhancing the farmers' grip on marketing by setting up cooperative sales organizations. This modernizing strategy entails four key issues farmers are confronted with. First, farmers have to decide whether or not to consent to risk investing in new milling equipment. Second, they are pressed to change their working strategies from minimal to optimal. Third, they are asked to support their cooperative presidents in efforts to work together with other cooperatives. Finally, they are confronted with the possibility of joining in a national union of olive growers, conforming to a modernizing strategy. Deciding these four issues is not easy. Three obstacles exist that have confused the issues and hampered execution of the modernization strategy: market structure, cooperative structure, and state-sector relationships.

The first obstacle to modernization was that members of the boards of cooperative oil mills realized they could sell their oil to only a few industrial companies that completely dominated the market. These tendencies were already visible during the 1960s (López Ontiveros 1978). By 1970 eight firms managed to control more than 70% of the market for olive oil in Spain, and by the end of the 1980s this number had decreased to five firms. As these firms have interests not only in olive oil but in other vegetable oils as well, the strategies of most of them are geared towards selling low priced, competitive olive oil. Against these few firms more than 3000 olive oil mills are unable to make a significant impact on the price of the oil. As a consequence, the dominant marketing conglomerates have kept prices for quality oil down relative to standard quality. Mill leaders have therefore been unable to guarantee returns on modernizing investments to their members. This has led to strains in the relations between mill managers and members. Especially in the 1970s and 1980s, as prices for inputs and labor kept rising and the government suppressed full compensation for the producers, the majority of olive growers were only interested in the price they could get from the mill. Furthermore, this gave rise to a sharp competition between the mills for suppliers.[8] This competition is diminishing the chances of setting up stable groups of cooperatives that make an attempt at marketing their own oil and forcing the commercial firms to pay better prices. The oligopsonic market structure has thus so far thwarted efforts to establish a firm modernizing drive based on new mills and collective marketing arrangements.

The second obstacle continues in this line. The membership link between cooperative mills and olive growers is easily severed in Andalusia. This has to do with the historical development cooperatives have undergone. Most Andalusian cooperative oil mills were constituted after the Civil War (1936-39) in an attempt by the state to pacify relationships between elite farmers and the peasantry (Sevilla Guzmán 1979). During the 1950s and 1960s cooperative mills pushed many private mills out of business. As most of these private mills were owned by elite farmers themselves, they tried to hold on to their power by becoming the presidents of the cooperatives. In the role of presidents they were able to dominate the sale of large amounts of oil, which came to be the most important task of the cooperatives. Most olive growers, though, were not interested in a cooperative endeavor; their only interest was a secured channel to sell their olives. In the course of time the majority of cooperatives did not develop alternative services, like cooperative buying of fertilizer, that would have strengthened the ties between mill and members. Without these selective incentives the great majority of minimal farmers and cost-effective farmers today feel free to choose the mills that offer them optimal results. It is clear from the discussion on management styles, that cost-effective and minimal farmers will choose those mills that do not make any demands with respect to plague control and harvest procedures.[9]

Finally, an important obstacle is the strained relationship between the farmers' organizations and the Spanish government. During the 1980s the agrarian elite in Andalusia (in coalition with farmers' organizations around the country)[10] were involved in a struggle with the socialist government over the establishment of a corporatist form of state-sector relationships. This system of interest representation would have been used to present the models of modernization and development popular among both the elite and the professional medium-sized farmers, and to coordinate state expenditure and legislative activity with the goals the farmers' organizations had set for the agrarian sector. Instead, the socialist government has kept the farm groups at a distance, trying to constitute a socialist organization of farmers. This government strategy has thwarted initiatives of the organized olive growers in Andalusia to set up collective arrangements to deal with the problems of modernization and marketing. The objective of the leaders was to use CAP regulations on producer aid to establish a national union of producer organizations that would handle all matters regarding the disbursement of the producer aid. This union would be entitled to use a small percentage of this aid for promotion, research, education and other activities that would promote the quality of olive oil. The administrative framework of this union could also be used for the constitution of necessary collective arrangements. This would entail the coordination of supplies to mills, collective marketing, modernization research, and improvement procedures. However, the Minister of Agriculture of Spain denied full recognition and effective responsibility to this union. This implied that no financial resources could be assembled for modernizing the sector.

The intermediate structures that connect olive growers in Spain to the wider economic and political environment are characterized by two relationships. One is the conflict between farmers' organizations and cooperatives with both commercial firms and the state, and the other is the resulting problematic link between the modernization strategy of the olive sector leaders and the majority of the growers themselves. CAP-induced activities take place on or above the mill level and are dominated by the modernization strategy followed by the elite. This strategy appears to be obstructed by oligopsonic marketing firms and inter-mill competition as a result of the management styles of the majority of the farmers. The uncooperative position of the state has, until the end of 1990, prevented olive growers from setting up a national union of regional organizations of growers, which would have created the administrative framework needed to overcome the problems of forming cooperative marketing groups and end the competition between cooperatives, factors severely hampering the strategy of the olive growing elite to react to the more liberal changes already introduced within the CAP in the last couple of years.

Farmers and the Intermediate Structures (II): Dairy Farming in the Netherlands

The significant changes which Dutch farmers have experienced since the 1960s highlight the prominent role of intermediate structures in Dutch dairy farming, a role completely different from the one in Spain.[11] In 1960 more than 180,000 dairy farmers existed in the Netherlands, which number had decreased to 60,000 by 1984. At the same time, the number of cattle increased from 1.6 to 2.5 million, implying a rise of almost 400% to a mean of 42 cows on each farm. The implied scale enlargement among the Dutch dairy farms was accompanied by a change in the way the farmers organized their productive activities. In the first place, the mechanization of dairying made it possible for farmers to keep greater numbers of cattle without resorting to hiring labor. In the second place, new methods were introduced in the production of maize and silage. In the third place, cow cubicle sheds and large deep-cooling milk tanks were innovations enabling farmers to rationalize tending cows and transporting milk to the milk factories (Maas and Kramer 1986: 7).

Styles of Farm Management

Mechanization of milking, feeding, and the production of raw fodder has enabled dairy farmers to increase their stock of cattle. More important, however, farmers in the Dutch dairy sector have become incorporated into a network of agents and have been compelled to take decisions with respect to the degree of interaction they will undertake with these agents. As in most agricultural sectors, the farmers are no longer left to themselves, but they are bombarded with technical advice, with knowledge on inputs, with innovations, with regulations, and with financial services. As Bolhuis and Van der Ploeg have convincingly demonstrated in their study on Italian dairy farmers (1985), the networks into which farmers have been incorporated create several distinct ways of organizing productive activities on the farm, correlated to distinct ways of handling the relationships with the external agents. Some follow the lines prescribed by government advice, follow the optimal use of fodder prescribed by agroindustrial firms, make regular use of veterinarians, have great need for capital from financial institutions and are highly integrated into input markets. These farmers specialize in milk production and they try to maximize economic results by striving for a high production of milk per cow combined with scale enlargement. They do this by implementing the methods and information made available by external agents. In recent Dutch literature on dairy farming these farmers are called forerunners (Van der Ploeg 1990). Others tend to keep all these influences at a distance, while striving to develop the milk yield of their cows by focusing on sound feeding practices and health. They maximize income without increasing the number of cows. These cow-farmers produce more of the fodder themselves and tend to be less integrated into markets for other inputs as well. Some double-goal farmers not only specialize in milk production but they also make cheese or sell their cows for meat (Maso 1986). This group of farmers relied less on outside information and more on their cattle raising experience instead.

Since 1984 dairy farmers have been confronted with milk quotas that have diminished their capacity to develop their holdings. As recent research has demonstrated (Van der Ploeg and Ettema 1990), different styles of management give rise to different reactive strategies and development chances. The forerunners develop their farms by intensifying and scale-enlargement, but since 1984 this is no longer possible without extra quotas. Thus, these optimal farmers often try to buy quotas on the open market. Other farmers, like double-goal farmers, can easily divert milk to their secondary activities like cheese production or intensify raising cattle for meat. Their development potential is therefore larger. Quotas and their consequences currently provide the only example of CAP regulations directly influencing the strategies dairy farmers deploy to develop their holdings. But other influences of the CAP have been incorporated into such intermediate structures as the technological support network, the collective marketing arrangements, and the statutory organizations.

Intermediate Structures

Maso (1986) points to the process of incorporation Dutch dairy farmers have undergone since the Second World War and, especially, after 1970. He concludes that it is impossible to avoid the incorporation of the farmers into networks of agencies that tend to prescribe what farmers should do. In a first phase, dairy farmers were confronted with increasing labor costs, which they could no longer afford. This set off a period of increasing mechanization and a growth in the amount of external capital used by farmers. In a second phase, during the 1960s, pressures emanated from the dairy factories to lower the costs of milk processing. For the farmers this implied buying a milk tank that would make daily delivery to milk factories unnecessary and made possible the concentration of factories. As these milk tanks were very expensive, simultaneous pressures to enlarge the number of cows and, consequently, build new sheds arose. With the availability of cow-cubicle sheds farmers were in a position to enlarge their stock and mechanize milking and feeding procedures so as to keep labor costs down. To take advantage of this new technology farmers needed land redistribution and financing. Van der Ploeg (1991: 132-3) gives a very clear picture of the dairy farmers' position:

> [Within Dutch dairy farming] there exists a gigantic technological support network . . . in which institutional and economic interests, as well as political perspectives converge around and in a dominant technology-development. Such a technological support network . . . is very much capable of effectively exerting necessary influence. When the cow-cubicle stables emerged as a valid technological option interest subsidies, collateral funds and investment subsidies were invoked to make the factor capital as cheap as necessary to speed up the adoption of these stables. If the factors land and labor corresponded unsatisfactorily with this new model, for instance as a consequence of scattered strips of land, land consolidation was executed [my translation].

This quote illustrates the fact that the farmers are incorporated into a framework geared towards raising the productivity of labor, land, and cattle. Though several styles of management are possible within this framework, fundamental arrangements exist which provide Dutch dairy farmers with the means to maintain their incomes. Apart from the above mentioned technological support networks, these arrangements are characterized by collective marketing organizations, state-backed quality control programs, and stable and close channels of policy coordination connecting the sector with the government. These three supports are still crucially missing in the Spanish case.

Collective marketing associations have come to dominate the Dutch dairy sector in the course of this century. In 1900 industrial dairy production was in the hands of more than 900 firms, of which 50% were cooperatives. By 1980 the total number of firms had decreased to 62, of which four controlled more than 65% of the market. More than 90% of productive capacity is now under cooperative control (Van Waarden 1985). The four very large firms, all unions of cooperatives, are the hallmark of collective organizations with respect to quality control, distribution of milk supplies, and marketing and research. By concentrating their small surplus funds farmers can have essential tasks performed which would usually be impossible for individual farmers. Product innovation and marketing are especially out of reach of any individual farmer. By setting up unions of cooperatives means were created to control marketing of dairy products and to provide farmers with larger shares of the added value.

During the decades after 1900 some dairy farmers solved the problems of the quality of the dairy products like milk and butter. For example, Van Waarden traces the need for collective regulating arrangements to two circumstances that loomed large in the Frisian dairy sector at the turn of the century. In the first place fierce competition between the factories for milk suppliers resulted from the need to maximize prices paid to their members and thus to increase efficiency by using economies of scale. "In the past, factories used to compete continually, luring farmers away from one another with a high advance on the milk price" (Van Waarden 1985: 199-200). This incentive also undermined the possibilities of a strong quality regime, since factories would be tempted to relinquish controls in order to attract as many suppliers as possible. In the second place, the lack of trust between the members, who knew nothing about management and marketing, and the directors of the cooperative, prompted interests among the farmers in an organization, controlled by them, that would monitor the management of their cooperative. Several authors stress the point that a crucial step in the successful constitution of collective arrangements was the constitution of farmers' organizations (Van Waarden 1985: 201-2, 216; Bolhuis 1990: 45). One of the successful attempts was made by the Frisians:

[The Frisian union] succeeded in getting the power to determine which farmer should supply which factory. Furthermore, the Frisian union and other regional associations prescribe bookkeeping techniques, require that the accounts of the firms are monitored by the association, and regulate investment of member firms (Van Waarden 1985: 200).

The state government and national polities in The Netherlands also support innovation. The state has executed programs of land consolidation, and has provided financial backing and farm modernization (Maso 1986). In this, government officials helped Dutch dairy farmers to apply for CAP funds. Furthermore, the state has followed up on the Frisian scheme for quality control and made it the responsibility of statutory bodies, in which government and farmers' representatives work together (*Centraal Orgaan Zuivelcontrole*). All dairy firms are forced to submit to quality controls by this agency, and the standards are written down in Dutch law (Bolhuis 1990: 50-1). The state has thus backed up by law many of the collective arrangements that provide dairy farmers with a strong position on the market. It has helped "village cooperatives to grow into large internationally oriented firms with their own quality services" (Bolhuis 1990: 53). Finally, Dutch farmers' representatives are by law allowed to occupy seats in such corporatist institutions as the *Landbouwschap* and the *Produktschap voor Zuivel*, where policy proposals concerning the farming community at large and the dairy farmers in particular are debated before political decision making takes place. This arrangement, in existence since the beginnings of the 1950s, has been very important in furthering the development of Dutch agriculture.

GATT, 1992, and Management Patterns
Among Olive Growers and Dairy Farmers

In the fall of 1991 and the first months of 1992 the Ministers of Agriculture of the Community discussed the far-reaching plans of Commissioner Ray MacSharry for the renewal of the CAP. His proposal for lowering prices and diminishing support partly paved the way towards conclusion of the Uruguay Round[12] and the implementation of 1992-regulations. The above analyzed case studies have made it clear that it is by way of the CAP and related intermediate structures that pressures for change will reach the local-level farmers. Changes will imply further liberalization of trade in agricultural products, combined with a reduction in support levels and a harmonization of agricultural food regulations throughout the Community.[13] Liberalization will result in a drop in protective tariffs and a cut-back on export subsidies. Though at this stage of writing it is not yet clear to what level these cutbacks will bring prices down, it can be foreseen that EC consumers will be confronted with lower priced products from outside the EC, while at the same time exporting firms will be forced to deal with the necessity of bringing their prices more in line with world market levels. This will imply a struggle between agroindustrial exporting firms and processing industries on the prices paid for the goods. Depending on the position of these processing industries, potentially lower prices will result in downward pressures on the prices paid to farmers. More directly, income support levels connected to production will be lowered, implying an additional loss of income on the part of farmers. Finally, harmonization of food regulations will be carried out and the role of state control over contents and quality of elaborated food products will subsequently be diminished. This will amplify the processing and marketing possibilities, making food cheaper by using qualitatively inferior products. The feeble position of specialized quality products that must rely on protected production circumstances, will be undercut.

In the case of olive growing the GATT proposals of the European Commission imply a reduction in support of more than one billion ECU. In practice this will mean that olive growers will receive less producer aid (which is a lump sum to support income) and that both cooperative and private oil mills will be forced to sell their oil on the market more often, instead of selling it to the intervention agencies of the EC. In comparing the intermediate structures in the olive oil and dairy sectors, it is clear that a crucial determinant of the responses of olive growers to the current pressures emanating from EC-level decision making is and will continue to be the absence of viable collective arrangements with respect to marketing and quality. As I elaborated above, a limited group of elite farmers, leading farm groups, and cooperative oil mills have recognized these problems during the 1980s and elaborated a strategy based on the development of collective marketing groups and the modernization of olive oil mills. This strategy was clearly inspired by existing CAP regulations. The problems they have encountered are remarkably similar to the ones experienced by, among others, Frisian dairy farmers at the turn of this century. In that period competition that existed between dairies threatened to undermine the care for the quality of milk and cheese, and some farmers took the initiative of setting up farmers' associations that could solve these problems by arranging collective structures that could be trusted by the farmers (Van Waarden 1985: 201).

The strategy formulated and partly implemented by the dominant elite in Andalusian olive growing, based on the constitution of an all encompassing union of collective marketing organizations, will be the instrument that will determine the changes that will take place among the olive growers. In their perspective, this strategy is the only way of confronting the dangers they perceive in the oligopsonic position of the multinational food concerns, the policies advocated by the socialist government, and the liberalization of market regulations in the wake of the GATT and 1992-negotiations. When support levels go down, food legislation is liberalized, and the market is opened up, multinationals compete for market shares by offering cheap products, as they are doing now in Spain (Hoogveld and Jurjus 1990). The farm group leaders may try to prevent prices from falling by organizing their own marketing channels through their cooperative structures, as happened in the Dutch dairy case where two giant cooperatives control almost 70% of the dairy sector. An important factor that has positively influenced the Dutch development, though, is as yet missing in the Andalusian case: constructive state backing and ready assistance in solving organizational and financial problems. In the years to come, therefore, the farm group leaders will press the government to intervene on behalf of unions of cooperatives and authorizing cooperatives to regulate the work of their farmers. I thus foresee considerable pressure emanating from the agrarian elite, as well as cooperative (and possibly private) mill managers, on the olive growers to adapt their farm work to the exigencies of quality production. The cost-effective and minimal farmers will especially have to be persuaded to change their management patterns. Whether this will succeed will also depend on whether these unions of cooperatives will prove to be stable organizations. If not, and if the multinational conglomerates retain their control over marketing, the strategy of the Andalusian elite is bound to fail, and the pressure will come to bear on the optimal farmers, who will be forced to turn into cost-effective or minimal farmers, thereby forsaking the goal of quality production. The role of the Spanish government will prove to be crucial in deciding which course will be taken.

In the Netherlands liberalization will not result in any pressures for change in the management patterns of dairy farmers. Though prices for milk are expected to decrease, the collective marketing facilities have the funds to develop new products and new strategies in order to keep up market shares and drive other less competitive producers out of the market. The common objective of Dutch dairy farmers to enhance productivity will no doubt be reinforced successfully, given the existence of a politically backed technological support network.

Conclusions

In this chapter I set out to argue that developments taking place on supranational levels influence courses of action taken by farmers on the local level, but that this influence is not determined by those supranational developments alone. Instead, these influences are mediated by the structures connecting local level actors with higher level decision makers. These intermediate structures ensure that political decisions made at the EC level to liberalize agricultural trade and diminish support for farmers are not disaggregated into uniform pressures on farmers throughout the EC. Distinct intermediate structures result in distinct pressures. These structures comprise socioeconomic and political linkages that process higher-level decisions into concrete pressures for change on farmers. Even then actual changes are not determined, since distinct management styles tend to produce different reactions.

Spanish olive growers are going through a period of uncertainties. Decisions with respect to "1992" and the GATT are becoming clear and the alternative consequences for their positions are being brought home to them by their representatives. Depending on the position the Spanish government will take with respect to the development strategy formulated by the Andalusian farming elite, the resulting pressures will either come to bear on cost-effective and minimal farmers to bring their ways of producing in line with the exigencies for top quality olive oil, or on the optimal farmers who, in that case, will have to seek ways of making production cheaper. Dutch dairy farmers, on the other hand, will be reinforced in their strategy of improving productivity, albeit that some styles of management will more easily be adapted to the strains of the quotas.

Studies of rural areas in the EC seem to be dominated on the one hand by social scientists focusing on policies for rural areas without due attention to farmers' behavior (see, e.g., Cloke 1990; Haney & Almas 1991), and on the other hand by anthropologists who, with few exceptions (see, e.g., Wilson 1989), describe the collective meanings among farmers and social interaction between them (see, e.g., Giordano 1987; Shutes 1987). As I see it, in both cases policy makers are at a loss as to the linkages that exist between their policies and the responses of farmers. A focus on intermediate structures should help to solve at least part of the remaining puzzles. I have stressed farmers' endeavors to organize themselves and their attempts to capture the benefits of the policies set up by the EC. It is in this process that farmers come to attach meanings to the EC and the CAP and develop norms on how best to operate their farms. The understanding of intermediate structures that make up the arenas where farmers and their representatives on the one hand and policy makers on the other hand meet, can also contribute to explaining sociocultural change in rural areas.

Future anthropological research in and of the EC could focus on the identification and analysis of the intermediate structures that appear to play an important role in the linkages between local developments and national or supranational influences. In this way anthropologists can contribute fundamentally to an understanding of the varieties of behavior we observe on the local level. At the same time we can supply policymakers, in the New Europe of the EC, with knowledge and understanding of the effects their supranational policies have on local actors.

Notes

1. Many introductory studies on the CAP are available. The reader is referred to Tracy (1989), Neville-Rolfe (1984), and Harris et al. (1983). For studies on the processes of decision making at the EC level on agriculture, see Senior-Nello (1984), Petit et al. (1987) and Moyer and Josling (1990).

2. Especially during the 1970s many studies appeared on Spanish rural communities and culture. See for instance Brandes (1975) and Aceves (1976). During the 1980s this paradigm was not challenged. For a single effort to change dominant ways of analysis, see Harding (1977). The dominant view on modernization of rural life and agriculture in Spain can be traced in Lieberman (1982). For a critique of these views, see Jurjus (1988).

3. In Andalusia 29% of the farmland is used for the cultivation of olives (in the province of Jaén more than 65% of the farmland is taken up by olive growing, and in the province of Córdoba this figure is 37%). These data are from the *Censo Agraria 1982*, Tomo II.

4. In this village of some ten thousand inhabitants I spent three months in the summer of 1986, doing fieldwork for my masters degree. Agricultural activity dominated economic and social life. In the 1980s more than 2000 families depended on agriculture for their livelihoods. Of these families around 1000 owned or rented land. Olive growing was practiced by some 800 families, the majority (80%) on a small-scale basis (less than 500 trees, i.e. approximately 5 hectares).

My research focused on a dozen families whose organization of economic activity I studied and on the local cooperative that processed the olives of all growers, with the exception of only a few. Through interviewing I gained insight into the key issues in economic activity and the role of the cooperative oil mill. My central question was in what way state programs for developing agriculture had influenced, during a period of twenty years, the strategies of the farmers, both small and large scale. This issue was researched by studying the archives of the local cooperative and the two state bureaus, the Camara Agraria and the Agencia de Extension Agraria. This was complemented by interviewing officials of these agencies.

5. This research was financed by the Commission of the EC. Its central question was in what way the olive oil sector of Andalusia could be reformed using instruments available under the CAP. The problem facing Andalusian olive growers is the overall bad quality of their olive oil. This study was not an ordinary anthropological one, conducted in a community, on the local level. For eight months in 1989-1990 I studied people acting on higher levels of integration in society. Political and economic aspects were very important elements in this study. Some of the results are published in Hoogveld and Jurjus (1990).

The farmers' organizations I studied were ACEA, ASAGA and ASAJA, so-called pressure groups. OPRACOL, UNAPROLIVA, IBEROLIVA, FEDEPROL and its national group FEDEPROL-ESPANA were organizations of olive growers, some of which were connected to ACEA and ASAGA. The majority of these organizations were based in the city of Córdoba, ASAGA was based in the province of Sevilla, UNAPROLIVA in the province of Jaén. Information on these organizations was gathered through interviews with key staff members and active farmers, and research of archives. All organizations in the research took part in a survey on such topics as organizational strategy, goals, and management. The study of olive oil mills was based on a survey among 60 Andalusian mills. I received help from the mill associations INFAOLIVA and UCAE in setting up this survey. They announced my visits to the mills and supported me in asking the mill owners and managers to participate.

6. Among agricultural economists it is not yet common to allow for alternative forms of farm management. Based on the idea of the rational entrepreneur, only minimizing costs is accepted as a viable way to develop a farm. For further information on the idea of several equally viable ways to manage and develop an agricultural holding, see Bolhuis and Van der Ploeg (1985).

7. Though these terms are mine, the practices described by them are recognized by both farmers themselves and the people working in the olive oil sector.

8. During my stay I witnessed a dispute between the president and a member over slight price differences that existed between this cooperative and one in a neighboring town. On other occasions, mainly during the stay in 1989-1990, I had the opportunity to talk to interested farmers and cooperative staff about the fact that growers are not at all interested in sound management as long as prices are in line with the neighboring cooperatives and private mills.

9. This point was brought to my attention by an informant who is currently working to establish a group of cooperatives. He experiences these conflicts and thinks it impossible to make demands when the prices for qualitative olive oil are not high enough to give any return on the investments made by farmers to enhance the quality of their olives.

10. The Andalusian olive growing elite is organized in ASAJA, with strong provincial organizations in Sevilla, Córdoba, and Málaga. These provincial organizations were set up and led by elite farmers who had already played

significant roles in the formulation of agrarian policies under the Franco regime.

11. The data in this section on Dutch dairy farming are from research carried out by social scientists from the University of Wageningen. They have studied dairy farming by focusing on farmers' goals, the ways they organize their work, and the ways they participate in, use, and are influenced by intermediate structures. See Bolhuis and Van der Ploeg (1985), Long et al. (1986), Maso (1986), Van der Ploeg (1990, 1991), Van der Ploeg and Ettema (1990).

12. At the time of writing (March 1992) negotiations on CAP reform and the Uruguay Round were not yet concluded. It was expected that the GATT talks would either be concluded before April 19, or would be suspended until after the US presidential elections. That would give the EC Ministers more time to make a deal on liberalizing the CAP.

13. See the report *Steunvermindering in de Europese landbouw. Het GATT-voorstel van de Europese Commissie onder de loep* of the Dutch Institute of Agricultural Economics (November 1990). Also see Bolhuis (1990) and Hoogveld and Jurjus (1990) for developments in the dairy sector and the olive oil sector as a consequence of 1992.

References

Aceves, Joseph B., ed. 1976. *The Changing Faces of Rural Spain*. Cambridge: Schenkman Publishing Company.

Bolhuis, E. 1990. "Zuivelproduktie: het krachtenveld rond kwaliteit," in J. D. van der Ploeg and M. Ettema, eds., *Tussen Bulk en Kwaliteit*. Pp. 45-54. Assen: Van Gorcum.

Bolhuis, E., and J. van der Ploeg. 1985. *Boerenarbeid en stijlen van landbouwbeoefening*. Leiden: Leiden Development Studies.

Brandes, Stanley H. 1975. *Migration, kinship, and community: tradition and transition in a Spanish village*. New York: Academic Press.

Censo Agrario 1982. Tomo II, Andalucía. Madrid: Instituto Nacional de Estadística.

Cloke, Paul J. 1990. "Community Development and Political Leadership in Rural Britain." *Sociologia Ruralis* 30: 305-22.

Giordano, Christian. 1987. "The 'wine-war' between France and Italy: ethno-anthropological aspects of the European Community." *Sociologia Ruralis* 27: 56-66.

Haney, E., and R. Almas. 1991. "Lessons on European Integration: Watching agricultural policies from the fringe." *Sociologia Ruralis* 31: 99-121.

Harding, Susan Friend. 1977. *The Village and the State in Spain*. Ann Arbor: Xerox University Microfilms.

Harris, S., A. Swinbank, and G. Wilkinson. 1983. *The Food and Farm Policies of the European Community*. New York: John Wiley and Sons.

Hoogveld, A., and A. Jurjus. 1990. *Olive Oil in Spain: strategies and prospects*. Nijmegen: Institute for Social and Behavioral Studies.

Institute for Agricultural Economics. 1990. *Steunvermindering in de Europese Landbouw. Het GATT-voorstel van de Europese Commissie onder de loep.* Den Haag: Dutch Institute for Agricultural Economics.

Jurjus, André. 1988. *Small farmers and the state in Southern Spain. Levels, linkages and strategies as tools in the analysis of change in local agriculture.* Unpublished M.A. Thesis. Nijmegen: Catholic University.

Lieberman, Sima. 1982. *The Contemporary Spanish Economy.* London: George Allen & Unwin.

Long, N., J.D. van der Ploeg, C. Curtin, and L. Box. 1986. *The commoditization debate: labor process, strategy and social network.* Wageningen: Agricultural University Wageningen.

López Ontiveros, A. 1978. *El sector oleícola y el olivar: oligopolio y coste de recolección.* Madrid: Ministerio de Agricultura.

Maas, J., and J. Kramer. 1986. *De toeleveranciers in het Nederlandse melkveehouderijcomplex.* Nijmegen: Geographical Institute.

Maso, B. 1986. *Rood en Zwart. Bedrijfsstrategieën en kennismodellen in de Nederlandse melkveehouderij.* Wageningen: Agricultural University Wageningen.

Moyano Estreda, E. 1984. *Corporatismo y Agricultura: Asociaciones profesionales y articulación de intereses en la agricultura española.* Madrid: Instituto de Estudios Agrarios, Pesqueros y Alimentarios.

Moyer, H.W., and T.E. Josling. 1990. *Agricultural Policy Reform. Politics and Process in the EC and USA.* New York, London: Harvester Wheatsheaf.

Neville-Rolfe, E. 1984. *The Politics of Agriculture in the European Community.* London: Policy Studies Institute.

Petit, M., M. de Benedictis, D. Britton, M. de Groot, W. Henrichsmeyer, and F. Leshi. 1987. *Agricultural Policy Formation in the European Community: The Birth of Milk Quotas and CAP Reform.* Amsterdam: Elsevier.

Ploeg, J.D. van der. 1990. "De betekenis van bedrijfsstijlen. Van pioniers en fanatieke boeren." *Spil* 89-90: 35-42.

_____. 1991. *Landbouw als mensenwerk. Arbeid en technologie in de agrarische ontwikkeling.* Muiderberg: Coutinho.

Ploeg, J.D. van der, and M. Ettema, eds. 1990. *Tussen bulk en kwaliteit. Landbouw, voedselproduktieketens en gezondheid.* Assen: Van Gorcum.

Senior-Nello, S. 1984. "An Application of Public Choice Theory to the Question of CAP Reform." *Review of European Economics* 11: 261-83.

Sevilla Guzmán, E. 1979 *La Evolución del Campesinado en España.* Barcelona: Ediciones Península.

Shutes, Mark. 1987. "The Role of Agricultural Production in Social Change in a Rural Irish Parish." *Social Studies* 9: 17-28.

Swann, D. 1988. *The Economics of the Common Market.* Harmondsworth: Penguin Books.

Tracy, M. 1989. *Government and Agriculture in Western Europe, 1880-1988.* New York, London: Harvester Wheatsheaf.

Waarden, F. van. 1985. "Varieties of collective self-regulation of business: the example of the Dutch dairy industry," in W. Streek and P. C. Schmitter, eds., *Private Interest Government: Beyond Market and State*. Pp. 197-220. London: Sage Publications.

Wilson, Thomas M. 1989. "Large Farms, International Politics, and the Local Arena: The Irish Tax Dispute of 1979." *Human Organization* 48(1): 60-70.

7

Rural Communities
Without Family Farms?
Family Dairy Farming
in the Post – 1993 EC

Mark T. Shutes

One of the crucial concerns of the chapters in this volume is to show how the analytical techniques of anthropology can be usefully applied to situations where social change is taking place at a transnational, macro-level. Certainly it can be argued that the Single European Act (SEA) has the potential to produce more dramatic social change more quickly than any other event in the history of the European Community (EC), and that the completion of the Internal Market (IM), which is primarily concerned with the processes of economic integration, will affect all areas of productive enterprise within the EC, from the smallest farm to the largest corporation.

Given the magnitude and scope of such events and their obvious potential to produce changes in all areas of life within the EC, the predominantly micro-level analytical perspective offered by anthropology might be viewed as being too narrow to be of any immediate use in understanding the social consequences of those changes, and a stronger preference might be accorded to those disciplines that rely predominantly upon macro-level analytical techniques, such as political science, economics, sociology, systems analysis, and jurisprudence. Certainly this assumption is validated by the popular perception (even among the practitioners of the above-mentioned disciplines) of the anthropologist as one who toils endlessly in the attempt to unravel the cultural complexities of a single remote community.

Many anthropologists would themselves support such an assumption, since our discipline has been strongly influenced by structuralist principles to view individual cultures as historically unique geographic, linguistic, and behavioral units, which can only be compared at the narrow points of contact between one such bounded unit and another (Voget 1975: 360-399). From this perspective, an anthropologist studying a community involved in massive and rapid transnational changes would be more likely to evaluate the impact of those changes upon the local community in order to understand how outside elements had affected the local cultural patterns, and would eschew any attempt at predicting the outcome of the changes in advance, by means of some macro-level theory, as being outside the purview of their discipline (Barth 1967). In point of fact, however, modern anthropological theory has become informed by broader ecological, rural sociological, neo-Marxist and world systems approaches to change, which have seriously challenged the idea of uniquely bounded cultures by showing that groups which share common productive strategies and common economic and political networks are subject to similar kinds of behavioral processes and changes, despite the fact that they are geographically and linguistically distinct (see, e.g., Voget 1975: 676-696; Wolf 1982; Goodman and Redclift 1982; Long 1984; and Chase-Dunn and Hall 1991).

In this chapter, I demonstrate that when the anthropological analysis at the local level focuses upon the ways in which social relationships are affected by changing ecological, economic, and political constraints upon the productive strategies of dairy farmers, it is possible to extend that analysis to other dairying communities where similar constraints exist. In other words, it is possible to offer a general predictive model of what will happen to dairy farm communities within the EC because of the same structural constraints. This analysis suggests that a market strategy based principally upon dairying generates a common set of capital and labor requirements for European family farmers, who must also share a similar set of pricing and market constraints.

In the following sections I shall (1) summarize the present condition of the local southwestern Irish dairying community in which I have studied; (2) examine evidence which suggests that similar conditions exist for family dairy farm communities within Ireland as a whole and in a number of other EC member states; (3) identify a general set of ecological, economic, and political constraints which can be used to explain such coterminous developments; and (4) suggest what will happen to these kinds of communities when the IM is completed in 1993 and beyond.

Consistent with the goals of this volume, I am attempting to push the limits of anthropological perspectives in order to demonstrate both the efficacy of the discipline's micro-level methods, and to generate potential scenarios for future examination. Such predictions may later prove to contain inaccuracies, but such early efforts will at least allow us to better evaluate the changes that will be experienced in the localities and regions of the EC in the years ahead.

Local Conditions

Beginning in the early 1970s, the rural community which I study in Southwestern Ireland underwent a transition in production strategy from mixed-farming with an emphasis upon cattle and milk production to one which was based solely upon the mechanized production of milk. Taking advantage of the numerous grants and low-cost loan schemes offered by the EC, and the highly subsidized price for milk, these farmers willingly transformed their economy and their community in an effort to become more modern "Euro-Farmers" (Shutes 1991: 3-9).

My analysis of the economic and social conditions which existed in 1986, and still exist to date, shows that EC membership has resulted in the growing lack of control by local farmers over their productive relations, which increasingly limits their decision-making choices. Despite a substantial increase in income during the initial years of membership, the fact remains that complete dependence upon dairying has made them extremely vulnerable to the vagaries of both the world market and the local environment. Few farmers were able to escape the lean years of bad weather, recession, and production quotas which marked the 1980s without encountering some form of additional debt that has severely curtailed their future development, and massive butter surpluses in the EC place them in the position of being the least efficient producers of that product in a glutted market. They have not been able to successfully compete even in the highly subsidized environment that presently exists (but which will also change because of the EC farm policy reforms agreed by the member states in 1992) and it is likely that many farmers, including those with larger holdings, will be driven from full-time to part-time farming, with some being driven out of farming altogether. Their heavy investment in specialized dairying equipment and their total income dependence upon milk production offers them few production alternatives for the future. It is milk, or it is nothing.

On the social side of this new round of changes, small farmers in the Southwest of Ireland are being systematically stripped of their sense of identity and purpose. Had they been less skilful in managing their small enterprises in the past, and less willing to respond to market conditions, they might have been more secure today. In short, their participation in EC plans and policies punished them for exhibiting the very behavior that such membership was supposed to enhance, and now increasingly threatens the very reproductive potential of their community. Local farmers are angered and disillusioned by such events, but are more determined than ever to keep hold of their land at any cost (Shutes 1991: 13-15).

Conditions Within the EC

The above findings were based upon the micro-level analysis of the changing ecological, economic, and political constraints that affected the productive decisions of the farmers in a single community, and the ways in which the changes in production strategy affected the social conditions within that community (Shutes 1987, 1989). And yet there is evidence from macro-level analysis to suggest that similar conditions exist for small family dairy farm communities throughout the EC.

In his examination of the impact of the Common Agricultural Policy (CAP) upon milk production within the EC, Bowler (1985:137) says that "milk is the main problem commodity" and the primary source of expenditure of the Agricultural Fund in terms of price supports and the disposal of surplus product. The reasons for high price supports and the resulting massive surplus are primarily due to existing social conditions. In his words (1985: 137):

> For social reasons, the price of dairy products can be reduced only slowly in real terms: a large number of farmers (nearly two million) depend wholly or mainly on milk for their income; milk producers tend to occupy the smaller farms in the Community on which opportunities for alternative forms of production are severely limited.

Although Bowler is quick to point out that there are developing regional variations to this pattern and that some member states have a greater number of family dairy farms than others (Bowler 1985:140-143), clearly large numbers of family farms within the EC have undergone similar transitions to specialized dairying under the CAP and are experiencing similar problems to those I identified in a local community in Ireland. Let us now look at some specific examples from different member states examined at the macro-level.

As might be expected, the outlook for family dairy farming within Ireland as a whole is quite similar to that which I found in my local case. Hannan and Breen (1987:64) believe that further reductions in the milk price support system, or the implementation of further milk production quotas will be the most damaging to the developing dairy farmer, particularly if they have borrowed to support their technological expansion. They view these farmers as being in a "highly vulnerable position" with little opportunity for further expansion and facing the very real possibility of elimination. In their words (1987: 65):

> The future points to continued concentration of production and incomes at the top, at the same time a process of withdrawal from production, dependence upon off-farm income, or direct income-maintenance payments will continue for almost half of the farm population. . . . We hesitate to end on the same pessimistic note as a recent report . . . by Kelleher and O'Mahony (1984:113), but it appears highly appropriate: "State intervention functions in such a way as to reproduce the very conditions which call for State support in the first place."

Family dairy farms in Denmark are faring little better than those in Ireland. Bagen (1987:140) describes the income conditions from the mid 1970s through the 1980s as being low to very low, and yet family farms had to continue to invest in technology in order to remain competitive with larger concerns. The result was the accumulation of a massive debt which stopped any future expansion on developing family farms and "brought the agricultural community to its knees". According to Bagen (1987: 141):

> There is an overall tendency towards farms either becoming industrialized agricultural units, or becoming part-time or spare-time occupations. This process leads to a state of permanent economic pressure on small, full-time farms. . . . The Danish crisis . . . had its specific national causes, but it was also inflicted by factors of a more general nature. In this sense, the Danish crisis may be a first sign of what might happen in other countries in the future.

In the former Federal Republic of Germany, Planck (1987:179) identifies a similar process of transformation on family farms, wherein, given the inducements of EC managed price supports for milk and the ready availability of low cost loans and grants, farmers rapidly increased milk production and invested heavily in specialized technology to carry out the increases. Under the conditions of declining price supports and production quotas that typified the 1980s, such farmers became strapped with debt and unable to finance further expansion. In Planck's view (1987: 185):

Since the 1970's, incomes on cropping farms have been rising much faster than on livestock and dairy farms, where most of the family farmers operate.

As wages and income demand climb, labor processes employing capital-intensive, high level technology . . . become more significant. . . . Because of their relatively small size, this sort of investment is only possible under certain conditions. The adoption of such technologies in an effort to utilize the available work force causes increased production on family farms. Under certain circumstances this may lead to surplus production and falling prices. Such conditions, in turn, especially impact upon small farmers that have low liquidity. Therefore continued investment becomes the fate of the family farm. . . . Larger farms had income advantages based on the fact that they could more easily raise and accumulate capital with which to improve their farm operations. . . . Most farmers saw no possibility of accumulating capital. Many go so far as to draw on the substance of their property or from their off-farm income to invest in their farm.

For family dairy farms in Great Britain, Gasson argues that the milk price support system of the CAP rewards the larger producers (which she calls "larger-than-family farms") at the expense of the small, and have made it increasingly difficult for the family dairy farmers to compete without incurring an unmanageable debt burden (1987: 23). In her words (1987: 29):

Size related differences in income within types of farming can be very great indeed. . . . Differences between types of farming compound the disadvantage of the family farm. Since the 1970's, incomes on cropping farms have been rising much faster than on livestock and dairy farms, where most of the family farmers operate. . . . Many family farmers in Britain, therefore, have reason to feel dissatisfied if they compare returns for their labor with wages and salaries in other occupations. . . . Yet without higher incomes these farmers find it difficult to expand their businesses . . . and . . . expansion has been the key to economic survival.

Given these conditions, Gasson believes that the future of family dairy farming within Great Britain "appears increasingly questionable" (1987: 23).

For France, Lamarche (1987:206-211) documents a similar process of the rise of "elite" large farmers during the 1960s and 1970s, the subsequent loss of relative income on the smaller family farms, and their need to expand production through investment in order to remain competitive. This did not become problematic until the industrial recession years of the 1980s, when it no longer became possible for debt-ridden marginalized farmers to sell off their land and seek better paying industrial jobs. Since the 1980s, says Lamarche (1987: 212):

The problem differs for marginalized farmers. . . . they must find solutions to their agricultural marginalization and to obtain an 'acceptable income'. It is a question of their survival.

The most common solution, according to Lamarche, has been to move to part-time farming.

Although less comprehensive, there is also some evidence to support a similar process taking place in the more remote areas of rural Spain. In a regional study of a rural district in Cantabria in northern Spain, anthropologist de la Peña Reddy (1986) documents a similar transition from mixed farming to specialized dairying beginning in the mid-1970s, which has accelerated since Spain became a member of the EC. Today, the villages in this region are suffering from the same over-dependence upon milk as the primary source of income, and Reddy concludes that many farms will become abandoned altogether should the price of milk be reduced any further.

Generalization, Cause, and Prediction

Clearly my local level analysis in Ireland, which focused upon ecological, economic, and political constraints on production in one small community, produced analytical results comparable to those identified by macro-level analysis both for Ireland as a whole and for other EC member states. Both levels of analysis identified the common set of problems confronting family dairy farming within the EC, that is, under-capitalization and the resulting over-production within a price-supported market place has lead to falling prices and price quotas, massively increased debt, and a decreasing ability to compete with the larger non-family dairying enterprises. This in turn has lead to an increasing dependence upon outside income on the part of family farmers and, hence, an increase in the number of part-time farmers or those who quit farming altogether, with all of the social disruptions to local farming communities that such processes imply.

It is at this juncture, I believe, that the anthropological perspective offers researchers far greater precision in their analysis of family dairy farming within the EC. For the micro-level perspective not only correctly identifies the general set of problems that are afflicting such farmers, but also enables us to demonstrate the specific set of ecological, economic, and political factors that are at the source of the problem, and to do so from the point of view of real farmers having to make real decisions in a rapidly changing production climate.

What anthropologists have failed to do in the past is to move from the specific to the general, that is, to move our level of analysis up a notch and attempt to produce a set of more generalizable factors that might apply to any family dairy farm community which shares them. Such a procedure would allow us to offer a hypothetical set of interrelated factors from which we could predict possible outcomes should those factors change. What follows, therefore, is not simply a list of the factors which explain the present conditions of the dairy farm community within which I worked, although a more limited and specific set of them certainly do apply to that case. Rather, based upon my own field experience and my readings of the statuses of other such communities, I herein attempt to identify a more general set of ecological, economic, and political factors which impinge upon many family dairy farm communities within the EC which share some of these factors.

I fully recognize the risks inherent in any such procedure, but I am encouraged to attempt it for a number of reasons. Firstly, although I have not examined every possible case, the striking similarity of conditions between my own field site community and those that have been described for family dairy farm communities within the EC in general, with specific examples from Ireland, Denmark, Germany, Great Britain, France, and Spain, certainly suggests that the problems are wide-spread and warrant a common explanation. Secondly, if anthropologists are unwilling to generalize beyond the local case, then predictions about the outcomes of events that are transnational in scope, such as those commencing in 1993, become impossible. Some (or all) of the factors that I identify may prove to be wrong-headed, and so the predictions that I base upon them may prove to be erroneous. But at the very least we can learn from such mistakes and work to improve the predictability of our models. Finally, the causes of the present problems in the Irish community where I work are transnational in origin, and the solutions to them must also be sought at the transnational level. If, as an anthropologist, I am unable to address the community's problems at that level, then I am reduced to the passive alternative of documenting, albeit in accurate detail, the ultimate demise of that community.

Ecological Factors

Two factors stand out as being most important: the distribution of fertile soils and the geographic location of the community. Typically there is an even distribution of small amounts of high quality soil with the remainder of the soil being of very poor quality. Historically this condition tends to produce a distribution within the community of predominantly moderate-sized farms (40-80 acres), with very few "marginal" farms, few, if any, larger farms, and no possibility of large-scale cereal grain production or beef fattening. The most common location for such characteristics to occur would be in mountain/valley areas, although lowlands areas with inadequate drainage would also produce similar distributions.

Prior to World War II such areas would be relatively remote from larger urban centers, not simply because of geographic distance but also because of the lack of an adequate transportation infrastructure. Communities may only have been a few miles from urban centers but were "remote" because of these transportation difficulties. This problem was particularly acute for those communities located in mountain/valley areas. These conditions combined to produce a predominant production strategy which I refer to as "mixed- farming," which involved the small-scale production of beef and milk, principally for cash needs, combined with the production of cereal grains and/or root crops, principally for home consumption. Typically such a strategy might also involve the production of eggs and poultry and some small number of pigs and sheep, which would meet both cash and home consumption needs. The goal of such a strategy was to find the best short-term mix of cash and subsistence needs for any given year, and to allocate their limited number of high quality land parcels accordingly. Transportation problems made the total dependence upon cash products risky to the extreme since their relative isolation produced both a lack of familiarity with the pricing structure of the market and a very real inability to deliver to such markets in a timely fashion.

A mixed-farming strategy produced the perfect conditions for what is generally known in the EC as the "family farm." Low cash availability and a dependence upon subsistence crops made such enterprises heavily labor-intensive and tended to select, therefore, for large single families as the principal production unit. But the labor tasks also required intense periodic dependence upon non-family members, and so the system would also support a relatively large population of landless agricultural laborers. The relative equality of farm size, combined with the labor-dependency between landed and landless and the unpredictable market conditions, produced, in turn, a very stable set of social relationships, where the prevailing values emphasized maintenance of the family unit as the primary goal for production and the "egalitarian" community as the ideal social unit.

Economic Factors

The most significant economic factor to affect this mixed-farming strategy was the massive and rapid re-industrialization of Europe immediately after World War II, which created a high demand for industrial labor. The proliferation of higher-paying industrial jobs resulted in the loss of cheap agricultural labor due to urban migration and the virtual disappearance of the landless class in these communities. The increasing urban population created, in turn, a markedly higher demand for agricultural products. Major investments in transportation infrastructure facilitated the outflow of labor and agricultural products from heretofore "remote" rural communities to developing urban centers and the inflow to those communities of manufactured goods. With this bi-directional flow also came a growing awareness of, and greater dependence upon, the external market economy (Clout 1984:18-67).

The loss of cheap labor, combined with easier access to dependable markets, jointly fuelled the move away from a mixed-farming strategy in these communities towards an increasing specialization in existing cash-oriented enterprises, principally beef and milk production, with milk taking the dominant position because it provided a greater source of cash. Loss of available labor forced an investment in machine technology which was financed by the subsequent increase in cash-oriented production that such technology provided. The labor-intensive production of goods for home consumption rapidly disappeared and more and more food-stuffs were purchased with cash. In this fashion, the move towards specialized market production, more specifically milk production, was initiated.

Some disruption of community values was the inevitable effect of such changes. As ties to urban areas increased, and landless laborers and those with very small marginal farms were gradually eliminated from the community, the notion of the local place as being an ideal "egalitarian" social unit was virtually abandoned. But, since the changes in agricultural production had strengthened the income position of the majority of the family farms, and since most farms still had options to choose short-term market strategies, most of these changes actually reinforced the older values which stressed farming as a way of maintaining the family unit, rather than viewing farming as a business.

EC membership accelerated the move to specialized dairying through subsidization of milk prices and through offering a system of grants and loans for dairy farm improvement on a scale that no single nation state could have accomplished. What resulted was a massive over-production of milk products, which lead to the introduction of milk production quotas in the 1980s. We have seen above the impact of these quotas on family dairying farms. They were dependent upon the continuing expansion of production to overcome their investment debt, and the imposition of quotas brought that expansion to a halt. The net result was that development on these farms ceased in the late 1980s with farmers trapped in a pricing structure that was sufficient only to maintain their debt. There was little hope of working their way out of that debt, and, since they had invested so heavily in technology specifically related to dairying, little chance of moving into other production strategies. For the first time since World War II, this process has lead to the dissolution of some moderate-sized family farms or, more frequently, to the movement from full-time to part-time farming, with a growing dependence upon off-farm employment and state welfare mechanisms.

This last round of changes strikes at the heart of family farm values, threatening, as it does, the very security of the family on the land. Not surprisingly, the most common response has been to seek off-farm employment as a means to maintain the family farm unit. Even those farmers who have chosen to go out of production entirely in return for a yearly stipend have not left the land. With few production options and little capital for major changes in present production strategies, many farmers see themselves as having been betrayed for doing what they were encouraged to do, and are now preparing for a long fight to keep their families on the land by any strategy available.

Political Factors

The idea of the family farm is a politically potent one in Europe, symbolizing as it does a number of desirable characteristics such as a stable family structure, independence, self-sufficiency, ecological balance, and a strong community support network, all of which seem to be diminished by the demands of complex urban living. The notions that one must "get back to the country" to refresh and renew the spirit, and that rural peoples somehow retain a core of crucial values, are widely held by the urban classes of Europe, whether or not they themselves have roots in such places.

In addition to this symbolic importance in the political arena there is a very real numeric importance as well. Family farming on moderate-sized holdings is still the predominant form of agricultural production in the EC. The median farm size for EC member nations varies between 40 to 80 acres, with the vast majority falling into the 40 acre category. Rural constituencies, therefore, wield considerable influence in the electoral process, since they account for eighty percent of the land area and more than half of the total population within the EC (European Communities – Commission 1991:12), and family farmers constitute a significant percentage of that rural electorate.

Immediately following World War II, given the large number of small to moderate agricultural holdings, the low level of technological development, and the highly variable soil quality on those holdings, it would seem only logical for European politicians to have initiated a rigorous policy of land consolidation. Such a policy would have included the mandatory sale of marginal holdings to farmers with greater development potential, the resettlement and retraining of those farm families that were displaced, and the pursuit of rural community development programs that would provide rural community members with economic alternatives to farming. But it is precisely at this point that the double-edged sword of symbolic and numeric potency attached to family farming came into play.

As we have already seen, post-war urban migration had a severely disruptive impact within rural communities with predominantly moderate-sized holdings; but it had a devastating effect upon those communities with predominantly small holdings, including the abandonment of entire villages and hamlets. Family farmers viewed any attempt at mandatory land consolidation as a direct threat to their families and communities, and had the evidence of such abandonments to support them. The suffering and anomie that was produced in these marginal areas also had an enormous emotional and symbolic impact upon urban dwellers, who either had their roots in such places and/or feared the loss of something fundamental and important to national ideals and values. Such people objected to mandatory land consolidation policies with their votes, and very few national political parties could muster the "will" to carry them out without fear of losing their grip on governance (the Netherlands may be an exception here). The maintenance of the family farm had become the "sacred cow" of European political parties.

The result of all of this was the widespread adoption by national governments of an "Indirect Solution" to agricultural development. Price subsidization and low cost loan and granting schemes were offered to farmers as an incentive to increase production through technological investment. Direct social welfare payments and special development funds were allocated to the more marginal rural communities, who remained on their land, but were, in effect, made wards of the state. The problems of land fragmentation were "solved" through rural industrialization schemes which offered incentives to industries that would locate plants in rural areas in the hope of attracting more marginal farmers off their land. Community development programs were also initiated in an attempt to lure non-productive farmers into other rural economic enterprises and out of farming. Given the political and economic climate in Europe after the war, such policies seemed to produce one of those rare moments for national politicians, a time when they were perceived to be able to please nearly everyone, although few of the long-term problems of land consolidation were ever directly addressed.

It is perfectly clear that these national "indirect" agricultural policies were at the heart of the CAP that went into effect with the establishment of the original European Economic Community (EEC) in 1957 and which were eventually made explicit during the meeting of agricultural experts at Stresa in 1958 (Planck 1987:155-156; Hill 1984:20-22; and Fennell 1979:11-12). By 1968, the EEC's total commitment to such policies became vibrantly clear when the so-called Mansholt Plan, which was severely critical of the CAP and recommended the removal of some five million people from agriculture between 1970 and 1980, was greeted with such hostility that "politicians – ever wary of the voting power of farmers and harried by the agricultural lobbies – found the plan embarrassing, so much so that it was never formally discussed by the Council of Ministers" (Hill 1984:38-40).

The economic impact of this "indirect" policy upon moderate-sized family farms has already been discussed. Price supports are inherently regressive in nature, and differentially reward those larger farms where development has already taken place. Family farms can only support development through increased production which leads to eventual market surpluses and price reductions which increase debt and stifle further production. The administration of the CAP at the supranational level only served to accelerate this process for family run dairy farms.

In addition, the attempt to provide alternative employment within rural areas and the provision of social welfare to farms of marginal size and productivity have worked at cross-purposes to those of agricultural development, since both have served to keep families on the land. In the former case, available off-farm employment has lead either to the "one-man" farm, wherein a farmer's children work off the land and contribute income to the farm now worked solely by the parents, or to part-time farming which uses the extra off-farm income to assist in the maintenance of the farm unit. In the latter case, a conscious effort is made to maintain farm families on marginally productive plots through direct welfare payments, which offers little incentive for such families to give up their land. In both instances land consolidation is thwarted, and the gap between the productive capacity of family farms versus larger corporate farms increases.

Rural development schemes suffer a similar fate, for when they are initiated in areas where moderate-sized family farms predominate, the farming members of the community often oppose those projects which would deplete agricultural holdings, such as the addition of tourist amenities and hotels, and view other activities, such as village beautification or historic preservation, as useful but time-consuming projects better left to others. Given the lack of available land resources, it is simply not in the self-interest of full-time family farmers to empower the non-farming segment of the community, particularly when there is a conflict of interest over the use of land and water resources (Curtin and Varley 1989) and/or an inadequate non-farm infrastructure for general rural development (Reynolds and Healy 1991).

EC membership and the adoption of a CAP has magnified the problems inherent in the "Indirect Solution" by raising the level of the debate to the supranational level. In Brussels, political coalitions of farmers unions and cooperatives regularly lobby the EC to maintain and/or increase the price subsidies on agricultural products, and national governments become more concerned with the total levels of their subsidies than with the on-going problems of agricultural planning within their own national boundaries (Hannan and Breen 1987). In effect, the "Indirect Solution" has become the favored solution, and agricultural subsidies have become the political stumbling block between the EC and other agricultural exporting nations, as is evidenced by the recent breakdown of the General Agreement on Tariffs and Trade (GATT) talks. The politicization of the agricultural sector within the EC has obscured the very real problem, particularly acute among dairy farmers, of too many moderate-sized family farms with too few production options, and has simultaneously strengthened the resolve of family farmers to retain their holdings and their way of life.

Implications of 1993

The completion of the IM will, in itself, require a massive input of capital on the part of the EC member states, considering that the plans include the elimination of all tariff boundaries, the initiation of a common currency, the equalization of working conditions and pay across state boundaries, and the initiation and funding of major new programs in environmental protection and in rural, urban and regional development. The CAP is again experiencing major difficulties with mounting surpluses of agricultural products, particularly dairy products, which have prompted the EC Commissioner for Agriculture to propose major reforms in the existing price support system during the run-up to 1993. In addition, the EC is also under tremendous pressure from other GATT nations to reduce and/or eliminate the direct market subsidy given to EC farmers for their products. Finally, the recession which began in the United States is now being severely felt within the EC in terms of rising unemployment and stagnant market conditions.

Given all of the above, it is quite likely that family dairy farms will experience a significant decrease in the price supports for their products over the next few years, and, hence, a loss of real income from their enterprises. Indeed, some farming interests claim that the proposed CAP reforms alone will result in the loss of hundreds of millions of dollars in uncompensated income during the first year (MacConnell 1991). The following is what I believe to be the logical outcome of such price support reductions for family dairy farmers in the EC.

As should be clear from what has been discussed above, any decrease in real income at this present juncture would have disastrous consequences for family dairy farms. With their ability to increase production severely curtailed by quotas, many of these farmers are currently operating at marginal levels of profit, and much of that profit must go to service the debt from previous technological expansions. Loss of price supports would most probably result in large numbers of family farms moving to part-time farming status and into the ranks of those seeking alternative employment. Others may opt to accept payment from the EC to go completely out of production for a specified time, in schemes similar to those that have operated in the United States. And many of the smallest family dairy farms would be forced onto the roles of state welfare assistance.

The reductions in price supports would not lead immediately to the abandonment and sale of family owned farms, and so would not lead to greater land availability for the more progressive producers. EC supported programs of rural social welfare and subsidies for non-production, together with the long-established rural values associated with maintaining the family land at any cost, mediate against such an outcome. In addition, given the number of farms going out of full production at once, it is quite likely that the price of agricultural land would decrease, particularly in the more remote areas, which would be a further disincentive for land sale on the part of the family dairy farmer. And even if cheaper land were to become available to the more progressive family dairy farmers, it is unlikely that many would be able to afford its purchase, given their present debt structure.

The resulting decline in family farm milk production would greatly increase the market share of the larger milk producers, who, as we have seen, are better able to weather such price support reductions. An increased market share would further enhance the ability of the larger milk producers to control both the cost of milk to consumers and the price per gallon paid to producers, enabling them to drive the remaining family farms out of the market by selling at a level that no family farm could afford to match. This market environment would likely mean the demise of full-time family-run dairy farming within the EC, since those who took a "wait-and-see" attitude through reduced production would never be able re-enter the market with prices at lower levels than those which drove them out in the first place.

Farmers seeking alternative employment in an effort to maintain their farm holdings would be doing so under three readily apparent handicaps: (1) Most would be seeking jobs close to their holdings, which limits their employment opportunities to regional rural towns, many of which are already suffering from severe unemployment problems which would only be made worse by the reduced income of their former farmer-customers. (2) Although the economic integration plans include major allocations for general rural development and the enhancement of non-farm employment opportunities, such plans have been slow to develop, as we have already seen, in those areas where community life is dominated by family farms, and so it is unlikely that many new jobs would be available immediately. In the long run, corporate tourist interests would be in the best position to take advantage of the funds available for general rural development and this would mean that the vast majority of the jobs eventually available to locals would be of the low-pay service variety and/or seasonal in nature. (3) Even if rural towns and redeveloped rural areas could provide significant employment opportunities, farmers would be entering the market at precisely the same moment in time that the restrictions on labor migration within EC members states will have been eliminated as part of the economic unification plan, which means they may find themselves competing for jobs with urban migrants who would demand less pay and would have higher levels of industrial and urban skills. In the short run, therefore, it would be very unlikely that many such farmers would be able to solve their income problems, and still maintain their farm holdings, through access to alternative labor.

Faced with a "no-win" situation for their family farms and an increasing impoverishment in life style compared to their urban counterparts, these farmers would eventually be forced to sell their land to corporate farm and/or tourist amenity interests, and family farm oriented rural communities would become a part of European history, just as such places have become a part of the history of the United States. In addition, the resulting increase in corporate farming and tourist amenities would result in water and soil pollution problems and a major change in the basic ecological balance in Europe, which is so predominantly rural, and in continuous battles between such interests on the one hand and farmers and environmentalists on the other (Allen and Jones 1990).

The social consequences of these changes are perhaps the most serious. After having experienced the early positive aspects of increased income and a reinforcement of their life-styles, rural family farmers are now faced with the loss of their farms and an ever-diminishing importance placed upon their enterprises. These farmers have undergone more changes in their strategies and taken more risks than any rural generation in the history of Europe. They have done everything that they believed was required of them to become modern "Euro-Farmers," secure in the notion that the system was supportive of their activities. Now they are faced with a continuing decline in their standard of living, a massive debt structure, and little hope of producing their way out. Worse yet, in their minds, is their growing sense of their failure to achieve their primary goal, which was to maintain their families on the land.

Out of this frustration and anger has come a tenacious commitment to stay on the land at all costs, taking advantage of every political action and economic program that will sustain this goal, even at the cost of going out of production altogether. Given the circumstances outlined above, it is likely that the disappearance of the family farm community within the EC will become a slow and agonizing war of attrition, involving a massive expenditure of economic and political capital that could very well frustrate the long-term success of the Community itself.

Conclusions

Direct price supports for agricultural products combined with rural welfare and development schemes have been at the heart of what I have called the "Indirect Solution" in European agriculture before and after the formation and expansion of the EC. Such measures have radically transformed the moderate-sized family farm from mixed-farming to market farming, principally the production of milk and milk products. Participation in the CAP has served to dramatically accelerate this process of transformation, and has resulted not only in the development of massive milk and butter surpluses, but also in a solidification of the policies of the "Indirect Solution."

The inherently regressive nature of the direct price support policies has produced a crisis in production for the moderate-sized family dairy farm, such that further reductions in price support will have disastrous consequences for these enterprises and the rural communities of which they are a significant part. Under a variety of pressures outlined above, the EC is being forced to move away from direct price subsidies and to examine a variety of non-market compensations. According to Brendan Kearney (1991: 12):

> The great debate now taking place centres on what might happen to the main features and structures of farming as we have known them, if the form and level of supporting agriculture is significantly changed. The main characteristic of that change is that support prices would be reduced and producers would receive compensation, but, within limits. Ironically, in some ways it is favouring the American system. The issues now causing concern in the rural economy include the effects of CAP reform and GATT on farm structure, agricultural employment, farm viability and farm incomes. . . . How they will affect the aspirations and enterprises of that small core of younger farmers, who normally contribute to the essential dynamics of agriculture, will be crucial to the vitality of those rural communities which hitherto had been mainly dependent upon market agriculture.

Based upon a radical extension of the anthropological analysis of an Irish dairy farm community, validated by the findings from other such EC member communities, it is my conviction that the "aspirations and enterprises" of another generation of EC family dairy farmers cannot be sustained. Rather, as both Kearney and I have suggested, agriculture within the EC seems to be moving irrevocably towards the agribusiness model of the United States. To view the present facts otherwise would be to assume that the values and life-styles of farmers can somehow be maintained in a rural environment where such people no longer actually farm. It is perhaps the ultimate absurdity of the EC-administered "Indirect Solution" that the stated goals are to preserve and protect rural life and yet the policies seem designed to frustrate the very productive activity from which that life has sprung.

References

Allen, Robert and Tara Jones. 1990. *Guests of the Nation: the People of Ireland Versus the Multinationals.* London: Earthscan Publications.

Bagen, Torben. 1987. "Family Farming and the Agricultural Crisis in Denmark," in B. Galeski and E. Wilkening, eds., *Family Farming in Europe and America.* Boulder & London: Westview Press.

Barth, Fredrik. 1967. "On the Study of Social Change." *American Anthropologist* 69: 661-669.

Bowler, Ian R. 1985. *Agriculture Under the Common Agricultural Policy: A Geography.* Manchester: Manchester University Press.

Chase-Dunn, Christopher, and Thomas D. Hall. 1991. Comparing World Systems: Theoretical and Empirical Issues. Paper presented at the Annual Meeting of the American Sociological Association. Cincinnati.

Clout, Hugh. 1984. *A Rural Policy for the EEC?* London: Methuen.

Curtin, Chris, and Tony Varley. 1989. "Brown Trout, 'Gentry' and Dutchmen: Tourism and Development in South Mayo," in C. Curtin amd T. M. Wilson, eds., *Ireland From Below: Social Change and Local Communities.* Pp. 207-223. Galway: Galway University Press.

Curtin, Chris and Thomas M. Wilson, eds. 1989. *Ireland From Below: Social Change and Local Communities.* Galway: Galway University Press.

de la Peña Reddy, David. 1986. *Cultural Adaptation to the Effects of Migration and Agricultural Change in a Rural Spanish Community.* Unpublished Doctoral Dissertation. Department of Anthropology, University of Florida.

European Communities – Commission. 1991. *The European Community: 1992 and Beyond.* Luxembourg: Office for Official Publications of the European Communities.

Fennell, Rosemary. 1979. *The Common Agricultural Policy of the European Community: Its Institutions and Administrative Organisation.* London: Granada Publishing Ltd.

Galeski, Boguslaw, and Eugene Wilkening, eds. 1987. *Family Farming in Europe and America.* Boulder & London: Westview Press.

Gasson, Ruth. 1987. "Family Farming in Britain," in B. Galeski and E. Wilkening, eds., *Family Farming in Europe and America.* Boulder & London: Westview Press.

Goodman, David, and Michael Redclift. 1982. *From Peasant to Proletarian: Capitalist Development and Agrarian Transitions.* New York: St. Martin's Press.

Hannan, D.F., and R. Breen. 1987. "Family Farming in Ireland," in B. Galeski and E. Wilkening, eds., *Family Farming in Europe and America.* Boulder & London: Westview Press.

Hill, Brian E. 1984. *The Common Agricultural Policy: Past, Present and Future.* London: Methuen & Co.

Kearney, Brendan. 1991. "CAP and GATT Combination Will Affect Farming Structures." *Irish Times* 13 November: 12.

Kelleher, C., and A. O'Mahony. 1984. *Marginalization in Irish Agriculture.* Dublin: Economic and Rural Welfare Research Centre.

Lamarche, Hugues. 1987. "Family Farming in France: Crisis and Revival," in B. Galeski and E. Wilkening, eds., *Family Farming in Europe and America.* Boulder & London: Westview Press.

Long, Norman, ed. 1984. *Family and Work in Rural Societies: Perspectives on Non-Wage Labour.* London: Tavistock Publications.

MacConnell, Sean. 1991. "MacSharry Disputes Fall in Income." *Irish Times* 13 November: 1.

Planck, Ulrich. 1987. "Family Farm in the Federal Republic of Germany," in B. Galeski and E. Wilkening, eds., *Family Farming in Europe and America.* Boulder & London: Westview Press.

Reynolds, Brigid, and Sean Healy, eds. 1991. *Rural Development Policy: What Future for Rural Ireland?* Dublin: Conference of Major Religious Superiors.

Shutes, Mark. 1987. "The Role of Agricultural Production in Social Change in a Rural Irish Parish." *Social Studies* 9(2):17-28.

_____. 1989. "Changing Agricultural Strategies in a Kerry Parish," in C. Curtin and T. M. Wilson, eds., *Ireland From Below: Social Change and Local Communities.* Pp. 186-206. Galway: Galway University Press.

_____. 1991. "Kerry Farmers and the European Community: Capital Transitions in a Rural Irish Parish." *Irish Journal of Sociology* 1:1-17.

Voget, Fred W. 1975. *History of Ethnology.* New York: Holt, Rinehart, and Winston.

Wolf, Eric R. 1982. *Europe and the People Without History.* Berkeley: University of California Press.

8

The Face Behind the Door: European Integration, Immigration, and Identity

Gary W. McDonogh

In June, 1990, in a Catalan television debate over immigration, labor organizer Salomon Suleyman angrily challenged officials: "You want to rebuild the Berlin wall at Algeciras." Suleyman, a Maghrebi immigrant, shared the concerns of many non-European commentators who have seen "fortress Europe" as the harbinger of radical exclusion towards outsiders (El Malki 1990; Rincón 1991; See Whitney 1991). Yet immigrants already settled in European cities, whether workers or refugees, also have faced repeated violence which signals exclusion as a potential facet of everyday life. Germany alone – a major focus for those seeking political asylum – witnessed one thousand attacks in 1991 (*ABC Nightline* 17 December 1991). Such eruptions of racism and riot have become:

> a measure of the dimensions of a time-bomb facing Europe in the Nineties and its inability to cope with the mushrooming immigrant ghettos on the outskirts of every major city. Experts at the European Commission say that every day their number are being swelled by thousands of North Africans and huge numbers of gipsies and other minorities from Eastern Europe. Almost without exception, the fear of violence, ghetto youth gangs and their rivals is all pervasive in Europe's major cities (Rollnick 1991).

As Europeans have examined the problem of the Other in the

European Community (EC), they have sought to explain the phenomena associated with immigration, identity and racism in a variety of ways. For some, reactions to immigrants are identified with right-wing politics both as a continuing heritage and as a more diluted appeal to xenophobia in a crisis: "Many politicians are starting to think, and a few to say, that Europe is already full, with an estimated 10,000,000 immigrants, and that the need to harmonize immigration policies is now urgent" (Rice 1991:13; See Raspail 1973; Harris 1990; *Europ* 1992). Others have viewed racism through the dark mirror of the United States. In June 1991, for example, deadly clashes in French industrial suburbs between North African immigrants and locals spurred Interior Minister Philippe Marchand to swear "There will be no Bronx in France." He explained that police would patrol tense suburbs to avoid more violence, shortly before Prime Minister Edith Cresson inaugurated sweeping deportations and other controls (Massonneau and Masurel 1991:54; Lebaude 1991). Similarly, a commentator greeted 1989 incidents in Spain with the claim, "This is Not America" (Nadal 1989), Germans have discussed links between neo-Nazis and the Ku Klux Klan and *The Economist* evoked the U.S. and the U.S.S.R to frame Europe as it worried that "Racism's back" (16 November 1991:15-16). Responses to immigration also are related to philosophical and ethnological process of categorization and "otherness" in Julia Kristeva's *Etrangers à Nous Memes* (1988), Tzvetan Todorov's *Nous et les Autres* (1990), and Tomás Calvo Bueza's ironic *Los racistas son los otros* (1989). Finally, such a discourse intertwines with statements on other urban problems. Thus in 1991, Jacques Chirac noted that "Notre probleme, ce n'est pas les étrangers, c'est qu'il y a overdose." The association of immigrants and drugs was extended by Jack Lang, spokesman for the government, who claimed that Chirac "se shoote a la drogue dure du racisme" (Frappot 1991). German neo-Nazis have claimed their expression is only part of a drive for national identity while Umberto Eco has labelled the African influx as the cause of a "worldwide genetic mutation." (*The Economist* 28 April 1990). Despite their divergences, the language of such statements has reinforced an image of dangerous others even whether or not such rhetoric spills into the streets.

All these linkages of European identity to migration from outside challenge anthropological analysis of contemporary immigrants, their descendants and the response of host populations in a new urban Europe. As the EC has become an increasingly unified confederation, it appears to offer sophisticated pluralist models. Official programs sustain and disseminate European cultural traditions, fostering a new status for nationalities without states, as several papers in this volume explain. While national prejudices remain, an integrative ethos prevails in political rhetoric and is exported as liberal democracy for the Third World. Yet what does this mean to non-European (or non-EC) minorities? Are they to be excluded by new walls, defining strict boundaries of European citizenhood? Will Europe distinguish between new arrivals and those who, while marked as different, have settled there for decades? And what do institutional and policy decisions mean in the streets, factories and shops where "incidents" emerge, as both citizens and immigrants seek to manipulate social and cultural categories? Indeed, can categories of immigrant or race conceal other issues of class, gender and political control even in discussions of legal and illegal immigration, nation-state policies, the status of refugees or the nature of constraints on movement which have evoked particular concern for 1992 (Weil 1990; Wieviorka 1991; Baldwin-Edwards n.d.)? If boundaries and migration pose special themes for the integration of 1992, both the relationships of European states with colonials (and former colonials) and the presence of significant populations of color within Europe suggest ongoing challenges for anthropological research.[1]

Indeed, anthropology faces an important task in disentangling and yet relating strands in complex European, national and local questions. Problems of immigrants, for example, have become increasingly apparent in urban Europe among people and institutions often ignored in EC scholarship. Like Smith's contribution, however, this chapter is particularly concerned with urban interactions and the demands for policy response, whether in Barcelona, with a relatively limited foreign population or Amsterdam, which Philomena Essed suggests might reach 50% non-white by the year 2000 (1990:39).

Clearly, the dismantling of Europe's economic and cultural internal boundaries raises questions about the definition of identity and exclusion. This dialectic of Europe and the Other has long historical origins which evoke the multiple meanings of 1992 which Wilson discusses in his introduction. As 1992 celebrates the integration of the EC, it also recalls five centuries of contact with the New World, millennia of contact with Africa and Asia and the European development of both internal and global colonialisms (Said 1978; Temprano 1990; Todorov 1990). Despite the presence of national minorities and others who are culturally-distinguished as racial groups for centuries in the case of Gypsies and Jews, in the past, distance often transformed the experience of multi-racial society; the colonized were to be ruled, studied or enshrined in a cabinet of curiosities, whether a museum or a theater (Lebow 1976; Lester 1986). In late 20th century Europe, however, the localization, experience and meaning of the other have changed. Decolonization and neo-colonialism towards former possessions have fostered metropolitan settlements of Asian, African and Caribbean immigrants in Britain, Holland, Belgium and France. The economic power of Northern Europe demanded workers who arrived first from the countries of the fringe – Spain, South Italy, Ireland, Portugal, Yugoslavia and Turkey (Buechler and Buechler 1981; Prada 1990; *The Economist* 28 April 1990). With the incorporation of some of these states into the EC, coupled with a falling birthrate throughout Europe, immigration has extended further afield while destinations have become diffuse. Third-world immigrants without metropolitan colonial ties now fill labor demands in countries which previously exported labor, such as Spain, Italy and Greece. Meanwhile, some *Others* now reside in Europe, settled in metropolitan colonial centers for decades where they have raised families and established institutions. They see themselves as European as well: "Afro-Europeans," "Arab-Europeans" and "Asian-Europeans" (Husband 1982; Ben Jelloun 1984; Grillo 1985; Gilroy 1987). Thus, this chapter, like that of Varenne, focuses on processual aspects of the redefinition of a European *self* for the redefinition of the *other*.

Moreover, in experience and organization, as well as in culturally-constructed responses, the situation of each immigrant group and setting differs: to be Vietnamese in Paris, even in a population divided in political loyalties (Bousquet 1991) differs from the embattled status of Vietnamese left behind in East Germany by the fall of the Communist regime. To be a third-generation Muslim in France, whose 3,000,000 Islamic adherents form the largest such population in Europe (*The Economist* 9 February 1991), is to differ from an illegal Moroccan caught in a marginal life in Barcelona (McDonogh 1992 a, b). While mass media reports often conflate immigrants, significant cultural, economic and social differences still distinguish them. In fact, as groups establish institutions and identities for themselves they may increase differentiation of class and culture, whether or not these distinctions are apparent in the eye of the host. Furthermore, these groups now include generations of metropolitan Asians, Arabs and Africans who have emerged as voices in the analysis and representation of their own situation. Films such as Hanif Kureishi's and Stephen Frear's *Sammy and Rosie Get Laid* (Kureishi 1988) reverberates with works such as Mehdi Charef's *Le the au harem d'Archi Ahmed* (1983), Amryl Johnson's *Sequins for a Ragged Hem* (1988) and Inongo-Vi-Makamé's *España y los Negros Africanos* (1990), which show Europe as the locus of orientation of writers of color taking charge of their own experience. The task of anthropology must be to pay attention to the differences and similarities among these experiences as well as examining comparative patterns and

policies, and to make recommendations based upon such an understanding
This chapter provides a recognition of these complex problems with regard to 1992. It draws on field materials from Barcelona, interviews and travel in other contemporary European cities, and extensive analysis of press, cultural media and published studies. From these, it examines the questions raised by new EC immigration between two worlds and European responses, both for 1992 and for generations beyond.

Immigration and Racism in a European Context

Estimates of immigrants of "color" in Europe range from 7 to 13 million, roughly 2-4% of the total EC population. These include 4.5 million in France, 2.5 million in Britain, 1.8 million in Germany and 800,000 in Spain (Callovi 1990; Riding 1990; Pereda et al. 1987; Corachán 1991; *The Economist* 1 June 1991). The presence of numerous illegals in submerged economic niches complicates any accurate enumeration, as does the status for those who seek asylum, whose numbers have soared from 14,000 in 1973 to 500,000 in 1990 (Rice 1991:13). Germany, for example, hosts more than half of the refugees of the EC, who often fade into the population while their status is decided (*Der Spiegel* 30 September 1991; Whitney 1991).

Refugees, however, are clearly not the only marked population in Europe. One of the deaths by racially-motivated violence in German riots, for example, was a youth of Turkish immigrant parents who had lived all his life in Germany. The second and third generation of color, who may have citizenship from birth or result from mixed marriages, enlarges populations of "Others" by as many as 2 million in France alone (Calot et al. 1991) as well as incorporating vast differences of integration and status.

Responses by European citizens, however, may overlook such distinctions. The French-Arab novelist Tahar Ben Jelloun has cited with alarm a *Le Monde* survey that showed 35% of all European citizens think that presence of third world immigrants is bad, with percentages of disapproval reaching 52% in Belgium, 47% in Denmark, 44% in France and 43% in Germany (*Le Monde* June 16,1989, cited in Ben Jelloun 1990:407). Robert Melcher (1991) notes that 94% of the French think racism is present in their country and 84% feel they "understand it." Work by Calvo Bueza (1990a, b) in Spain; Essed (1990) in the Netherlands; Grillo (1985), Weil (1991), Wieviorka (1991) and Bousquet (1991) in France; and Willis (1977), Kureishi (1988), Sivanandan (1990) and others in Britain have shown how racist attitudes have been transmitted to and transmuted by younger citizens of color and other indigenous respondents, boiling over into riots. Other studies underscore the ways in which a discourse of "race, " "color," "culture" and "immigrant" is used among citizens and immigrants to explain everyday actions (Reeves 1983; Miles 1989; Essed 1990, 1991; Todorov 1990; Van Dijk 1991; Wievorka 1991). This raises the question of race and racism as appropriate labels. Miles (1989) has warned of the complexities of the term. Yet Essed (1990) has tellingly suggested how the absence of discussion of racism leads to false construyal of social phenomena where other causes may be internalized by those who experience prejudice. In general, I follow her focus on categorization and power as foundations of racism, while recognizing the corollary need to study class, gender, and cultural variation.

It is also important that the experience of new immigration, differentiation and conflict has become in a profoundly new way, a *European* phenomenon. A *New York Times* report observes: "For the moment, with millions of Europeans out of work, a labor shortage is not apparent. In several places, immigration is even blamed for unemployment. But immigrants are needed to do the menial or low-paid jobs that out-of-work-locals refuse to do." The French demographer Jean-Claude Chesnais adds "A number of countries may be about to enter a long cycle of dependency on migration even though a large proportion of public opinion and of the political class is violently hostile to the idea" (Riding 1990). *The Economist's* 1990 "Italian Survey" notes that:

> Just as Catholic Italians are becoming more and more like Protestant northern Europeans in their attitudes to the numbers of children they want, so are they like northern Europeans in shunning dirty and tedious jobs. There will be a demand for immigrants in hospitals in the fields, in domestic jobs and so on (26 May 1990:25).

Anna Cabré of Barcelona's Universitat Autónoma has reached similar conclusions about Catalonia as a country "addicted to immigration" throughout its modern history to the point that it may face a crisis if "no habrá moros para todos" – if there are not enough Arabs to go around" (F. García 1991). The magazine of a marginal downtown zone in Barcelona added an ironic twist: "We now form part of the European Community. We are now Europeans, and as such we now have our own blacks and our own moors. What kind of Europeans would we be if we did not?" (Martínez 1991:9).

Similarly, responses have been both local and community wide.

Controls on external immigration are instituted through agreements such as the External Frontier Convention. Deportations and labor sanctions have reinforced policies, especially in areas such as Spain which have been seen as lax; rights of residence and access to citizenship may be restricted. One of the intriguing questions, in fact, of 1992 concerns the movement of those without papers across state boundaries within the EC (Baldwin-Edwards, n.d.: 9-10). New controls on immigration will not alter all relations of class, color and movement. Immigration must still account for reunification of legal immigrants with their families as well as political refugees (*The Economist* 1 June 1991:45; Baldwin-Edwards n.d.). Moreover, formal controls cannot immediately deal with the flow of illegal immigrants especially in the Southern, "gateway" nations of the Mediterranean (Baldwin-Edwards n.d.; *The Economist* 28 April 1990: 26). Meanwhile, established legal immigrant and refugee populations grow in numbers, complexity, and demands for rights. And riots as well as acceptance define a gamut of local informal responses.

Europe also has sought to change relations with the third world, keeping race and class international, through EC policies and investments. *The Economist* notes:

Encouraging people to stay at home is a popular remedy among Europeans. But it costs money, and the money may not achieve much. The commission calls for the EC to pay for big, labour-intensive public-works projects in the Mediterranean countries. . . . But the community will not open its markets to the most competititve exports – fruit and vegetables and textiles – that these countries produce (1 June 1991:46).

Euro-parliamentarian Simone Weil noted in remarks to a Barcelona conference on Mediterranean migrations: "given the lack of sufficient natural resources and foreign investments, differences in the level of life can only become worse, just as labor problems force youths to go into exile to find means of subsistence" (1990:48-9). Moreover, this aid must face colonial and cultural ties. Thus, a writer from Bogotá concludes "It is hard to understand why Spain, Latin America's main link with the EC, would forget about Latin America just as the world turns to celebrating the 500th anniversary of Christopher Columbus' discovery" (Rincón 1991:14).

All these ramifications of immigration, cultural categorization and policy demand anthropological and perhaps linguistic perspectives as well as policy responses. Yet any issues which may be "resolved" by 1992 must also be linked to populations perceived as problems which both antedate and transcend simple divisions of historical experience. Here, Barcelona, in its comparative framework, illustrates the social and

150

cultural complexities of immigration and identity for both those who
arrive and those who greet them.

Immigration and Response in Modern Catalonia

Barcelona has been the center of the struggle of Catalans for national
identity within the Spanish state, especially with regard to Francoist
oppression. Its integration into the EC has renegotiations with the
nation-state as well as transnational support for Barcelona as an
international city. Nonetheless, the quest for Catalan identity and voice
must be juxtaposed to the lives of culturally distinctive immigrants in
Barcelona and its environs as a comment on the experience of Europe as
a whole.

Spain and Catalonia have emerged from the complex and
multicultural history of the pluralist medieval Iberian peninsula of
Arab, Jew and Christian, which was brought to a bloody conclusion in
the process of national unification and religious integration. The
experience of New World, African and Asian colonial outposts,
however, continued to bring the exotic into Spanish life. Furthermore,
gypsies in Spain and Catalonia long have evoked vivid responses to
otherness which have been translated into genocidal politics or cultural
imposition (San Román 1986; Calvo Bueza 1989; Pi-Sunyer n.d.). Calvo
Bueza's recent surveys found gypsies to be more discriminated against
than any other group by students and teachers in many areas (1990a,b;
San Román 1988). I found similar prejudice expressed against them by
other Spanish aliens who felt the gypsies had not chosen to integrate.
Gypsies also act as a key symbol of dangerous people for national
racism, and, ironically, as a key excuse within deracialized discourse.
Thus when a lawyer in provincial Catalonia defended a client who had
refused to serve blacks, he queried "Would they let a gypsy enter the
Hotel Ritz?" referring to an elegant hotel in Barcelona (See McDonogh
1992a, b).

Today's immigrants have arrived after centuries of decline in which
Spain lagged behind the industrial development of Europe. In this
period, Catalonia and the Basque provinces, whose national histories
and distinctive languages and cultures straddle the Pyrenees, found
support for their renewed nationalism in industrialization and economic
power. These areas, in turn, were constrained by struggles against the
state, contributing to divisions in the Spanish Civil War (1936-39), and
the repression of the Franco dictatorship (1939-1975). Under Franco,
regional economies based in Barcelona and other Northern cities
recovered, but Spain became an exporter of cheap labor – a country of

the South, whose workers found both money and prejudice in Northern European industrial centers. Catalonia, however, already had received Spanish immigrants for decades. In the 1960s and 1970s, this massive immigration resulted in conflicts over local integration and Catalan linguistic and cultural integrity (Candel 1964, 1986; DiGiacomo 1984; Woolard 1989; F. García 1991; P. García 1991). Slowly, however, these immigrants have been absorbed into Catalan society with its relatively low natality, representing today a significant portion of the total population. Language, residence and affiliation have all become primary markers, however ambivalent, of Catalan identity for immigrant and native alike.

Spain's acceptance into the EC in 1986 recognized the state's political transition from fascism. Its economic reorganization in the 1980s has spurred continuing development in which EC policies have had direct impacts on investment, exchange and the international status for Barcelona and the autonomous region of Catalonia. These range from support for the 1992 Olympics, to recognition of Catalan as an official EC language and talks among "rich regions" within the community. Affiliation also has converted Spain, like other Mediterranean members, into a "gateway" into Europe. Wealth, opportunity and access in this European Spain have attracted those from poorer or war-torn areas of Africa, Asia and Latin America whether or not prior colonial ties existed with the Spanish state.

In the 1990s, these people constitute many of Spain's 700,000 legal and illegal foreign residents, along with an increasing number of second-generation descendants (Pereda et al. 1987). Catalonia's 6 million inhabitants include as many as 100,000 Arabs, 50,000 Latin Americans, 40,000 Filipinos and other Asians, and 25,000 Africans. Numbers vary according to periods of control, sources of information and political utility. A 1991 news report, for example, notes 407,671 legal and roughly 256,051 illegal immigrants in Spain. The 88,500 illegals in Catalonia included 22,000 Filipinos, 6,500 Central Africans and 15,000 Moroccans (Corachán 1991). More recently 110,000 illegal immigrants in Spain have sought regular status under new amnesties (Duva 1991). Such reporting, however does not indicate the size of "ethnic" populations nor their perception within Barcelona society which was phenotypically much more homogeneous only a decade ago.

Many immigrants have arrived in the last three decades and have escaped slowly from marginal occupations, housing, and social status. They still may be lumped together as illegals or problem groups within press coverage or uneasy co-residence. In order to facilitate comparison, I have separated immigrants into three groups: Asians, including Filipinos, Chinese, and Indians; Maghrebis (including

Moroccans, Algerians and other Arabs) and Sub-Saharan Africans. Each provides a springboard to reflect on other EC areas.

Latin Americans also merit attention for the Spanish case although this is a distinctive situation for Europe as a whole. Latin Americans have assimilated more easily because of their shared language, religion and history and have special rights as Spanish immigrants. They are also not clearly "racially" marked. In the past, the added cachet of being political refugees, often with professional training, aided assimilation to the nation-state and to its middle class. Even in this neo-colonial case, problems have emerged, with poorer immigrants from the Spanish Caribbean and Andean zones. In summer 1991, for example, authorities decried Peruvian gangs composed of illegal immigrants who used delinquency as both a source of funds and as a means of avoiding deportation through legal loopholes (Corachán 1991), while some Uruguayos have been linked to prostitution (*El Pais* 8 December 1991). Latin Americans' special residence status represents an interesting point of negotiation for all colonial ties after 1992 (Baldwin-Edwards n.d.). It may also be interesting to compare these groups with the ambivalent situation of poor Caribbean immigrants as recent colonials in Great Britain and as "jeunes, noirs et 'francais de papiers'" in France (*Le Monde* 11 December 1991).

Asians, by contrast, represent an exotic presence in Spain. Although Spain controlled the Philippines for centuries, contemporary Asian immigration lacks direct colonial continuity. Instead, Asians have developed specific niches in Barcelona; their ethnic stereotypes shape labor segmentation. Thus Filipinas have been recruited for domestic service, which demands single, young females (85% of the immigrants) with or without legal status, primarily residing with their employer, increasing their dependency. Recruitment and the Spanish urban cultural image of the clean and docile Filipina both limit expectations. These Filipinas become frustrated because of lack of family, job over-qualification, and limited mobility (Pereda et al. 1987). Their situation recurs elsewhere in Europe despite reports that "in Brussels, Poles are replacing Filipinas as maids in yuppie households" (*The Economist* 1 June 1991:45). Roughly 10,000 other Asians, including Chinese and Indians, have achieved an ambivalent if successful status in Barcelona, with a limited range of visible occupations, including restaurants, tourist stores and small urban groceries. In their individual histories, they show complex manipulations of international opportunities and networks, whether in North America, the Persian Gulf or Europe. While predominantly male, many have imported spouses and relatives and dedicated themselves to family businesses. According to Caritas surveys, they feel little discrimination; they are seen as exotic rather than excessively competitive (Pereda et al. 1987). Race is eclipsed by quiet success as well as some facets of assimilation (McDonogh 1992a). Discussions that Cindy Wong and I held with various Barcelona friends in 1991, however, suggested the impact of Orientalist imagery on these limited Asian communities. Stereotypes of physiognomy, language and other traits are strong, whether formed by mass media or popular culture. These rarely include knowledgeable distinctions among Asians: "Para nosotros, todos son chinos" (For us, everyone is Chinese). Even a star of popular magazines with some Filipino heritage, Isabel Preysler, was nicknamed "La chinita." Others have suggested that a search for "invisibility" may be part of Asian strategies of disappearing into a united Europe (See Kureishi 1988; Bousquet 1991).

Nonetheless, the varied reception of Asians betrays other intersections of race, cultures and class. Nowhere is this more apparent than in the remarkable absence of the Japanese among general reports on racism. While jokes are made about tourism, a Japanese school has been well-received in the Barcelona metropolitan community, and the Catalan government devoted an issue of its periodical, *Mon Laboral*, to Japanese work culture in Catalonia, underscoring stereotypic similarities as well as opportunities in increasing investment (Furriol 1990). Arabs, by contrast to Asians, have a long history of antagonistic contact with Spain, from Moorish Granada to 20th century involvement in Moroccan colonial wars whose impact often shook Spanish governments. In 1939, when Franco invaded the peninsula from the Canary Islands, beginning the Civil War, he was accompanied by North African troops whose "racial" visibility figured in popular representations of wartime terrorism (See Lester 1986 for similar responses in Germany; Hughes 1956:352-5 for an American black's reaction to the categorization "moro"). Until 1956, Moroccans could emigrate to Spain as citizens of its protectorate while the Moroccan monarchy enjoyed close ties with Franco. The Spanish fortress enclaves of Ceuta and Melilla on the northern coast of Morocco still act as permeable gateways to the North. Illegal immigrants may cross the Straits of Gibraltar by boat; the press speaks of Europe's "boat people" (See Raspail 1973).

In the late 1960s and 1970s, Maghrebis supplied cheap, unskilled male labor. In 1987, Caritas found 1/3 of those surveyed earned less than $300 per month (Pereda et al. 1987:118), an economic situation highly sensitive to the labor market. Joining the EC stimulated both Spanish growth and the use of the state as a gate – often closed – to the North. Thus, Algerians and Tunisian refugees have diversified the previously Moroccan population, although their presence underscores Spain's participation in the Mediterranean basin.

Most of these Arabs form an urban/suburban and industrial lower working class population. Although predominantly male, some have formed families with local women or Arab women who have become uneasily incorporated into Spanish life. Arab women themselves have sometimes entered the workforce as domestics or factory workers at the expense of their traditional roles, increasing likelihoods of divorce (Losada 1988). Mosques and other associations have become meeting places and voices in local affairs and relations with Morocco. Arabs, like Asians, are categorized according to cultural stereotypes which combine old and new. Teresa Losada, a Franciscan nun who has worked with Arabs in Barcelona and nearby provinces, has found Orientalist images of criminality, dirt and disease raised against the immigrants (1988; personal communication 23 January 1989). These pressure immigrants to assimilate, even as mosques have sprung up throughout Catalonia as centers for religion and culture. However, grand mosques in capitals like Madrid (Cristobal and Alvarez 1990) or in elite resorts are patronized by wealthier Arabs, confusing panoramas of class and ethnicity.

Blacks also show ambiguities of adaptation and acceptance. After losing its slave possessions in the New World, Spain lacked a visible black population even in large cities. Since the 1980s, however, black Africans have come to represent a small but highly salient presence in Catalonia, set apart by phenotype as well as cultural imagery of Africa. They are primarily young males engaged in unskilled rural agricultural work rather than seeking urban employment, although street vendors are as common as they are through the rest of Europe. Most are illegal, but political asylum is rarely granted (Pereda et al. 1987; De la Torre 1988). Until 1989, Barcelona's African community was centered in the portside Raval neighborhood around racially-oriented bars, a cultural center, and an Afro-beauty shop. In the 1990s, Barcelona's African presence has become more dispersed, perhaps as a reflection of urban reform (McDonogh 1986, 1991; P. García 1991; Martínez 1991). Agricultural settlements tend to be limited to crowded barracks or familial clusters.

Ideologically, however, blacks occupy an intensely contradictory cultural position. As Calvo Bueza has pointed out, Spanish textbooks and popular thought have shared a general European vision of discrimination against blacks as the paradigmatic case of racism in the U.S. or South Africa (1989). Yet as in the exoticism on the 1930s, Africans remain associated with primitivism. Folklore, children's books and toys reinforce these associations, while news media in Spain, France and Britain, link Africans and other immigrants to AIDS, prostitution, drugs and crime – a dangerous sexual other. While each group has its own heritage, niches and experiences of responses in the city, common features also have emerged among new immigrants of color in Barcelona. For example, all have faced elusive choices of integration and division. The nuclear as well as extended family has been an area of support as well as conflict. When migrants form families, however, the presence of wives and children may be perceived as an "invasion." Mixed relationships face other social problems. Further pressures on marriage, as noted, arise from erratic work opportunities and the sexual division of labor. Formal and informal groups serve to sustain and develop community identity among immigrants, creating institutions for a measured integration. Some immigrant organizations in Catalonia have focused on labor rights as a response to discrimination, at times uniting diverse immigrants as in other parts of Europe (Sivanandan 1990; Désir 1991). Yet cries for employment rights can emphasize competition between old and new residents of poor neighborhoods, exacerbating tensions which will be expressed through racism. Religious and cultural centers have also become a focus for immigrants, whether in the conversion of a Spanish Catholic parish by Filipinos or the mosques of Pakistanis, Arabs and Africans. They have fostered language and culture as well as spiritual bonds, but may also separate immigrant groups more from each other. By comparison with other European centers of established non-European communities, public celebrations of ethnic diversity seem uncommon in Catalonia, despite many invited *foreigners* sponsored by Olympic patronage. Even the diversities of food, music and culture which immigrants might bring seem to face resistance among Barcelona residents whom I know. What may be significant here, however, is missed potential of more public venues in the formation of inter-collective cooperation and identity (see Cohen 1980; Beriss 1990). Barcelona's racially marked groups remain discrete and, in some cases, hostile to each other: Africans and gypsies have battled in urban gang wars.

These social formations among relatively recent immigrants only suggest the complexities of older and more varied European populations. Yet they underscore the multiple meanings of immigrants of color in the formation of new European urban societies after 1992. These formations, however, cannot be understood without examining responses – cultural, institutional and individual – which deal with these new populations.

Integration and Response

The impulses of immigrants towards integration, however, also face individual and institutional reactions in the host society. In Catalonia, the immigrant population preceded many formal controls. Policies have responded to EC concerns as much as local perceptions of "problems." Nonetheless, authorities charged with preparing for 1992 have been charged with extreme severity, including plans for "eliminating all illegals and minimizing even the legal immigrants" (*Avui* 6 November 1990).

Elsewhere, the slower development of policy may have had confusing impacts. Even before 1992, for example, Philomena Essed notes that systematic policy in the Netherlands have changed radically from colonial status for Surinamese under a policy of assimilation in the 1950s to cultural tolerance in the 1960s and 1970s to integration in the 1980s after the arrival of those escaping the travails of independence (1990:39-40; Castles 1986). Despite some successes Essed provides compelling personal evidence for the racism that remains in everyday life.

Quite apart from formal policies which the EC as political body will deal with, other institutions and actions reproduce patterns of racial identification and prejudice which face both immigrant and resident of color in Europe. Despite the exploration of immigrant issues in European media, for example, Spanish headlines have screamed "Delinquency is the only source of income for Africans in Barcelona" (Capdevila 1988) or offer apparently sympathetic yet victimizing evaluations, such as that "Africans Suffer from a Persecution Complex, says the Mayor of Santa Coloma de Farners" (Bouis 1989). Despite wide diversities in coverage and attitude, a 1987 Caritas survey concluded that the intensity of media attention fostered for the public "*an image of the immigrant in Spain and a suspicious and anti-social person*" (Pereda et al. 1987). Similar claims have been made for coverage in other parts of Europe (Smitherman-Donaldson and Van Dijk 1988; Van Dijk 1991; Murray 1986). Voices of immigrants remain limited or channeled through "spokesmen" and stereotyping.

The police and other institutions of urban social control (including electoral rhetoric) reinforce negative cultural perceptions of difference among urban communities. Lack of training and opportunities have in fact led some new immigrants to drugs, crime and prostitution. However, Inongo-vi-Makomé also writes of the administrative controls which criminalize immigrants as he higlights the humiliations which surround arrests of Africans: "If someone asks for an explanation (never the detainee), they respond they are fulfilling the law. It is a psychological warfare, that the police utilize, hoping that the immigrant loses his dignity, becomes disheartened and returns to his homeland" (1990:156); Africans and Arabs with whom I spoke recapitulated these views and experiences. By contrast, even Barcelonans in marginal neighborhoods often espouse a rhetoric of alien guilt and security to defend police actions (McDonogh 1992b). While this situation remains polemic, my impression in the field has been that both police and administration act severely in dealing with those markedly different in appearance, style and class reflecting and reproducing a wider European urban culture of fear among citizens and immigrants (Bridges 1983; Gilroy 1987; Kureishi 1988).

The reproduction of immigrant communities in cities and their periphery, however, underscores another focus for anthropological research on immigration and its impacts: schools and neighborhood groups through which urban youths, immigrants and hosts, learn to deal with each other. Social service workers and teachers in Barcelona's immigrant neighborhoods have stressed their concern with both immigrant adaptation and the reproduction of racism across generations. Losada describes a second generation of Maghrebis in Catalonia who parallel many experiences of their contemporaries elsewhere in Europe:

also called "the sacrificed generation", "generation zero" or "Negative beings (Seres en negativo)", with a formation riding between two cultures, confronted with two opposed, conflictive and often negative realities. The efforts to assimilate the culture of the host country causes the young immigrant to break his frames of reference. The identity his parents propose is disconnected from life. He underuses the mother tongue and constantly speaks his adopted language. The effort to feel equal to his companions makes him hide differences" (1990:243).

Partial acceptance in everyday life may still mask rejection through benign stereotyping or it may fail to assuage fears of rejection.

Spain's educational reform since Franco has stressed a widely accessible liberal public education as a reply to Francoist religious indoctrination, which would seem to be an ideal conjuncture to incorporate new groups. Yet reform also has led to a strained and unequal distribution of goods and services amidst a range of new demands from Catalan to computers. Since immigrants are often forced into housing in marginal neighborhoods, their schools and schoolmates are likely to be those that face the most difficulties in facilities and staff even before dealing with a new diversity of languages and cultures (See McDonogh and Maza n.d.). As Paul Willis has pointed out for working-class England, such school settings can reinforce antagonisms and attitudes of class, internalizing limitations for both immigrants and local students (1977; See Grillo 1985:163-217 on France).

Within the classroom, texts may reinforce racial divisions and self-doubts among immigrant students, whether through benign neglect of history or the propagation of ethnic and cultural stereotypes. Calvo Bueza has underscored how gypsies are relegated to history, literature or folklore in Spanish texts (1989:9-68) while racism is denatured by discussion in the abstract only, or with reference limited to distanced settings: "Thus our xenophobia against others is attenuated and reduced to immorality, while the stereotype that 'the racists are the others' is massively reinforced" (1989:198-199). Pi-Sunyer has confirmed both representations and silence which structure the learning of history (n.d.). Thus, unless critically reexamined, these complement media imagery of savagery, danger and exoticism (Calvo Bueza 1989, 1990a; Foster 1989). Within the school, Inongo-vi-Makomé has signalled other causes for scholastic failure among African immigrant children, including the work life of the family, the ambience of racism in schools and wider social images and the lack of a strong tradition of self to be passed on. Thus he carefully observes that class opportunities and scant resources are critical challenges to meet, even while dealing with racism and its impact on both immigrants and local citizens (1990: 177-184).

Complementary institutions have been generated by immigrant communities in search of their own identity outside of schools or social services or in response to the prejudice of cultural media and state controls. However, these centers face ambivalent interpretations amidst volatile debates such as language identity and ideology in Catalonia (DiGiacomo 1984; Woolard 1989). Many African immigrants, for example, speak some French, Arabic or English and languages of their nation-state before arriving in Europe. In Catalonia, their interests in language are linked to economic success and mobility as much as to new local roots, which may become a source of antagonism. Learning Castilian rather than Catalan, for example, facilitates mobility throughout the state and perhaps the EC, but may be challenged by nationalist hosts. Here, a critical concept of the Afro-European who makes EC-based choices must be balanced against other models (McDonogh 1992b).

Reforms in education, like analytic investigation, cannot overcome the legacy of relations of race and power which pervades European culture. Yet these areas of response underscore the need to focus on younger generations influenced by new racism who present a special challenge for a uniting Europe. Racism among skinheads and neo-nazis, or among quiet complainers about competition and a lack of opportunities who are attracted by a resurgent right, are problems as serious as those of disenfranchised youths attacked at school, in work and on the streets. Indeed, in readings and interviews in 1991 and 1992 I have been concerned by the torturous internalization of projected values in this generation, whether in the Arab-Spanish youths who criticize other "shiftless" Arabs even as they distance themselves from stereotyping and the daily prejudice they encounter, or in the *beurs* in France who cling to a French nationality while seeing it may have no place for them. This area would seem to be a primary area for anthropological contributions to EC policy, both in deconstructing cultural stereotypes and in a more socio-economic analysis of the impacts of immigration and residence of people of different cultures as well as colors in Europe after 1992.

Conclusions

The challenges of immigration, resident populations of color and responses within the EC represent a continuing expression of power relations as well as a changing phenomenon linked to particular groups, settings, and beliefs. By concentrating on Barcelona and Catalonia, where local and nationalist traditions have been strengthened by incorporation into Europe, I have suggested the pervasiveness and importance of dealing with the challenge of immigration, identity and racism in Europe as a whole. It is significant that immigration in Catalonia – as in Italy, Greece and Germany – has been transformed by its participation in Europe as well as by the attractions of work opportunities for those outside. At the same time, the heritage of European culture in fundamental areas of categorization and Orientalization as well as events in England, France and Germany also shape Catalonia's range of responses within the Spanish state and the EC.

In many cases, in fact, the boundaries between ethnicity, nation, class and race in the Europe of the 1990s have been called into question by cultural commentators and popular actions as much as government policies. In 1988, Jean Baudrillard's compared the unspoken mixing of France to America's violent shock of Europeans and other races:

All our immigrants are, at bottom, *harkis*, living under the social protection of their oppressors, to whom they can oppose only their poverty and their de facto sentence of transportation for life. Immigration is, admittedly, a hot issue, but the presence of several million immigrants has not made its mark on the French way of life nor changed the face of the country. That is why, when you return to France, the dominant impression is a clammy sense of petty racism, of everyone being in an awkward, shameful position. The sequel to a colonial situation, in which the bad faith of both colonizer and colonized persists, whereas in America, each ethnic group, each race develops a language, a culture in competition with and sometimes superior to the 'natives' and each group symbolically rises to the top (1988:82-83).

In four years, the problems of France have not "disappeared", given both the continuing impetus of uneven development and the growth of diversified populations of immigrants who are now citizens of color in EC states. These have made their mark, and the cities of Europe demand creative and thoughtful solutions as the French SOS-Racisme president Harlem Désir notes:

I don't think we should count on a miracle recipe. We must avoid fashionable effects: for six months, it is thought that the solution is urbanism, then for the next six months, education and republican values, then one discovers employment. Why not sport? I believe that long term actions should be built patiently on all fronts and that the problem is . . . a choice of political and budgetary priorities by society and the State.

The alternative is "the rise of violence, of communal responses, of racism, of anti-semitism. . . . a hatred of all against all since each is the scapegoat of the other" (1991).

For anthropologists, the unity and diversity of Europe suggests foundations for comparative work and policy. While France, Britain and Germany have had recent riots, for example, the Netherlands have shown more success in integration of colonial immigrants, even if incomplete. The experience of Spaniards and Italians as emigrants might be balanced against the experience of Spain or Italy as hosts, within shifting frameworks of clas, ethnicity and nation. All studies, finally, should be linked to work outside the EC, in immigrant homelands as well as among other hosts.

Baudrillard points again to the United States, where decades of policy decisions, discussions and citizen action in this century have identified racism as a problem and sought to change it, while slowly recognizing the imterlocking impact of class, color, gender and other differentiations of power. As both areas the EC and the U.S. face new outbreaks of interracial violence, the creative dialogue this volume embodies for other issues takes on additional importance. Europe in 1993 and beyond urgently poses important questions about the economic, social and symbolic presence of people of color in the United States. Meanwhile, America's transformation from long-established isolation to a host for world immigrants suggests the importance of understanding Europe's colonial experience and its contemporary changes.

The comparative examination of the social and cultural processes of racism in the United States and a united Europe is compelling in terms of the human cost of discrimination and the increasingly recognized need for creative solutions. Anthropologists are well-prepared to analyze how "traditional" groups worldwide de-individualize aliens as part of their struggles over rights, resources and identities. Such social and cultural divisions in a complex modern Europe merit equal attention, balancing local categories and comparative study. Thus the discipline can facilitate an awareness of problems and solutions among scholars in a variety of fields, among policy-makers, and among immigrants and citizens of a New Europe.

Notes

Funding for fieldwork specifically related to this analysis has been provided by the American Council of Learned Societies, the New College Anthropology Endowment, and the New College Alumni Association. In Barcelona I have been aided by Jose M. Gallart, Carles Carreras, Josefina Roma, Jim Amelang, Xavier Gil, Joan Pujadas, and Dolors Comas d'Argemir as well as the family Garcia Aleman, Floren, Cristina, and Juan de Retana and others. Data first were assembled for a 1989 UC-Berkeley conference and later discussed at a Council for European Studies Workshop on 1992 integration at CUNY in October, 1991. The project has profited from comments by Oriol Pi-Sunyer, Susan DiGiacomo, David Beriss, Richard Price, Susan Rogers, Lawrence Saunders, Gisele Bousquet and Jill Dubisch.

1. This research springs from two longstanding projects. Research in Savannah, Georgia since 1982 has examined the contradictions of race, class and religion among black Catholics (McDonogh n.d.). My fieldwork since 1976 in Barcelona has looked at class and culture in the constitution of urban life (McDonogh 1986; 1991) concentrating since 1986 on city planning, education and marginal zones of the downtown. This work has been conducted since 1986 with Gaspar Maza of the Centre de Serveis Socials Erasme de Janer and since 1990 with Cindy Hing-Yuk Wong. I have already presented a detailed overview of the Catalan situation (McDonogh 1992a; McDonogh and Maza n.d.). Research materials on Germany have been supplemented by investigations of my assistant, Peter Weiss in 1991-2. I leave aside considerations of the well-documented causes that have led to this immigration in the first place (see Roque 1990)

References

Baldwin-Edwards, Martin. n.d. Immigration after 1992, unpublished paper, author's personal file.
Baudrillard, Jean. 1988. *America*. London: Verso.

Ben Jelloun, Tahar. 1984. *Hospitalité française: racisme et immigration maghrebienne*. Paris: DuSeuil.

_____. 1990. "L'émergence des sociétés pluriculturelles," in M. A. Roque, ed., *Els moviments humans en el mediterrani occidental*. Pp. 405-409. Barcelona: Institut Català d'Estudis Mediterranis.

Beriss, David. 1990. Being French and Other: Making a Place for Caribbean Culture in Paris. Unpublished paper presented at the annual meetings of the American Anthropological Association, New Orleans.

Bouis, Pepa. 1989. "Los africanos sufren de mania persecutoria, segun el alcaldede Santa Coloma de Farners." *El País*. 10 January: 1.

Bousquet, Gisele. 1991. *Behind the Bamboo Curtain: The Impact of Homeland Politics in the Parisian Vietnamese Community*. Ann Arbor: University of Michigan.

Bridges, L. 1983. "Policing the Urban Wasteland." *Race & Class* 25(2) :31-47.

Buechler, Judith and Hans. 1981. *Carmen: The Autobiography of a Spanish Galician Woman*. New York: Schenken.

Callovi, Giuseppi. 1990. "Les migrations internationales, nouveau défi pour l'Europe," in M. A. Roque, ed., *Els moviments humans en el mediterrani occidental*. Pp. 67-86. Barcelona: Institut Català d'Estudis Mediterranis.

Calot, G., H. Long, and C. Milleron. 1991. "Un mise au point commune." *Le Monde*. 28 September.

Calvo Bueza, Tomás. 1989. *Los racistas son los otros: gitanos, minorlas y derechos humanos en los textos escolares*. Madrid: Popular.

_____. 1990a. *España racista?: Voces Payas sobre los gitanos*. Barcelona: Antropos.

_____. 1990b. *El racismo que viene: otros pueblos y culturas vistos por profesores y alumnos*. Madrid: Tecnos.

Candel, Francesc. 1964. *Els Altres Catalans*. Barcelona:62.

_____. 1986. *Els Altres catalans vint anys despres*. Barcelona: 62.

Capdevila, Carlos. 1988. "La delinqüencia es l'unica font d'ingressos dels africans a Barcelona." *Avui* 6 March.

Castles, Stephen. 1986. "The Guest Worker in Western Europe – An Obituary." *International Migration Review* 20 (4):761-777.

Charef, Mehdi. 1983. *Le thé au harem d'Archi Ahmed*. Paris:Mercure de France.

Cohen, Abner. 1980. "Drama and politics in the development of a London carnival." *Man* 15 (1):65-87.

Corachán, Jordi. 1991. "El Problema de los residentes clandestinos en España." *El Periódico*. 11 August.

Cristobal, Ramiro, and Fernando Alvarez. 1990. "La cultura islámica inaugura su capital europea en España." *Cambio16* 19 November:122-127.

De la Torre, Iosu. 1988. "España limita cada vez mas a la entrada de refugiados políticos." *El Periódico* 4 September.

Désir, Harlem. 1991. "Un entretien avec le président de SOS-Racisme." *Le Monde* 8 June: 2.

DiGiacomo, Susan. 1984. *The Politics of Identity: Nationalism in Catalonia*. Ph.D. Dissertation, University of Massachusetts.

Duva, Jesús. 1991. "110,000 personas han solicitado legalizar su situacion a tres días de que termine el plazo." *El País*. 8 December:22.

Essed, Philomena. 1990. *Everyday Racism.* Claremont: Hunter House
_____. 1991. *Understanding Everyday Racism.* Newbury Park:Sage.
Europ. 1992. "Extreme droite: La cote d'alerte." 64: Janvier-Mars.
Foster, Imogen. 1989. "Nature's outcast child: black people in children's books." *Race & Class* 31 (1):59-77.
Frappot, Bruno. 1991. "Madame Cresson denonce les propos de M. Chirac." *Le Monde.* 15 June 1991:1, 40.
Furriol, Eulalia. 1990. "Una nova cultura productiva a les empreses japoneses radicades a Catalunya." *Món Laboral* 11 (Segon Semestre): 7-19.
García, Fernando. 1991. "Cataluña está amenazada por la falta de inmigración extranjera." *La Vanguardia.* 8 August:15.
García, Pep. 1991. "Inmigración." *Som-Hi Raval* 1(4) junio-julio:3.
Gilroy, Paul. 1987. *"There ain't no Black in the Union Jack": the Cultural Politics of 'Race' and Nation.* London: Hutchison.
Grillo, R.D. 1985. *Ideologies and Institutions in Urban France: The Representation of Immigrants.* Cambridge: University Press.
Harris, Geoffrey. 1990. *The Dark Side of Europe: The Extreme Right Today.* Savage, Md: Barnes & Noble.
Husband, Charles. 1982. *'Race' in Britain: Continuity and Change.* London: Hutchison University Library.
Hughes, Langston. 1956. *I Wonder as I Wander.* New York: Hill and Wang.
Johnson, Amryl. 1988. *Sequins for a Ragged Hem.* London: Virago.
Kristeva, Julia. 1988. *Etrangers à Nous Memes.* Paris: Fayard.
Kureishi, Hanif. 1988. *Sammy and Rosie Get Laid: The Screenplay and The Screenwriter's Diary.* New York: Penguin.
Lebaude, Alain. 1991. "Les employeurs de clandestins seront plus severement sanctiones." *Le Monde* September 28.
Lebow, Richard. 1976. *White Britain and Black Ireland.* Philadelphia:ISHI.
Lester, Rosemarie K. 1986. "Blacks in Germany and German Blacks: A Little Known Aspect of Black History," in R. Grimm, and J. Hermand, eds. *Blacks and German Culture.* PP. 113-134. Madison: University of Wisconsin.
Losada, M. Teresa. 1988. "La inmigración arabo-musulmana en Cataluña en los últimos 20 años." *Boletín Informativo: Secretariado de la C.E. de Relaciones Interconfesionales.* 27 (October-December-1988):18-23.
_____. 1990. "Segunda generación de inmigración marroquí," in M. A. Roque, ed., *Els moviments humans en el mediterrani occidental.* Pp. 243-248. Barcelona: Institut Català d'Estudis Mediterranis.
McDonogh, Gary. 1986. *Good Families of Barcelona: A Social History of Power in the Industrial Era.* Princeton: Princeton University Press.
_____. 1991. "Discourses of the City: Policy and Responses in Post-Transitional Barcelona." *City & Society* 5 (1):40-63.
_____. 1992a. "Terra de Pas: Reflections on Immigration in Catalonia," in M.Azevedo, ed., *Gaspar de Portola Catalonia Studies Program Symposium on Catalonia, Europe and the World.* Berkeley: International and Area Studies.
_____. 1992b. "Bars, Gender and Virtue: Myth and Practice in Barcelona's *Barrio Chino.*" *Anthropological Quarterly* 65(1):19-33.

164

_____. n.d. *Black and Catholic in Savannah*. Knoxville: University of Tennessee Press.

McDonogh, Gary, and Gaspar Maza. n.d. "Chaval del Barrio, Hijo de la Ciudad." *Revista de Ciencies Socials*.

El Malki, Habib. 1990. "La place du facteur humaine," in M. A. Roque, ed., *Els moviments humans en el mediterrani occidental*. Pp. 95-98. Barcelona: Institut Català d'Estudis Mediterranis.

Martínez, Pepe. 1991. "Racisme." *Som-Hi Raval* 1(4): 8-9.

Massonneau, Valerie, and Laurence Masurel. 1991. "Philippe Marchand: Il n'y aura pas de Bronx en France." *Paris Match* 13 June: 54-5.

Melcher, Robert. 1991. "Racist Habits Taint the French." *The European* 29-31 March: 5,15.

Miles, Robert. 1989. *Racism*. London: Routledge.

Murray, Nancy. 1986. "Anti-racists and other demons: the press and ideology in Thatcher's Britain." *Race and Class*, 27 (3): 1-19.

Nadal, Rafael. 1989. "Esto no es América: Integración y racismo conviven en la geografía de la inmigración en España." *El País* 8 January.

Pereda, C., M. A. Pereda, and colectivo IOE. 1987. "Los Inmigrantes en Espana." *Documentación Social* 66 (I-III 1987).

Pi-Sunyer, Oriol. n.d. *The Absent Other*. Amherst:University of Massachusetts Press.

Prada, Miguel Angel de. 1990. "España, de país de emigración a país de inmigración," in M. A. Roque, ed., *Els moviments humans en el mediterrani occidental*. Pp. 232-42. Barcelona: Institut Català d'Estudis Mediterranis.

Raspail, Jean. 1973. *Le Camp des Saints*. Paris: Robert Laffont.

Reeves, F. 1983. *British Racial Discourse: A Study of British Political Discourse about Race and Race-related Matters*. Cambridge: University Press.

Rice, Robert. 1991. "Trying to Stem the Refugee Tide." *World Press Review* November: 13-14. Reprinted from *the Financial Times*, London.

Riding, Alan. 1990. "Western Europe, Its Births Falling, Wonders Who'll Do All the Work." *New York Times* 22 July.

Rincón, Juan Carlos. 1991. "Slamming the Door on the Third World." *World Press Review* 14 November:14. Reprinted from *El Espectador*, Bogotá.

Rollnick, Roman. 1991. "Europe's New Ghettos of Fear." *The European*. March 29-31.

Roque, Maria Angels, ed. 1990. *Els moviments humans en el mediterrani occidental*. Barcelona: Institut Català d'Estudis Mediterranis.

Said, Edward. 1978. *Orientalism*. New York: Random House.

San Román, Teresa, ed. 1986. *Entre la marginación y el racismo. Reflexiones sobre la vida de los gitanos*. Madrid: Alianza.

Sivanandan, A. 1990. *Communities of Resistance*. London: Verso.

Smitherman-Donaldson, Geneva, and Teun A. van Dijk, eds. 1988. *Discourse and Discrimination*. Detroit:Wayne State University Press.

Temprano, Emilio. 1990. *La caverna racial europea*. Madrid: Cátedra.

Todorov, Tzvetan. 1990. *Nous et les autres: La reflexion francaise sur la diversite humaine*. Paris: Du Seuil.

Van Dijk, T.A. 1991. *Racism and the Press* London: Routledge Kegan Paul.

Vi-Makomé, Inongo. 1990. *España y los Negros Africanos*. Barcelona: Llar de Llibres.

Weil, Simone. 1990. "Europa i la Mediterrania," in M. A. Roque, ed., *Els moviments humans en el mediterrani occidental*. Pp. 41-50. Barcelona: Institut Català d'Estudis Mediterranis.

Weil, Patrick. 1991. *La France et ses Etrangers*. Paris: Calmann-Lévy.

Whitney, Craig R. 1991. "Europe Looks for Ways to Bar Door to Immigrants." *New York Times*. 29 December.

Wieviorka, Michel. 1991. *L'Espace du Racisme*. Paris: L'Harmattan.

Willis, Paul. 1977. *Learning to Labour: How Working Class Kids Get Working Class Jobs*. New York: Columbia.

Woolard, Kathryn. 1989. *Double Talk*. Stanford: University Press.

9

Frontiers Go but Boundaries Remain: The Irish Border as a Cultural Divide

Thomas M. Wilson

One of the idealized goals of the completion of the European Community's (EC) Internal Market (IM) in 1993 is the creation of a "Europe without frontiers" (European Communities – Commission 1987). In most discussions of this process, the frontiers which are to be made redundant are seen to be the economic ones, i.e., all customs and legislative barriers between the EC's member states to the free movement of goods, services, and capital will be removed. But the realization of a true common market will also guarantee the free movement of information and people, which will have a number of ramifications in the social, cultural, and political spheres of each member nation. In fact, the creation of a New Economic Europe is clearly seen by the leaders of both the EC and the EC's states to be the prelude to a New Political and Social Europe. Although the configuration of this New Europe is very much in doubt, and the subject of heated post-Maastricht debate, it is becoming increasingly clear that the IM is a political transformation, which will certainly redefine the international borders between the EC's states but will not necessarily make these borders any less important, either for the communities and people who live there or for their nations and states. Economic frontiers may disappear but state borders and the symbolic boundaries which construct those borders will remain.

The transformations which these international boundaries will undergo are vital aspects of the EC integration processes and are sure to influence all future debates about the organization and expansion of the EC. Nevertheless, the impact and meaning of the EC among people who live at international borders is one of the least documented areas of the social science of the EC. This chapter explores some of the issues of the creation of an EC without frontiers by looking at a number of the ways in which the Irish Border may change, both physically and symbolically, due to and during EC integration in the IM. Its tentative conclusions support the hypothesis that the Irish Border will remain a cultural divide between the communities on either side of the international boundary, and, by extension, will persist as a barrier to sociocultural integration among the peoples of the Republic of Ireland (RI), Northern Ireland (NI), and the United Kingdom (UK). This situation may have resonances throughout the borderlands of the EC, but, at the least, is one possible arena in which the ECs' attempts at economic and political integration may or may not be successful.

There has been remarkably little anthropological research on and at the Irish land Border, and almost none on the "southern" side, i.e., in the counties in the RI which are contiguous to the six counties of NI. With few exceptions (see, e.g., Shanklin 1985; Taylor 1989) little ethnographic research in the RI has been near the Border or has viewed the Border as a cultural context. Perhaps not surprisingly, the majority of this work has also avoided the issues of the EC at local levels (Wilson 1984). In "the North" (as NI is most often referred to in the RI, "the South"), however, there have been a number of studies which address the issues of life in Border communities, most often in terms of class and religion (see, e.g., Bufwack 1982; Harris 1972; Leyton 1975; Vincent 1989), themes which reflect a more applied focus in NI ethnographic research (see, e.g., Donnan and McFarlane 1989) than exists in the RI. Although there has been some anthropological attention paid to the role of the EC at local levels in Ireland (Shutes 1991; Wilson 1989) as well as at regional and national levels (Kockel 1991; Ruane and Todd 1991), to date there has been no study in the sociocultural anthropology of Ireland which either investigates the impact of the EC on a Border community, or looks at the ways Border people are attempting to influence national and EC policy making.

This is understandable, given the dearth of anthropological interest throughout Europe in all things "EC" (some reasons for this are reviewed in this volume's introduction), but it is somewhat surprising because of the economic changes the EC has already effected in Border communities as well as the potential political changes which local and regional initiatives may effect through the EC. In the words of the leader of the major constitutional nationalist party of NI, EC integration might result in a situation where the "Irish border, like other European borders, will be no more in reality than a county boundary" (Ruane and Todd 1991:91). If this comes to pass, perhaps in a Europe of Regions espoused by the same politician, then the spinoff effects in the sociocultural lives of the people and communities living at these borders may be momentous. Simply put, if international borders are legally and/or functionally transformed due to state and supranational policies, then their roles in the day-to-day affairs of people who live and work at the borders will also be transformed. This, in turn, will redefine the meanings of those borders in the cultural construction of border communities' past, present, and future. Any economic and political changes which transform the Border in the future will resonate among those communities, North and South, who define themselves, if only in part, in terms of that Border. In NI alone this includes all those who see themselves as unionists, republicans, loyalists, Irish and/or British. A transformed Border will not only affect those NI people whose identities are dependent on their cultural constructions of the historical and contemporary Border, but will also manifest great changes in the everyday lives of all people who reside and labor at that Border.

This chapter's conclusions suggest that the Border will remain a fixed line as an international boundary in order to prevent criminals, terrorists, and illegal aliens from crossing it. In a borderland where the international boundary itself is disputed and at which there is a war which symbolically revolves around the presence of that Border (in which the definition of "terrorist" is also contested by many people of the local nationalist majority), the security forces' interpretations of free movement may become problematic in an era of "no frontiers." Thus, this chapter also explores ways in which the Border may be reinforced as a symbolic cultural boundary, which for hundreds of years, and certainly since the 1921 partition of Ireland into a twenty-six county Free State (now the RI) and a six county NI (a province still "loyal" or in "union" with the rest of the UK) defined some of the limits to local Border culture and community. For a great many people living on both sides of the Irish Border, and regardless of the hopes of many of their political leaders, EC integration may or may not result in a removal of economic barriers (the so-called EC frontiers) but its role in diminishing cultural boundaries is perceived to be marginal.[1]

The Irish Border as a Cultural Divide

Although there have been few anthropological analyses of the significance of the Border in the lives of its communities, since the 1970s there has been an increase in both scholarly and governmental interest in the Border as a region. This interest has been largely due to the resurgence of "the Troubles," i.e., the revitalization of nationalist terrorist responses to, at first, the violence of sectarianism, and then to the introduction of British military forces (for a review of the range of developments which have led to more scholarly interest in the Irish borderlands, see O'Dowd and Corrigan 1992). One seminal study, conducted by a geographer, predated both the present Troubles and the resulting academic and public sector attention. This study stressed the cultural significance of the Irish Border in the historical and political development of the British Isles, and it sought to place the Border within a comparative framework which would stimulate the study of other international boundaries as *cultural* divides between regions, nations, and states:

> Because of their appearance and course, because of the territories they give size and shape to, because of their impact on daily life, and above all because of the influences they exert upon the feelings of the people they unite or divide, boundaries form a fascinating theme. In the last resort they are symbols: they can stand for possession and loss, for hopes and disillusions, for patriotism and for oppression, for rights and wrongs. People may hate them and want them abolished and people may revere them, even long for them (Heslinga 1971:7).

The people and communities of the Irish Borderlands recognize the international boundary as both a fixed legal demarcation and a symbol of much that constructs the cultures which both integrate and separate them. They also recognize that their roles at the Border are taking on more significance than they did in the past, due in large part to EC interest in the potential impact of the IM on its borders and frontiers.[2] Reflecting this new Border awareness is a growing historical scholarship in Ireland on the role of the Border regions in the processes of nation building (see, e.g., Gillespie and O'Sullivan 1989).

The dialogic and dialectic relationships between local society and national centers is an arena of political economic relations that remains largely undocumented in the scholarship of nation building in Europe, and is almost wholly absent from the social science of EC-building. One area where these relations between local and national sociocultures is both clear and significant is at international borders. Following in the comparative tradition of Heslinga, Peter Sahlins has highlighted the importance of Border society in nation and state building in France and Spain:

both state formation and nation building were two-way processes at work since at least the seventeenth century. States did not simply impose their values and boundaries on local society. Rather, local society was a motive force in the formation and consolidation of nationhood and the territorial state. The political boundary appeared in the borderland as the outcome of national political events, as a function of the different strengths, interests, and (ultimately) histories of France and Spain. But the shape and significance of the boundary line was constructed out of local social relations in the borderland (1989: 8).

Although there have been many reasons why the Irish Borderlands' roles in similar processes have not been recognized by scholars and national leaders, this does not diminish Borderers' perceptions of the significance of their communities in the development of both their nations and their nations' roles in the EC. Such views of the Irish Border share the perspective that the legal border between the RI and the UK may only date from the 1920s but it has been a significant factor in the cultural divergence between communities on both of its sides. To many this increasing cultural dissonance is a reflection of diverging national trajectories, which have existed since the 17th century. To others the Border was a result of modern political machinations, still the cause of bitter debate in North and South, and it has created new causes of cultural disintegration. Overall, the people of the Border are aware that it will be altered in the future, but they are unsure as to the ways this will change what the Border means to them.

The processes of EC integration in the IM are intended to break down any barriers to the free movement of goods, people, and capital, but these same processes may be thwarted by the actual strengthening of border barriers throughout the EC because of concerns about security, immigration, and crime. Perhaps more significant to the EC will be the effects of integration on the symbolic constructions of borders. The borders of the EC will continue to mean something not only to borderland inhabitants but to all residents and citizens of the EC member states who recognize the importance of international boundaries to regional and national culture. These boundaries have a variety of functions, such as marking the limits to national sovereignty, defining the extent of, or the barrier to, national or regional culture, symbolizing a colonial or imperial past, or acting as a bulwark against the admittance of "others." In the Irish case the Border has come to symbolize many aspects of cultural cross-Border integration as well as cultural separation and divergence. The significance of EC-induced changes in local society at the Irish Border cannot be appreciated unless the wider contexts of cross-Border culture are explored.

Integration and Divergence

Many scholars conclude that the line drawn in 1921 which partitioned Ireland corresponds somewhat to a cultural division that has existed for centuries between the traditional province of Ulster in the north of Ireland and the rest of the island. This cultural borderland is important in the overall history of Ireland and Britain, and may be more usefully viewed as corresponding to a British north-south divide, i.e., northern Ireland may have more in common with Scotland and northern England than with "its" south, and the southern parts of both islands may be closer culturally than with their northern neighbors (Heslinga 1971:7-21). Traditional Ulster was also partitioned in the 1920s, with three of its nine counties remaining in the Free State. This was due in part to Unionists' demands to be the political majority in the only region of Ireland to remain loyal to the crown, but it also reflected the fact that the greater part of the province was home to historical, cultural, religious, and nationalist traditions not widely found elsewhere in Ireland. The core of this alternative "Irishness" was, and is, north County Down and south County Antrim, the areas in and around Belfast. To this day the majority of the people of NI are the descendants of colonists from Scotland, and are in large part Protestant or Presbyterian and Loyalist and Unionist, i.e., loyal to the British Crown and State and intending to maintain NI's union with the rest of the UK. These religious and nationalist traditions must be differentiated from sectarianism, which is religious bigotry and a tragic aspect of national and ethnic identity in NI. Ostensibly opposing this majority are those people in the province who are Roman Catholic and Nationalist, i.e., who claim affinities with the majority of the people of the RI. Perhaps the most important political ideology of this minority (who make up approximately one-third of the province's population of a million and a half) is republicanism, which in its most violent form, as promoted by the Irish Republican Army (IRA), seeks the unification of the two Irelands of North and South and the reversal of ethnic roles, i.e., in a thirty-two county socialist republic the Protestants of NI would be the national minority. This chapter is not a review of either the roots of the conflict in NI nor is it an analysis of contemporary political traditions. It is concerned with the ways the Irish Border symbolizes cultural dissonance in Ireland and the ways material relationships are changing at the Border, due in part to EC integration. Irrespective of the historical antecedents of the Border, the 1920s partition created, for the first time, an international boundary between nation-states on the island of Ireland. This fact has had major repercussions in local society and culture among the people of that island.

Thus, in many ways Border culture has had a short history in Ireland. Contrary to many stereotypes common outside of Ireland, and surprising even to the (other) British peoples, the legal demarcation between Ireland North and South has not proved to be a major barrier to many aspects of convergent culture, but it has proved to be an effective block to other aspects of a common culture. These functions will sustain the Border as a cultural divide long after the IM is implemented.

The key to cultural integration anywhere is communication. Perhaps the most important barriers to cross-Border communication are the political ideologies and overall political cultures which help define northern and southern Ireland. For example, until June 1992 the two major unionist political parties in NI had never formally met with representatives of the government of the RI, because doing so was seen by them to be a recognition of that government's right to be consulted on NI matters. The constitution of the RI, on the other hand, claims sovereignty over the counties of NI, i.e., one EC state claims another's territory. Unionists contend that such an arrogant claim prevents any meaningful dialogue. Any sort of negotiated peace in NI would be difficult because the various ideologies of unionism and republicanism are diametrically opposed. The groups of people from either side of the Border who adopt them are accepting historical constructions of ethnicity and nationality which make the integration of "the other" difficult if not impossible.

The provincial dominance of a Protestant majority belies the sociocultural realities of life at the Border in NI. In fact, most Northerners residing at the Border are Catholics, and perhaps have more in common with the people in the RI than they do with the majority of people in NI. This is also not to say that this NI Catholic minority are mostly republicans. But much of the IRA's support can be found in Border communities hit hard by the Troubles. Many of these people are certainly nationalists, but the ways to achieve a united "nation" of thirty-two counties, and the political configuration such a state would take, are hotly debated topics among the nationalists of the Border, and a subject worthy of much more ethnographic and political research than has heretofore occurred. But the fact that both "republican" and "nationalist" are the key political identities among the majority of the people at the NI side of the Border does not necessarily mean that they have much in common with their neighbors to the south. In fact, one would be hard pressed to find many supporters of the IRA in most places in the RI except in the Southwest, the cities, and the RI side of the Border, in the so-called "Border counties." Nonetheless, unionists fear an alliance between Northern and Southern republicans and have been attempting to thwart any political solutions to the NI situation which would include the RI government. The large banner hanging from the Belfast city hall reads "Ulster Says No." Although specifically addressing the Anglo-Irish Agreement of 1985, it also symbolizes Unionist rejection of any integrationist initiatives which might draw the province closer to the RI and/or further away from the UK, *even if* any of those initiatives come from the UK or the EC.

The basis for much of the political divergence between the communities across the Border comes from a strong belief in nationalism. The contested nationhoods of "Irish" and "British" make the integration of the nationalist minority difficult to achieve in NI, and make cross-Border cooperation difficult as well (for a review of the successes and failures of such cooperation, see O'Dowd and Corrigan 1992). As already noted, however, this has as much to do with entrenched politics on either side of the Border as it has with disputed meanings of "history," "nation," and "state." Since 1976 I have lived a good deal of my life in a town about thirty-five miles south of the Border. In all that time I have rarely heard anyone suggest that the unification of Ireland would be a good thing for the people of the South. Fear of terrorism, the economic costs of subsidizing the Northern economy, and the cultural distinctiveness of Northerners are the reasons most often given to me by the people of Meath as to why a thirty-two county republic is "just not on." Many Meath people are increasingly defining their nation as "the Irish" of the RI. They of course agree that all Northerners are Irish, even if some are more so than others, but that Northerners are so different that being Irish does not make them *the same* Irish as themselves (in ways reminiscent of so many cultural boundary studies done by anthropologists all over the world, including the British Isles, e.g., Cohen 1982). Nationalist attitudes are different yet again at the southern side of the Border, where many people resent the British security presence just across the fields from them, and fear for many of their friends and relatives who live across those same fields, on the northern side of the Border. In three counties of the RI there is also a shared Ulster heritage – these were the counties separated from the province at partition. Thus there is a strong republican sentiment in the Border counties of the RI, but even this is being challenged by the persistent images of indiscriminate IRA violence. In fact, on one isolated peninsula in the South the population publicly renounced support for the IRA after that organization assassinated a local farmer which it believed to be an informer (McCrystal 1991).

Terrorism, or in the words of some, the war of resistance, is thus another factor which prevents cross-Border communication and contact. Many people I know in Meath have never been to NI. Some are proud of this fact. Most contend that it is because of the violence. People at the southern side of the Border, especially at the eastern end of the Border where I am currently conducting field research, cross the Border all the time. In most cases this is to shop. Everyone I have interviewed considered the terrorist/security situation before visiting or living in the North. Some people deny that the security problem is important in their decision-making, but no one ignores it. In fact, the reasons one might travel North spring to most peoples' lips, because it is an excuse to discuss both the Border and the Troubles. As one Dundalk man told me, in regard to Southerners living or working in the North, "the only reason [Southerners] would emigrate North would be for love or money." But as one Armagh (NI) man countered, "there is precious little love left here." The offer of employment or the enticement of trying to collect a second dole may be motives for commuting North, but with the rising unemployment on both sides of the Border (with estimates running to over 25%) it is unlikely that there will be much south to north migration in the future.

The symbols of the Troubles are everywhere in NI. When crossing into the North on the main Dublin - Belfast road, one has to go through a security checkpoint complete with bunkers, sandbags, soldiers in flak jackets, policemen with automatic weapons, and barriers and ramps designed to slow up or isolate traffic. The precautions the security personnel take may be necessary – this checkpoint has been bombed twice by the IRA since 1991. Up and down the Border are a number of roads which are "unapproved," i.e., one is not supposed to take these roads across what may be the most "invisible" border in Europe. Many locals use these roads (which they consider to be *their* roads) often. When one is on them it is often impossible to detect if the Border has been crossed because there are very few signs announcing the transition (e.g., there are no mile markers or monuments so common at many European frontiers). Unless a traveller is used to the tell-tale signs – red or green post boxes, the surface of the road (good in the North, very bad in the South), characteristic road signs, and the design and care paid to houses and fields – one is apt to miss the change in national context. The color-coded symbols are sure to set the uncertain travellers right, when they encounter the red/white/blue or orange/white/green kerbstones, banners, and flags which mark the territorial limits of loyalists and nationalists respectively. Of course, battle-geared soldiers and police may also give it away. There is a war going on in NI, and no EC initiatives regarding the IM are going to change that sad fact.

Cultural stereotyping, which is not a far cry from sectarianism, also prevents cross-Border communication and integration. Such stereotypes are difficult to measure and impossible to quantify. To what extent does an offhand remark regarding the dress, the habits, and the speech of "the others" reflect either more serious forms of behavior or the commonly held beliefs of ones' comrades ("us," however defined)? Nonetheless, such cultural stereotyping is real, potent, and far from decline in Ireland and Britain. Some of this stereotyping may be laudatory – Northerners, both Catholic and Protestant, are often seen to be honest, precise, neat, god-fearing, and excellent business people – but it is also tied to negative images – humorless, unloving, and bigoted, for example. For better or worse these notions are commonly expressed, along with Northern versions of people and behavior in the RI, and they inform the beliefs and actions of many people who are reluctant to work towards closer integration of the many Irelands.

There have also been a number of economic barriers to cross-Border communication. Most of these have been customs and excise controls on the import-export trade. The economies of the towns of Newry and Dundalk, for instance, have depended on international trade as much as on local retailing and services. The completion of the common market is transforming most of these economic cross-Border ties because of the removal of customs checks at borders and the effects of the harmonization of taxes on retail prices. Suffice to say, these barriers are overcome by those who can afford to do so, and, as might be expressed by an EC free marketeer, commerce is a driving force behind cross-cultural and international communication.

Other forms of economics, on the other hand, tie communities to each other across the Border. As reviewed above, the Irish Border is an agent of integration itself in that it helps to construct, both materially and symbolically, relationships between people who might otherwise be divided by an international boundary. There are many agents of cultural integration which may transcend the Border but which seldom ignore it. Even the institutions of Church and sport which predate the creation of the international boundary in Ireland are now largely influenced by its presence. In short, a great deal of cross-Border and cross-cultural interaction goes on both because of and regardless of the Border. Much of this interaction may be affected by the EC moves towards the IM and monetary and political union.

An economic activity which is in great need of more research world-wide (among other aspects of the informal economy, see Smith 1990), and which is poorly documented at the Irish Border, is smuggling. As one Borderer put it in an interview with me, "around here smuggling is a cottage industry." Since the creation of the Border there has arisen a network of smugglers on both sides of the Border who smuggle whatever goods are in greatest demand and which offer the best reward. Since the 1920s these have often been farm goods, and since EC accession and the vagaries of farm subsidies and currency fluctuations across the Border such smuggling has flourished (Norton 1986). As I have often been told by people at the Border, it was not uncommon for the same load of wheat or cattle to be imported, smuggled out at night, and re-imported in order to collect the EC and state subsidies. In the 1980s, after the RI joined the European Monetary System and thus broke with sterling, the prices for consumer durables diverged considerably. Smugglers made many a profit bringing appliances, beer, spirits, and fuel into the South, in the so-called "boom" years for Northern retailers – years which were over by the end of the decade (T. Wilson n.d.). The unapproved roads were not just labelled as such for security reasons, but for the prevention of smuggling as well. When I recounted an embarassing adventure of being lost on the Cooley peninsula and finding myself in NI, my host reckoned I must have taken the "telly road" into the province, so named for the amounts of home appliances which made their way, unassisted of course, into the expectant hands of Southern consumers. Such smuggling is a common form of cross-Border linkage – after all, economics are seen to be a driving force behind culture by many people other than free marketeers – but its dimensions are difficult for a researcher to ascertain, for obvious methodological and ethical reasons. But long-term field research at any international border is sure to uncover many long-standing cross-cultural linkages (as, e.g., in the Pyrenees, see Douglass 1977), which are definitely not included in the plans for an integrated Europe. At the Irish Border, families and friends have long taken part in such illegalities, and they wonder what they will be able to smuggle in a future barrier-free, price-harmonized common market (besides drugs, armaments, and people, that is). They do not know what they will smuggle, but they know that they will find something.

Perhaps the most important form of face-to-face communication between communities at the Border in recent years has been cross-Border shopping. From 1979 to 1987, when the RI government attempted to stop the flow of its citizens to shops in the North, the towns of NI experienced an economic boom which transformed much of their infrastructure and brought Southerners to their communities in numbers unmatched in NI's short history (the economic dimensions to this period are reviewed in Fitzgerald et al. 1988). As I have detailed elsewhere (T. Wilson n.d.), these shopping forays ran the gamut from a few minutes' spin to a NI petrol station, to busloads of shoppers, on what might be an eight hour round trip, who would disembark from their coaches for a few hours of frenzied shopping for such things as spirits, small appliances, and toys. In Newry alone, where such shopping has fallen off since the introduction of travellers' restrictions in the RI, more stringent customs checks, and a return to price parity through the twin forces of tax harmonization and a UK inflation rate higher than that of the RI, merchants reckon that they are losing hundreds of thousands of pounds a year off the peaks of 1985 and 1986. But when this shopping was at its height, tens of thousands of Southerners overcame their doubts about terrorism and overlooked their stereotyped images of the North in order to buy cheap. Car parks in NI, from Derry to Newry, were full with RI registered autos. And although the consumer relationships which resulted were transitory, shopping brought people together who often came from great distances. Not surprisingly, until very recently Southern Border people continued to cross the line in order to buy less expensive petrol, spirits, cigarettes, and beer. As mentioned above, they have a number of reasons to view the Border differently from their countrymen, and so it is not the symbolic barrier it might be to others. Nonetheless, as prices converged since 1990, consumers have tended to stay on their own side of the Border. Northerners seldom shop south, except for weekend trips to buy Irish lottery tickets or to drink safely in a Southern pub. All of these face-to-face contacts, as ephemeral as they may be, help to break down cultural stereotypes and make the people on both sides of the Border question the images and notions they have learned regarding "them, the others."

Tourism functions in similar ways. Both day trippers and people on longer stays, whether heading north or south, help to break down barriers to cultural misunderstanding (this is not to deny the many obfuscations which result from tourist experiences and tourism images; for a review of NI tourism from an anthropological perspective, see D. Wilson n.d.). The importance of tourism has been recognized by the local governments of NI and the RI. Regional tourism initiatives, which define cross-Border regions (the tourist boards' construction of "St. Patrick's Country," which crosses the NI-RI Border, is a case in point) are some of the few areas where the governments cooperate. Both localities and governments are seeking to project images across the Border which will attract consumers. This important economic strategy has a great many sociocultural implications, one of which is its effect on bringing separated communities closer together.

Local government from both sides of the Border cooperate unofficially in a number of areas – road maintenance and sewerage are two – but there has been little to bring the provincial government and that of the RI together over the years, until the Anglo-Irish Agreement of 1985 established formal intergovernmental links. Since the resurgence of violence in NI in 1969, in fact, such relations have declined. This is not surprising given the political constituencies and philosophies reviewed above, but may appear a bit curious given the the convergence in political cultures between the two "states." People on both sides of the Border espouse the principles of parliamentary democracy, the rule of law, and nationalism (which, of course, cuts both ways). The UK and the RI are members of the EC and the UN. People in NI have the right to claim RI citizenship, and all Irish have the rights of citizens when resident in the UK. As Heslinga concludes "the British Isles in many vitally important respects still form a social unit" (1971:14). In a paradoxical way the political cultures of North and South in Ireland continue to both divide and bind. The impact of an integrating supranation is sure to become increasingly problematic at the levels of all cross-border political organizations and cultures throughout the EC.

Other organizations which bring their members together across the Border are churches and religions. Both the Roman Catholic Church and the Church of Ireland have parishes and dioceses which straddle the Border. People cross the Borderline when travelling to Church functions, such as baptisms and marriages, and recognize a comradeship which transcends any political demarcations. There has also been a growing ecumenical spirit in NI, fuelled by a number of atrocities perpetrated on the innocent by the "men of violence." Although the impact of such initiatives is often difficult to judge, especially among the nationalist enclaves at the Border, their significance for cross-Border cultural integration, both now and in the future, should not be underestimated. Like politics, religious culture may bring together people of the same religion and of different religions, or, in its sectarian aspect, lead to their murder.

More popular aspects of culture also transcend the Border. The Gaelic Athletic Association is the umbrella organization for traditional Gaelic games (hurling, Gaelic football, and camogie chief among them) in all thirty-two counties. Although associated with Catholic and Irish nationalism, the GAA's rather stringent and biased membership rules are all but a thing of the past (many people I interviewed in both the RI and NI remember the days when a young man was banned from playing Gaelic if he was even seen to pick up a soccer or rugby football). Nonetheless, few Protestants today play Gaelic sports, especially in NI. Rugby is another sport which is "country-wide," i.e., at international matches Ireland fields a team which represents the whole island (unlike soccer, which in international play has NI and RI teams). In terms of sports, the international boundary is hardly there, although sports also symbolize inclusivity and exclusivity, us and them.

Perhaps the most pervasive agents of cultural communication (which are almost impossible to study ethnographically, at least in terms of their reception) are the media. Newspapers, radio, and television provide the most important sources of cultural imaging because they present images of sameness and otherness, violence and peace, tragedy and humor. Their portraits of life on either side of the Border supply models of history, culture, and behavior that are difficult to dispute without first-hand experience. Because I live in both Irelands, I continually field questions about the corruption of RI politicians on the one hand, and about the ways people deal with all the flying lead which Southerners seem to think blocks out the sun in the North. Such images contain both truth and hyperbole, and owe much to the learning experiences of family, community, and the media. These media also break down the stereotypes and aid understanding and communication. But sex and violence still sell papers. As with any attempt to construct a cultural reality – as in writing an ethnography or this essay – the receiver of the words and images can interpret them as views of "us" and "them." These media images are the ones which most inform the cultures of the two Irelands today, a result of the fall-off in everyday contact across the Border, a situation which the EC may exacerbate.

As the above has demonstrated, there are many ideas, organizations, and relationships which both bring together communities from either side of the Border and keep them apart. The Border is both a material barrier to their discourse (e.g., as a customs stop) as well as a reason for cooperation (e.g., in smuggling). The Border is a symbolic barrier as well, behind which nations, creeds, and political parties can hide (where would republicanism and unionism be without it?), but also one which creates reasons for cross-Border communication. This Border, like many in the EC, has fashioned or influenced local society and culture in a number of ways which are certain to be influenced by EC integration. Both the Irish Borderers and I speculate on the ways this might occur.

The Irish Border in 1993 and Beyond

It is often difficult to judge the effects of public policy at local levels in the lives of most citizens, but even more difficult when many of the policies one would like to investigate have either not been decided yet or have not filtered down to the operational levels of local society and culture. Any analysis today (1992) of the ECs' goal of an IM in 1993 and beyond is thus constrained. But this chapter, and much of this book, seek to speculate about future sociocultural change, in much the same way as many people I have met throughout Ireland. They know the EC is coming, in the form if a single market, which elicits various responses of fear, curiosity, hope, and humor. The completion of the IM is judged by many people at the eastern end of the Border, in the rural and urban areas around Newry and Dundalk, as having an important impact on the quality of life of many Border residents. This material impact, which is locally discussed principally in economic terms, will probably change aspects of local employment, consumer culture, smuggling, and tourism. Many people recognize that it is sure to have other spinoff effects. The people on the NI side are more concerned with issues of sovereignty and security, which reflects wider concerns in the UK as a whole. As a result they do not want to see the "weakening" of the Border, i.e., they welcome the facilitated movement of goods, services, and capital, but not of people. But perhaps the most interesting result of EC integration at the Border may be its impact, or lack of one, on the symbolic constructions of the Border as a cultural boundary. Simply put, the economic changes are not likely to increase cross-Border traffic in people, and may diminish that form of communication. If so, then the Border will continue as a cultural divide, across which some will still go because of the networks they are already part of, but which will still act as the limits to many communities' self-defined notions of membership.

At present there are hundreds of people employed at the Border in jobs which may be made redundant after the completion of the IM. In the areas around the hubs of Newry and Dundalk, there are over two hundred people who work as customs agents, private customs clearing agents, and service personnel for the Border lorry traffic (e.g., in cafes and petrol and diesel stations). After 1993 lorries will no longer be required to stop for customs reasons (it is still unclear to what extent they will be stopped for security searches) which may have a devastating effect on workers and their families whose livelihoods depend on their commerce. Any unemployment is sure to have an important ripple effect in towns of over 20,000 inhabitants and 25% unemployment. Some jobs will remain after 1993. For example, some clearance agents will be operating computer links with ports of entry into the EC, clearing all paper work by phone and fax. But the majority of government employees and the lorry service personnel are pessimistic. Although both towns are lobbying their respective governments for both grants and employment schemes which will soften the shock of an IM, the state of their depressed economies does not bode well for local or regional fix-its. Nonetheless, the politics of EC integration at local and regional levels, and the dialectical relationships they have with national and supranational centers, is not only of interest to social scientists (as this book strongly suggests) but to EC citizens at local levels as well.

The goals of a common market include the harmonization of sales (VAT) and excise taxes among the member states, which has already been occurring at the Irish Border. Although economic integration of these sorts may help create economies of scale which will benefit the EC as a whole, it is important for all players (public and private sector decision-makers as much as scholars) to recognize that these changes will result in winners and losers at all sociocultural levels. Among the losers appear to be the consumers and some of the NI retailers at the Border. Without lower prices on either side, and at this stage there is almost complete parity, consumers will not cross the Border looking for much needed bargains in staple and luxury items. Newry town has already experienced the loss of revenue, as Southern cars come no further than a hundred meters into NI in order to buy some beer and fill up the petrol tank, saving just a few pounds in the transaction. Harmonized taxes and prices across the EC is sure to affect all those shopping zones specifically set up to attract the cross-border shopper (e.g., at the boundaries between France and Spain and Denmark and Germany). Such policies are also going to affect non-member states, as well as the statelets such as Andorra which depend on shopping. At the Irish Border less shopping will mean less travel and communication, perhaps making the international divide wider than it is today.

Smugglers are also wondering about the possible impact of the IM on their livelihoods. As noted above, their alternatives in an economy which limits or eliminates a lucrative but illicit trade in taxable goods would be to trade goods which are illegal in either or both countries. But the importation of weapons or drugs are not victimless crimes, a defence a few smugglers have made to me when discussing TVs or beer. And the British army or NI police will have no sense of humor if they catch anyone with these goods. Farm goods may still be worth the "midnight express" treatment, but the EC farm policy reforms and a Border which may be more heavily policed make such ventures increasingly unappealing to smugglers at the Border. As one old smuggler in a Border village told me, his greatest fear was walking into a SAS (British army counter insurgency force) ambush.

Many people in both the public and private spheres at the eastern region of the Border hope that a more truly integrated EC will boost tourism, through an increase in structural funds and the arrival of more continental visitors. To achieve this, the Border must not be seen to be a barrier or a boundary to warring communities. In most ways, in fact, tourism at the Border must deny that there is a cultural divide because if the tourist industry (i.e., government and businesses) does not succeed in dispelling the image of NI as the Lebanon of Europe, then NI tourism will be damaged. The IM is not reckoned locally to play a major part in the construction of regional tourism, but many locals are hoping that some of the cohesion funds which may accrue to Ireland in the next EC budget will be applied to the development of tourism infrastructure.

One of the most important issues for people on the Northern side of the Border, which is also part of most discussions about the IM, is that of increased security at the Border. As one anthropologist noted, when conducting comparative research on three EC borders, in NI "the opinion was widely held that as customs checkpoints are phased out . . . surveillance operations and police checkpoints will be reinforced" (Kockel 1991: 16). This stronger security also puts pressure on smugglers. In fact, rather than have a smaller customs presence at the Border, the British government recently built a new, more secure, customs station at Newry (Kockel 1991: 16). A number of people I spoke to said that on the surface this may appear to be "daft," because the UK was building a beautiful and expensive customs post at a time when customs checks were to be all but eliminated, but, upon further reflection, they thought that the post could easily be converted for security forces' use. Overall, however, there is great concern on the Northern side that the army and police will strengthen the Border through more checkpoints, roving patrols, and blocked unapproved roads. This last area of contestation, in which the British army blocks or dynamites unapproved roads in order to prevent terrorists' use of them, has become a major focus of local and national tensions. The more the roads are blocked the more local farmers use their tractors to clear them. This situation is especially tense at the western end of the Border (O'Dowd and Corrigan 1992:7-9).

Such security measures, fiercely debated throughout NI, may reflect the wider British fear regarding the loss of sovereignty in the EC. At EC levels, the UK has made it clear that the IM should not open up international borders to terrorists, criminals, and illegal immigrants (even though the Maastricht debates in Parliament demonstrate that many Tories, the "Euro-sceptics," are not convinced that the Government can guarantee the UK's borders in an era of economic and monetary union). The effects of the IM on security and crime at all EC boundaries are, as yet, unclear. Certainly the NI case has parallels elsewhere in the EC, most notably at the border between France and Spain. At this point in NI, many people both expect and hope that an increased security presence will make the Border less permeable to terrorist use.

Although most discussions about the IM, at the Border and elsewhere in Ireland, revolve around its potential economic and political effects, it will also have an impact on the Border as a symbolic boundary. As has been investigated by a number of anthropologists, in Britain and elsewhere in Europe (see, e.g., Cohen 1982, 1985, 1986), the symbolic construction of culture and community is largely concerned with the establishment of shared boundaries, which need not have physical or geographic referents but which are related to matrices of image and behavior. International boundaries often correspond to the symbolic constructions of those people who live at them, because these people had a role in their creation, and because the boundary has played a part in reconstructing local notions of national and regional culture. The dialectical relations between local and national society and culture which help construct national boundaries (see, e.g., Cole and Wolf 1974; Sahlins 1989) are being highlighted in current debates about the future structure and expansion of the EC. Anthropologists have much to offer in the analysis of the many cultural interfaces which occur at, and change the meanings of, international borders and frontiers (see, e.g., Driessen 1992).

Many aspects of Irish culture both integrate and divide people who live on the Irish Border, but all of these are liable to transformation through the intrusion of the EC. At this stage, it is likely that very little will happen, either through the EC or through national governments, to change the Border's role as a cultural divide. In fact, there is much to suggest, at the very least to the people who live there, that EC integration in the form of the IM may very well widen the cultural divide between the peoples at the Border, while at the same time helping their regional or national economies. In economic terms, the Irish Border may be home to a good number of losers in the game of EC building. The effects of this on Border life, and on the perceptions of the Border as boundary, are yet to be determined.

Conclusions

An anthropology of borders must take as one of its tenets the conclusion of an ancestor of modern political geography who suggested that "the border fringe is the reality and the border line is the abstraction" (Ratzel 1897:538, as quoted in Prescott 1987:12). The analysis of the changing abstractions which inform and construct local border cultures, and which, in turn, have an effect on nation and state, may be the most important contribution anthropologists can make to the growing scholarly interest in the changing contexts of international borders. The conclusions of this chapter should not be surprising to both the peoples of Ireland or to anyone, including ethnographers, who has lived and worked at international borders throughout the EC. Economic barriers may fall, removing some of the perceptions of international frontiers, but for the populations who live at the borders, and perhaps for those of their capital cities as well, the borders remain the physical and legal limits of the state's sovereignty and a symbolic boundary which helps define sameness and otherness, us and them.

This chapter has not been concerned with what the EC has achieved in Ireland through the processes of integration and the completion of the IM. It is too early for that. But it is about what may change and what may remain the same at the Border, almost in spite of the EC. Neither of these are as clear as some would suggest. Everything in the everyday life of local society and culture is vulnerable to outside influence. It is the role of the social scientist to investigate local level changes which are influenced by these external factors, among the peoples who after all constitute the *community* of the EC. Anthropologists should be ideally placed when conducting their long-term field research in Europe to investigate the many changing contexts of the EC in the lives of local and regional cultures. This chapter has explored some of the possibilities and probabilities of EC impact on one international border within the EC. In so doing it has sought to address the issues of symbolic boundaries and cultural identity which may be found at international borders worldwide.

Notes

The research this chapter derives in part from was funded by the United States National Endowment for the Humanities, the Wenner-Gren Foundation for Anthropological Research, the British Council, and the Queen's University of Belfast. I would like to thank Vincent Geoghegan, M. Estellie Smith, and Elizabeth Tonkin for critical readings of an earlier draft of this essay.

1. This chapter is based on field research I have been conducting since 1991 at the eastern end of the Irish Border, but it also reflects more than five years residence and research in County Meath, the Republic of Ireland, as well as residence in Belfast for the 1991-1992 academic year.

2. In this chapter I criticize the unproblematic ways in which the EC has used the term "frontiers" when referring to economic, political, and social barriers to free movement in an integrated economy of a common market. As is argued in the text, many political and sociocultural definitions of borders, or this Border in particular, will remain in the coming years. The term "frontier," although perhaps useful in both national histories and in evolutionary geography (see

Sahlins 1989:4), usually refers to the zone on both sides of an international boundary within which there is marked and ongoing international acculturation. To the people at the Irish Border, the term "the Border" refers to both the boundary line and the borderlands zone on either side of the legal divide. In this chapter I comply with this usage.

References

Bufwack, Mary. 1982. *Village Without Violence: An Examination of a Northern Irish Community*. Cambridge, MA: Schenkman.

Cohen, Anthony P., ed. 1982. *Belonging: Identity and Social Organisation in British Rural Culture*. Manchester: Manchester University Press.

_____. 1985. *The Symbolic Construction of Community*. London: Tavistock.

_____. ed. 1986. *Symbolizing Boundaries: Identity and Diversity in British Cultures*. Manchester University Press.

Cole, John W., and Eric R. Wolf. 1974. *The Hidden Frontier: Ecology and Ethnicity in an Alpine Valley*. New York: Academic Press.

Donnan, Hastings, and Graham McFarlane, eds. 1989. *Social Anthropology and Public Policy in Northern Ireland*. Aldershot: Gower.

Douglass, William A. 1977. "Borderland Influences in a Navarrese Village," in W. A. Douglass, R. W. Etulain, and W. H. Jacobsen, Jr., eds., *Anglo-American Contributions to Basque Studies*. Pp. 135-144. Reno: Desert Research Institute Publications.

Driessen, Henk. 1992. *On the Spanish-Morrocan Frontier*. London: Berg.

European Communities – Commission. 1987. *The European Community – 1992 and Beyond*. Luxembourg: Office for Official Publications of the European Communities.

Fitzgerald, J. D., T. P. Quinn, B. J. Whelan, and J. A. Williams. 1988. *An Analysis of Cross-Border Shopping*. Dublin: ESRI.

Gillespie, Raymond, and Harold O'Sullivan, eds. 1989. *The Borderlands: Essays on the History of the Ulster-Leinster Border*. Belfast: The Institute of Irish Studies.

Harris, Rosemary. *Prejudice and Tolerance in Ulster*. Manchester: Manchester University Press.

Heslinga, M. W. 1971 [1962]. *The Irish Border as a Cultural Divide*. Assen: Van Gorcum.

Kockel, Ullrich. 1991. *Regions, Borders and European Integration*. Liverpool: Institute of Irish Studies, University of Liverpool.

Leyton, Elliot. 1975. *The One Blood: Kinship and Class in an Irish Village*. St. Johns: Memorial University.

McCrystal, Cal. 1991. "The Vale of Tears." *The Independent on Sunday* 6 October: 3-5.

Norton, Desmond. 1986. "Smuggling under the Common Agricultural Policy: Northern Ireland and the Republic of Ireland." *Journal of Common Market Studies* 24(4): 297-312.

O'Dowd, Liam, and James Corrigan. 1992. National Sovereignty and Cross-Border Cooperation: Ireland in a Comparative Context. Unpublished paper. Annual Meeting of the Sociological Association of Ireland, Cork, 8-10 May.

Prescott, J. R. V. 1987. *Political Frontiers and Boundaries.* London: Unwin Hyman.

Ratzel, F. 1897. *Politische Geographie.* Berlin: Oldenbourg.

Ruane, Joseph, and Jennifer Todd. 1991. "Ireland – North and South – and European Community Integration," in Paul Hainsworth, ed., *Breaking and Preserving the Mould: The Third Direct Elections to the European Parliament (1989) – The Irish Republic and Northern Ireland.* Pp. 163-192. Belfast: Policy Research Institute.

Sahlins, Peter. 1989. *Boundaries: The Making of France and Spain in the Pyrenees.* Berkeley: University of California Press.

Shanklin, Eugenia. 1985. *Donegal's Changing Traditions.* New York: Gordon and Breach.

Shutes, Mark T. 1991. "Kerry Farmers and the European Community: Capital Transactions in a Rural Irish Parish." *Irish Journal of Sociology* 1: 1-17.

Smith, M. Estellie, ed. 1990. *Perspectives on the Informal Economy.* Lanham, MD: University Press of America.

Taylor, Lawrence J. 1989. "The Mission: An Anthropological View of an Irish Religious Occasion," in C. Curtin and T. M. Wilson, eds., *Ireland From Below: Social Change and Local Communities.* Pp. 1-22. Galway: Galway University Press.

Vincent, Joan. 1989. "Local Knowledge and Political Violence in County Fermanagh," in C. Curtin and T. M. Wilson, eds., *Ireland From Below: Social Change and Local Communities.* Pp. 92-108. Galway: Galway University Press.

Wilson, David. n.d. "Tourism, Public Policy and the Image of Northern Ireland Since the Troubles," in B. O'Connor and M. Cronin, eds., *Travel and Tourism in Ireland.* Cork: Cork University Press.

Wilson, Thomas M. 1984. "From Clare to the Common Market: Perspectives in Irish Ethnography." *Anthropological Quaterly* 57(1): 1-15.

_____. 1989. "Large Farms, Local Politics, and the International Arena: The Irish Tax Dispute of 1979." *Human Organization* 48(1): 60-70.

_____. n.d. "Consumer Culture and European Integration at the Northern Irish Border," in W. F. van Raaij and G. J. Bamossy, eds., *Cross-Cultural Issues in Consumer Research.* Amsterdam: Association for Consumer Research.

10

The Future of European Boundaries: A Case Study

Susan Parman

In the following chapter, data from Scotland are used to examine the conditions under which an ethnic group acquires class-oriented, nationalist political aspirations to breach existing nation-state boundaries. The purpose of using Scotland as a case study is to address the larger issue of how and when, in a world system, economic interdependence of ethnic groups is likely to diffuse nationalism – an issue that is at the heart of the future of European boundaries in the New Europe of the European Community (EC) and beyond.

The anthropological study of Europe was once primarily a study of peripheral, rural, small-scale, "ethnic" units, organized in "communities," whose value as anthropological subjects increased in proportion to the extent to which they were perceived as timeless, pure (undiluted by foreign influence and historical change), and unconscious. The historical, progressive centers of civilization and "Great Traditions," with their active decision-makers, were academically monopolized by historians, classical linguists, and archaeologists of Near Eastern civilizations and of classical Greece and Rome (Simmons 1988). Reed-Danahay and Rogers (1987:51) make the point that as more American anthropologists become interested in the study of Europe, they undergo "a radical rethinking of the anthropological 'other'." The "other" is not so much a passive member of traditional society (described in the traditional anthropological format of a community study) but an actor who negotiates meaning in multiple networks, the outermost boundary of which is the interdependent world system. This change in theoretical orientation is due not only to constraints imposed by the selection of Europe as an anthropological focus but to changes within the field of anthropology itself (Ortner 1984). It is likely that these changes, in turn, have made the study of Europe more acceptable within the overall field of sociocultural anthropology. It has also generated the need to develop theoretical models to describe and interpret events on multiple levels of a world scale. The purpose of this chapter is to discuss a model by which various levels of sociocultural organization and their interaction may be described and interpreted, to illustrate this model with examples from Scotland, and to attempt to use this model to speculate about the future of the EC after 1992.

One of the problems in studying complex societies is how to define and interpret the characteristics, boundaries, and relationships between the many levels of overlapping, intersecting social networks – kinship groups, friends, household, work group, church, community, ethnic group, nation-state, supra-national affiliation, and so on. The concept of social boundary system (Cohen 1969) is useful to describe networks of social relations, from dyadic networks to world system, as relatively firmly bounded or loosely bounded, in interaction with each other. A network is firmly bounded to the extent that persons and influences are excuded from it; internal unity is strengthened by reducing dissent in favor of consensus and by having rites of passage that govern admittance to the network. Firm boundedness is characterized by role performance within the network being independent of role performance in other networks, and by the ability of members to substitute for each other and assume each other's roles – a phenomenon called role transposability (Bott 1957).

A firmly bounded network tends to compete with those boundary systems that serve the same function, such as maintenance of social order, education, and the regulation of change. For example, a strongly bounded local community will compete, on the one hand, with family systems and friendship networks, and on the other with a nation-state (Cohen 1969:111-117), whereas a nation-state will usually not compete with a family system.

As societies change through internal development and external contact, their social boundary systems strengthen or weaken, and new social boundary systems may come into existence. The tightly knit, undifferentiated network of peasant communities (with high role transposability, emphasis on censensus, comingling of occupational, kinship, political, and religious roles) weakens as the centralized government of the nation-state becomes stronger. What we see happening today in Europe is the emergence of a new social boundary system, called the European Community. In the context of this new system, the social boundary systems of existing nation-states weaken, and previously weak systems, such as ethnic groups, become stronger.

Cohen's model enables us to describe the characteristics by which we might recognize a firmly bounded system, and to predict which systems are likely to compete structurally with each other; but it does not address the question of how new social boundary systems emerge (except as part of a general evolutionary trend reflecting improved technology). The following section addresses this issue.

The Boundaries of Ethnicity, Nationalism, State, and Nation-State

Ethnic identity is culturally constructed and dependent on historical factors. *Ethnos* is variously translated as people, culture, and race. An ethnic group is usually perceived to be a group of people having some identifiable geographic base within the boundaries of an existing political system, and identifying themselves as distinct from the broader population by virtue of their culture, language, history, religion, traditions, and political past.

As Barth demonstrated (1969), meanings (that define the boundaries between groups) are established through interaction. Ethnicity is one of the symbols of identity that may be negotiated. It is interpreted here not as a social category (which is socially neutral and usually imposed by other groups, as in census identifiers – "all people with Spanish surnames") but as a basis for recruiting members to a social group. Self-selected and associated with the existence of certain symbols of identity (belonging to a particular religion, occupying a particular residence, speaking a certain language, possessing characteristics such as second sight, and so on), ethnicity has the potential to organize feelings, thought, and action. When there are no organizing symbols and rituals by which ethnicity is defined, relations between ethnic categories become blurred.

Nation, like ethnic group, is culturally constructed and historically contingent; the term implies birth (L. *natio*, *nasci*) and shared territory. Unlike ethnic groups, nations possess their own territory and government. An ethnic group seeking to govern itself is undergoing a nationalist movement. Nationalism involves sentiments that the ethnic group (the "nation") should be congruent with the political unit (Gellner 1983). In bands, tribes, and chiefdoms (using Elman Service's [1962, 1971] cross-cultural classification of different types of social organization [also see Sahlins 1968, Sahlins and Service 1960, Service 1966 and 1975]), ethnicity and political unit are already congruent and the issue of nationalism does not arise. States, however, are large-scale forms of social organization that have come to incorporate many ethnic groups; in this context, nationalism emerges under certain circumstances. The emergence of states is associated with the development of centralized nodes of trade, communication, and government – which is to say, cities (See McNeill 1985 for a discussion of the relationship between cities and the development of ethnic diversity). There has been a remarkable movement during the past twenty years or so in which regionalized nationalist movements have developed in countries long thought to be integrated, and long thought to be dominated not by ethnicity and region but by class.

The state is a type of political system in which a centralized authority exists that has a legitimate monopoly on force. The distinctive function of the state is to regulate conflicts that arise among agencies such as the family, the village, the church, ethnic groups, and in general to maintain order. A nation-state based on industrialism (as are the members of the European Community) is a centralized political system composed primarily of people who share a common culture that is generated by a centralized system of education and communication (as Gellner argues, homogeneity is forged because a modern industrial state requires "a mobile, literate, culturally standardized, interchangeable population" [Gellner 1983:46]). "Ethnic groups" are a variety of minority cultural-political units within this system. These groups are not "natural units" destined to awake to their nationalist destinies; rather, they constitute the raw material of cultural diversity that may under certain circumstances crystallize into new nation-states. Gellner (1983:121) argues that

> ethnic groups were not nationalist when states were formed in fairly stable agrarian systems. Classes, however oppressed and exploited, did not overturn the political system when they could not define themselves "ethnically." Only when a nation became a class, a visible and unequally distributed category in an otherwise mobile system, did it become politically conscious and activist.

The EC has emerged as the result of numerous factors, including economic interdependency, political expediency, increased communication, and competition with other regions such as the Soviet Union, Japan, and the United States. The following section examines the characteristics of the Community as a social boundary system. I then examine the history of changes in social boundary systems within Scotland, paying special attention to nationalist movements and the role of Scottish crofters.

The EC as a Social Boundary System

According to the characteristics of social boundary systems discussed above, the nation-states of Europe, especially Britain, show signs of being firmly bounded, as indicated by powerful symbols of unity (e.g., Britain's adherence to royalist symbols of British identity, especially as reflected in the representations of the royal family on British money and stamps, and Britain's strenuous maintenance of a regal image in the eyes of an adoring American public – a source of genealogies and legends reinforced by books, magazines [e.g., *British Heritage*], films, and art shows) and resistance to transposability (particularly marked among the French and English).

A network is firmly bounded to the extent that persons and influences are excluded from it. Even after agreeing to the Single European Act in 1986, which specified that the European Community would become "an area without internal frontiers" by the end of 1992, Britain began planning a ten-million-pound immigration and customs-control facility to regulate and restrict entrance to passengers arriving from the Continent by train through the "Chunnel" (*The Sunday Times* 24 July 1988). Also, to the extent that dissent is tolerated within the EC, it is weakly bounded.

On the other hand, a new, supranational social boundary system called the European Community appears to be taking on the characteristics of firm boundedness, as indicated by role transposability – for example, various ministers of defense from European countries interchangeably playing the role of peacemakers for Europe in the Middle East and Yugoslavia – and by the emergence of unifying symbols – for example: a European Community flag, money, centers of government and banking; EuroDisney; the European University Institute in Florence (supported with grants from Brussels, dealing with a curriculum and concepts of a united Europe, whose intent is to produce people trained in economics and political science who can function in the new EC); jokes about Euro-categories (Eurosausage, Euro-pessimism, Euro-sclerosis); newspapers such as *The European*, journals such as *Contemporary European Affairs*, and news magazines such as *European Affairs: The European Magazine* (providing a "pan-European media platform" [February/March 1991:1]); and the rhetoric of people like Edgard Pisani ("More than a market, something other than a State: this will not be granted us, we must invent it and will it into being" [Pisani 1989:14]) and Jacques Delors ("what is at stake [in supporting the Single European Act] is the rise or fall of *our civilisation*" [Delors 1989:27, my italics]). Parliamentary methods of reducing dissent and encouraging consensus have emerged in the EC, and separate nation-states have made remarkable progress in agreeing to common legal and economic measures – in the process leading to changes that weaken the boundedness of their own systems and increase the strength of the Community as a social boundary system. At the same time, ethnic groups become stronger. The following section explores this idea by examining Scotland.

Scotland, Nationalist Movements, and the Role of Scottish Crofters

Keating (1989:160) defines Scotland, Northern Ireland, and Wales as "peripheral nations" within the United Kingdom, or "nations that have had their own distinct political concerns and where the balance of political forces has often differed from that in England." In this sense, the social boundary system of Scotland, viewed as a network of social relations of people engaging in political behavior, is distinct; but it has never been as firmly bounded as that of England. Although Scotland emerged as a kingdom in the 11th century from the amalgamation of four tribal groups, it formed political alliances with England that led to English claims to sovereignty over Scotland. The Scottish and English crowns were united in 1603, and the parliaments were united in 1707. Although the United Kingdom has no written constitution or code of public law, its statehood is based on the English principle of parliamentary sovereignty, or Crown-in-Parliament (Keating 1989). After unification of the parliaments in 1707, in a process that Michael Hechter refers to as "internal colonialism" (1975), Lowland Scots participated more extensively in the political and economic structures of the expanding British Empire, sent their children to English public schools, and modelled their intellectual, artistic, and literary life on English patterns – in effect submerging their separate cultural identity in a single national culture. In London, Scotland is often referred to as "North Britain," and the economic problems of Scotland are not referred to as Scottish but as problems affecting certain economic regions in the UK.

On the other hand, Scotland as a social boundary system remained distinct. It retained its own Church of Scotland, Scots Law, Scottish education, and local government; it possessed a distinctive dialect and a sense of shared history. In particular, it possessed the Gaelic-speaking Scottish Highlands and Western Islands that had been excluded from the prosperity that affected the Lowland Scots after the union of parliaments in 1707. This region of Scotland became a locus of ethnicity that, once linked with distinctive socioeconomic status, played a role in the formation of social boundary systems associated with nationalist movements. At times this region has been linked with Scottish nationalism; new networks of social relations, such as the Scottish Crofters' Union, are forming in the context of the EC.

Before the union of crown and parliament, the pastoral clans of the Highlands were strongly bounded systems that competed with the less strongly bounded central government – in effect, avoiding the attempts by the weak crown to subdue them, either as political vassals under feudalism, or as tax-paying whiskey-makers. In the Hebrides, the competitive, warring clans were united under a Celto-Norse kingship ruled by clan Donald that emerged in the 14th century and by the 15th century controlled a third of the land of Scotland. The "Lord of the Isles" held court, granted charters, and negotiated treaties with foreign powers (Cregeen 1968:156). The house of Argyll, senior branch of the clan Campbell, rose to prominence during the 15th and 16th centuries by attacking and destroying this competitive political structure (Cregeen 1968), thus strengthening the Scottish crown. The Scottish crown became the British crown when James VI of Scotland became James I of Scotland and England in 1603.[1]

Economic changes eroded clan social organization in the 17th century (the current concept of Scottish clans is supported by military organization and tourism). By the middle of the 19th century, the former system of land use under pastoral clans in the Highlands and Islands (common pasture for grazing cattle, and poor arable land rotated among its members in run-rig) had been almost entirely converted to crofting tenure (Devine 1988, Hunter 1976, Parman 1990). Crofting as a system of land use reflects the trends toward consolidation of land and land reform that swept through Europe in the 18th and 19th centuries; communally held arable land was divided into individually held strips, croft houses were built on these strips rather than clustered together in a hamlet (*clachan*), and undivided hill grazing (not suited to arable cultivation) continued to be used communally. But crofting as a locus of ethnic identity stems from events in the 19th century (such as mass emigration, the Clearances, poverty, the Disruption of 1843, the Irish troubles, radical political philosophy, and increased Scottish nationalism) that led up to the Crofters (Scotland) Act of 1886 and its subsequent amendments and interpretation.

A series of economic disasters in the 19th century devastated the Highlands, leading to mass emigration, mass evictions of people from the land to make way for sheep (a process that began in the 18th century, and became identified as the Clearances), and horrendous poverty. The strongly bounded clans had long since disappeared, their final scream (in the abortive support of some clans for the Jacobite

Pretender, Bonnie Prince Charlie) having been choked off at the Battle of Culloden and then artificially reproduced in the ethnic shrine of the Celtic Twilight from the late 18th century on. The central British government was pursuing an active social policy in the poverty-stricken Highlands (Day 1918), which included having government commissions report on the plight of crofters in the Highlands and Islands. Strong nationalist sentiments within Scotland encouraged the British government to appoint a secretary for Scotland in 1885 (this position had existed before but had lapsed in the 18th century), and the Scottish Office was instituted to administer UK statutes in Scotland.

During this period, a link was forged between crofters, romantic elements of Highland-Scottish history, the Free Church, Scottish nationalism, and Gaelic – a new synthesis of Celtic ethnicity. This synthesis is often rationalized by referring to romanticized versions of Highland history, but it is obvious that the conditions that produced the strongly bounded militant, pastoral clans, the Celto-Norse Kingship of the Western Isles, the weak Scottish crown, and the Jacobite Rebellion were quite different from those that produced crofting townships. The Free Church was associated with anti-landlordism and supported the crofters (it was created during the Disruption of 1843 over the issue of lay patronage vs. election of ministers; lay patronage, by which landlords appointed ministers rather than allowing the congregation to elect them, was imposed by Parliament in 1712, in violation of the Act of Union of 1707). The problems of Highland crofters were seen to be unique to Scotland and requiring specific types of land reform. Crofters, believed to embody the essence of democratic, egalitarian "Scottish democracy" by virtue of possessing remnants of the "primitive communism" of the Highland clan system (Keating and Bleiman 1979: 28), formed a political party called the Highland Land Law Reform Association (later the Highland Land League) that presented Highland issues to parliament. As part of its platform, the Highland Land Law Reform Association promoted Gaelic as the language of Scotland. Although less than 2% of the population today speak Gaelic (vs. 30% in 1707 and 5.2% in 1891 after the central government pursued a long-standing policy of repressing this "barbaric" tongue), it plays a stronger role today in defining the new Celtic ethnicity than it did in the past, serving as one of the markers of membership in the social boundary system of the crofting community and in some cases playing an important role in Scottish nationalism.

The Napier Commission Report of 1884 was followed by the Crofters Holdings (Scotland) Act of 1886 that provided security of tenure, hereditary succession, and fair rent, thus providing crofters-cum-"Celts" with the land to which they were believed to be fanatically attached, and also striking a blow for radical political philosophy. It also established a precedent for treating crofters as a special network that kept them from being submerged in the centralized bureaucracy of the British government. Although crofters were removed from special status and merged with all British smallholders in an act passed in 1911, a new Crofters Act passed in 1955 resurrected them after the Taylor Report of 1954 argued that crofting communities "embody a free and independent way of life which in a civilisation predominantly urban and industrial in character is worth preserving for its own intrinsic quality."

The Crofting Reform (Scotland) Act of 1976 was intended to rationalize the use of land and, like the 1911 act, to return croft land to nonspecial status. The Act made it illegal to create new crofts, provided crofters with the statutory right to become owners rather than tenants of their crofts (thus attacking a fundamental contrast within the crofting community by turning the crofter into a laird), and provided conditions under which land could be decrofted, or taken out of crofting tenure. However, just as the Taylor Report rescued crofters from the 1911 Act, events within Scotland and the European Community appear to be giving new life to the crofting community. The important network that seems to be playing a significant role as the locus of 20th century Scottish Celtic ethnicity is not the Western Isles Council (which I expected when I first started writing this chapter) but the recently formed Scottish Crofters Union.

To explain these events, and how they affect the formation of new social boundary systems, it is important to understand agricultural policy within Britain and Europe. In Britain in the 1940s and 1950s, grants and subsidies were intended to maximize production, and many grants were provided to promote amalgamation of farms, mechanization of agriculture, and general intensification (just as in Europe, the Common Agricultural Policy was originally devised to increase farm production). In 1947 the Department of Agriculture suggested that crofts be amalgamated into larger units as part of the post-war policy of expanding farming within the UK, and the Crofters Commission, formed in 1955, promoted the same goal. They were both stopped by the powerful symbol of the Clearances, and by the organization of crofters into voluntary associations to fight them – initially the Federation of Crofters, and recently the Scottish Crofters Union[2].

The major opportunities provided by the EC are in the Common Agricultural Policy (CAP), and in the funds provided through the European Investment Bank, structural Funds, and other financial resources. Now that surplus is a problem within the EC, the goal of the

CAP is to diversify the economy, protect small farms, enhance quality of life, and preserve the environment – goals which the Scottish Crofters Union say the crofting community embodies.

The EC pamphlet, *A Common Agricultural Policy for the 1990s* (1989:30), explicitly states that in areas designated as "least-favoured," it is not enough to strengthen farming; emphasis is placed on diversified economic development, or "integrated" programs (funds for which have been available since 1979) that promote a combination of agriculture, food processing, tourism, crafts, training, and general regional infrastructures. Targeted for such integrated programs were the Western Isles of Scotland. In the Western Isles today, the Integrated Development Programme (IDP) is an important source of outside funding that has infused EC capital into the region and given the region an alternative to the centralized funding from London. It has also legitimized crofting, which has always been a diversified economic system.

Structural Funds are used to fulfill various structural policy objectives (established by the EC in 1988 and effective from January 1, 1989), including the development of rural areas (Objective 5b). This objective is recognized as particularly important, for rural areas constitute about 80% of the total area of the EC and house more than half its population, and implies

> an entire economic and social structure which, quite apart from its function of providing people there with a living, is also *vital in preserving the ecological balance* and offering room for recreation. The main objectives here are to preserve the family-run farm, to create permanent and economically viable jobs outside agriculture through diversification and *to ensure greater protection of the rural environment* [italics mine] (European Communities – Commission 1991:13).

The emergence of the European Community as a social boundary system provides new conditions that affect the strengthening or weakening of old boundary systems, or the emergence of new ones. The role that the crofting community is beginning to take in the context of the EC may be illustrated by a newspaper quote describing a meeting of the Scottish Crofters Union in 1989:

> The image of a Highland crofter as a simplistic figure with outmoded values, popularised in patronising pulp fiction received a knock last week, when the third annual conference of the Scottish Crofters' Union at Benbecula attracted mass media attention, capacity attendance and speakers of international renown. After centuries of national neglect and even outright attack, crofting

is being thrown to the forefront of European priorities, following an incredible shift in social and environmentalist demands (*Oban Times* 23 March 1989:1).

The conference described the assets of crofting. As more land comes out of production, diversification is seen as the key to survival; crofters had previously been told to think like farmers, but farmers are now being told to think more like crofters. James Hunter, Director of the SCU at the conference, argued that "Crofting now supports more people to the hectare than any other non-urban land use now available in Scotland, more than farming, more than forestry and more than sport."

The meeting was attended by a conservationist from London who urged them to attack forestry, encourage tourism, and sell the image of the remote Highlands with its romantic history. Dr. James Hunter, the author of *The Making of the Crofting Community* (1976) and former Director of the Scottish Crofters Union, has attempted to link crofting with environmentalist issues in his new book (1991a), and the Scottish Crofters Union has allied itself with the Royal Society for the Protection of Birds (the SCU has about 4,500 members, whereas the Royal Society has more members than the entire Highlands and Islands). The alliance intends to produce a joint policy document arguing that crofting is environmentally sound (Hunter 1991b).

The Scottish Crofters Union has also allied itself with the Federation of Family Farms, a new organization that represents about 40,000 small farmers in the Scottish Highlands, England, Wales, Northern Ireland, and the Irish Republic and will be represented in Brussels

where its officials will have the job of demonstrating to the European Commission, now embarking on fundamental reforms to the EC's Common Agricultural Policy, that smallholding agriculture of the crofting type conforms precisely to EC Agriculture Commissioner Ray MacSharry's vision of the rural future (Hunter 1991b).

Nationalism and Europe 1992

The anthropological perspective which informs this chapter combines network, semiotic, motivational, and historical analysis. If we adopt the position of Marshall Sahlins, as adapted by Sherry Ortner (1984), the structure of society (as defined here in terms of social boundary systems) is created and organized in relation to dominant meanings and values. In the creation of a valued social life, the social actor (as individual or as collective social types) negotiates meanings and in effect creates culture. Radical change occurs not when groups come to power with alternative views of the world, but when there are "changes of meaning of existing relations" (Ortner 1984:155). As conditions change, both in the short term and long term, actors respond within the limits and opportunities provided for them; and when meaning changes, so do structural relationships (as defined by the strengthening or weakening of social boundary systems). For example, economic opportunities provided by the European Community may affect how ethnic groups define themselves (e.g., certain historical symbols may become significant), leading to changes in the strength or weakness of ethnic, national, and supranational social boundary systems. Historical symbols are frequently resurrected, changed, and recombined with current events to redefine existing relationships.

The works of Gellner, Hechter, and others imply that if centralized systems of communication and education continue in the EC as a consequence of effecting successful economic union, the process of nationalism will lead to a rewriting of the identity of Europe and eventually the world to forge a new social boundary system from the detritus of previous systems. Just as currently recognized nation-states are historical creations fused from the detritus of former "ethnic groups," what is now "supranational" will become "national." A hundred years from now, I predict a world social boundary system in which less firmly bounded regional units are involved with the interdependent exchange of resources. Only when an ethnic group within this larger system becomes a class, "a visible and unequally distributed category in an otherwise mobile system" (Gellner 1983:121), does it have the potential to become politically conscious and separatist in its political activism – as happened with crofters. When that happens, the creation of meaning can take many forms – the return of Naziism, Islamic jihad, Japanese warlords pursuing their divine destiny – in which case prediction remains focused on the past, and the future belongs to the accidents of history.

Notes

1. An interesting cartographic footnote: In 1540, after 26 years of being king of Scotland, James V visited the Hebrides for the first time as part of an attempt to subdue the unruly lords of the Western Isles. His pilot, Alexander Lyndsay, apparently made detailed notes of the coastline in a rutter, or book of sailing directions for seamen. Somehow this rutter fell into the hands of a French map-maker – a Nicolay d'Arfeville, called "Cosmographer of the King of France" – who prepared a marine chart that he presented to King Henry II in 1559, who promptly used it to attack Scotland. The Nicolay map, published in 1583 in Paris, was one of the most accurate maps of Scotland in existence.

2. Within Scotland, reorganization of local government in 1975 established the Western Isles (Outer Hebrides) as a region, replacing the previous, divisive form of county organization that linked portions of the Outer Hebrides with the mainland. The Outer Hebrides, with the largest number of Gaelic speakers and the most active crofting townships, provide an important locus of Celtic/crofting ethnicity. The Western Isles Council (in Gaelic, *Comhairle nan Eilean*), the unit of local government for this region, has been affected by relationships with the European Community (recently, and most disastrously, the Council invested EC money with BCCI and lost twenty-four million pounds, in the process contributing to negative stereotypes about Gaels and islanders). Although it is a perfect candidate for a social boundary system strongly bounded by exclusive rites of passage (speaking Gaelic, becoming a crofter), the Western Isles Council is not turning out to be a strongly bounded network (it is fraught with infighting, unpredictable in its politics, not allied with the Scottish Nationalist Party nor with any other party). Instead, the Scottish Crofters Union is emerging as an important network and locus of ethnicity. They had little chance of being more than a symbolic punching bag until recently, when changing economic conditions and opportunities provided by the European Community have led to important changes.

References

Barth, Fredrik, ed. 1969. *Ethnic Groups and Boundaries: The Social Organization of Culture Difference.* Boston: Little, Brown and Co.

Bott, Elizabeth. 1957. *Family and Social Network: Roles, Norms and External Relationships in Ordinary Urban Families.* London: Tavistock.

Cohen, Yehudi. 1969. "Social Boundary Systems." *Current Anthropology* 10(1):103-126.

Cregeen, Eric. 1968. "The Changing Role of the House of Argyll in the Scottish Highlands," in I. M. Lewis, ed., *History and Social Anthropology.* Pp. 153-192. New York: Tavistock Publications.

Day, J.P. 1918. *Public Administration in the Highlands and Islands of Scotland.* London: University of London Press.

Delors, Jacques. 1989. "Europe: Embarking on a New Course." *Contemporary European Affairs* 1(1/2):15-27.

Devine, T.M. 1988. *The Great Highland Famine: Hunger, Emigration and the Scottish Highlands in the nineteenth Century.* Edinburgh: John Donald.

European Communities – Commission. 1989. *A Common Agricultural Policy for the 1990s.* Luxembourg: Office for Official Publications of the European Communities.

_____. 1991. *The European Community – 1992 and Beyond.* Luxembourg: Office for Official Publications of the European Communities.

Gellner, Ernest. 1983. *Nations and Nationalism.* Ithaca, New York: Cornell University Press.

Hechter, Michael. 1975. *International Colonialism: The Celtic Fringe in British National Development, 1536-1966.* Berkeley: University of California Press.

Hunter, James. 1976. *The Making of the Crofting Community*. Edinburgh: John Donald.

____. 1991a. *The Claim of Crofting: The Scottish Highlands and Islands, 1930-1990*. Edinburgh: Mainstream.

____. 1991b "Staking a Claim of Right for Crofting." *The Scotsman* 5 September:13.

Keating, Michael. 1989. "Territorial Management and the British State: The Case of Scotland and Wales," in Joseph R. Rudolph, Jr. and Robert J. Thompson, eds., *Ethnoterritorial Politics, Policy, and the Western World*. Pp. 159-179. Boulder: Lynne Rienner Publishers.

Keating, M., and D. Bleiman. 1979. *Labour and Scottish Nationalism*. London: Macmillan.

McNeill, William H. 1985. *Polyethnicity and National Unity in World History*. Toronto: University of Toronto Press.

Ortner, Sherry B. 1984. "Theory in Anthropology Since the Sixties." *Comparative Studies in Society and History* 26(1):126-166.

Parman, Susan. 1990. *Scottish Crofters: A Historical Ethnography of a Celtic Village*. Fort Worth, TX: Holt, Rinehart and Winston.

Pisani, Edgard. 1989. "Europe: Neither Market nor State." *Contemporary European Affairs* 1(1/2):11-14.

Reed-Danahy, Deborah, and Susan Carol Rogers. 1987. "Introduction." *Anthropological Quarterly* 60(2):51-55.

Sahlins, Marshall. 1968. *Tribesmen*. Englewood Cliffs, N.J.: Prentice-Hall.

Sahlins, Marshall, and Elman Service. 1960. *Evolution and Culture*. Ann Arbor: University of Michigan Press.

Service, Elman. 1962. *Primitive Social Organization: An Evolutionary Perspective*. New York: Random House.

____. 1966. *The Hunters*. Englewood Cliffs, N.J.: Prentice-Hall.

____. 1971. *Primitive Social Organization: An Evolutionary Perspective* (2nd ed.). New York: Random House.

____. 1975. *Origins of the State and Civilization: The Process of Cultural Evolution*. New York: W.W. Norton.

Simmons, William S. 1988. "Culture Theory in Contemporary Ethnohistory." *Ethnohistory* 35(1):1-14.

11

Cultural Values and European Financial Institutions

Charles J. M. R. Gullick

Anthropology, with its interest in the translation of cultures and its study of organizations, has a significant contribution to make to the study of banking. Because of their expertise in cultural phenomena, anthropologists are beginning to play a major role in the study of the intercultural relations of organizations. The bulk of this research demonstrates that a far wider range of sociocultural factors needs to be considered in trans-cultural situations than is normally considered in management science. Such factors include kinship, social networks, folklore, the social environment, reciprocity, and concepts of social space and time. This chapter explores a few of these, but a longer and wider study of the culture of banking in an expanding European Community (EC) should consider them all.

In order to demonstrate the importance of cultural factors in the organization and perception of some European financial institutions in the run up to the completion of the EC's Internal Market (IM) in 1993, this chapter concentrates on four aspects of banking culture in Europe. These are the changing concepts of banks and banking, the perceptions of time held by bankers, the globalization and regulation of banks, and the relationship between banks and clients. These four factors are highlighted herein because they bring to the fore the tensions which both unite and divide EC banking practices. For example, at the ideological level changing ideas about banking are drawing together institutions, while other cultural values, such as those associated with time, tend to make financial integration more difficult. While other concepts are considered, the following discussion of the cultural constructions of time, and the social structures based on networks and action sets, highlight some of the ways in which intercultural relations are important, and to a great extent undocumented, aspects of financial organizations in the EC. In the context of EC banking, the British – German divide is particularly important as these countries play important roles in changing European banking styles. Their banking cultures, on the other hand, are markedly different from those of southern Europe.

The Changing Concepts of Banks and Banking

The changing categories of what constitutes a bank in the EC reflect changing social organizations. Traditionally the main business of banking was taking deposits and making loans, but banks have expanded into other fields. As financial intermediaries in the EC, banks may offer a whole range of other financial services such as insurance, credit cards, and foreign exchange. As a consequence the remit of a bank has become more complex than in the past (Maidment 1990). While the expansion of banking has been explored by social historians (Born 1983), anthropologists can also play a significant role in the discussion of the way in which the concepts of banking have changed in parallel with this expansion.[1] In general in recent years, the nature of banking has changed throughout the EC; Britain and Germany can serve as models of the ways the ideas and structures of banking reflect wider sociocultural configurations.

The main types of banks in Britain are still public and private banks, but the categories are merging. Public banks are limited companies and deal with the general public as individuals and as organizations. Private banks are mainly merchant banks and/or discount houses. They tend to be partnerships and to deal almost exclusively with industrial finance and foreign trade. Merchant banks raise funds for industry both at home and abroad. The division between commercial and private banks does not apply to Germany, the Netherlands and Switzerland. Their universal banks combine the majority of the roles of both commercial and merchant banks. They can also take equity stakes and help manage businesses to which they lend money. While theoretically French *banques d'affairs* should be similar to universal banks they tend to concentrate on the investment aspects of banking and as a consequence the system is more like the British. The Italian *banca d'affari* are a hybrid of the merchant and investment banks. Other financial intermediaries include building societies, savings banks, hire purchase companies, insurance companies, and investment trusts. Savings banks, *Casses d'Epargne*, and *Sparkassen* accept interest bearing deposits of small amounts. When used specifically for the purchase of housing these are called building societies in Britain.

In the EC many of these differences are becoming blurred. Many commercial banks now own insurance companies and merchant banks, and as a consequence have become similar to universal banks. Similarly one German universal bank has taken over a British merchant bank. As a result it has much in common with the British financial conglomerates that have developed in the last decade. Some insurance and building societies have merged to become similar conglomerates. These mergers partially result from the changing rules for financial institutions in the EC, but also to perceived synergies. Other areas in which bank centralization is claimed to be advantageous include their increased capital and information technology.

The Perception of Time Held by Bankers

The changes in the financial institutions in the decade leading to 1993 can be seen as converging evolution with (a) German universal banks taking on merchant bank roles, (b) British commercial banks combining with insurers and merchant banks, and (c) British insurers forming alliances with building societies. While at the organizational level German and British banking are drawing together, there are major cultural differences, as are demonstrated by their disparate views of time. Bankers' concepts of time range from mono-time to poly-time, from cyclical to lineal time, from backward to forward looking and from long to short-term. Mono-time (m-time) is used to describe working methods in which one task is done at a time and is the normal approach for northern Europeans. In contrast Poly-time (p-time) denotes practices when more than one activity is undertaken simultaneously. The study of this dyad owes much to the work of Hall (1959, 1966) and has been usefully explored in studies of Latin American managers (see, e.g., Harrison 1983; Condon 1985). P-time predominates in southern Europe: for example in Malta, where I have conducted field research, one may be undertaking more than one transaction in a bank with a bank official, who is also dealing with other unrelated tasks. P-time tends to occur in areas where networks are important and this partially explains the southern European preference for relational, as opposed to transactional, banking.

In banking literature and in my discussions with bankers their predominant model of time is lineal. However, in some areas a cyclical perspective underlies analyses of economic cycles and industrial cycles, which can be used to determine lending and investment policies. Discussions with bankers in which a lineal view of time came out mainly center around two phrases: "evolution" and "M & A" (mergers and acquisitions). By the former they mean *sui generis* growth and by the latter, expansion through combining with other organizations. While the development of many banks involved a mixture of evolution and M & A, their current perceptions of the future concentrate upon alliances and merging in the build-up to 1993. This approach means that they can spread rapidly into the whole of the EC, and (where thought relevant) gain the appropriate cultural expertise. For example British bankers are sometimes aware that their foreign experiences have been mainly in the Commonwealth and that this may not be directly applicable to the EC (Gullick 1990a: 131). In general the awareness of cultural factors depends upon the chosen niches and markets. Banks and insurance firms (and/or sections of large financial institutions) that concentrate upon large corporate clients are less worried by cultural inputs than those dealing with mass consumers.

The dyad of backward and forward orientations brings out the differences between North American and British concepts of time. The British tend to look more to previous occurrences and Americans to the future. This generalization does not, however, apply to British bankers who are more future oriented. This is currently demonstrated by the decision of the Standard Chartered Bank to remove all its mementoes of a colonial past from the reception areas of its headquarters. Perceptions of earlier events differentiate British banking from banking on the continental mainland. A factor that colors much of German financial management is the memory of hyperinflation between the two world wars. German bankers appear more aware of socioeconomic history than British bankers. German awareness of previous events is more centered within social history, while British financiers frequently propagate charter myths. Thus one of the textbooks on merchant banking describes most of the sagas commissioned by British bankers as "historical novels" (Clay and Wheble 1976: x). As a consequence Stanley Chapman in one of the few historically-based British accounts of banking points out that "the better sort of business history . . . has been written on the continent or in the U.S.A. and consequently is not directly concerned with the situation as seen from the City of London" (Chapman 1984: ix). I would add the caveat that some studies connect banking to railway expansion (see, e.g., Mitchie 1992), but these are exceptions, and that the best historical accounts are still produced in Germany and to a lesser degree France.

At one level the recent history of banking has followed trends that frequently started in the USA. Norrington (1989) went as far as to compare bankers with lemmings and Shreeve (1991b:1) called their decisions "sheep-like." Thus there was the phase during the 1970s in which banks over lent to "Third-world" states. The ensuing debt crisis forced banks to write off many of these debts. This was followed in the 1980s by the lending of funds with property surety during a property boom. This produced problems when property markets crashed (especially in the UK, USA and Japan). Other trends in banking which emanated from the USA and elsewhere included globalization, information technology, and transactional banking. But because of the cultural construction and perception of these trends, they have led to varying developments in the banking institutions of Europe.

In contrast to the histories and charter myths of banking which consider relatively long periods of time, most bankers have a shorter view of the future. Despite this it is possible to differentiate between the long-term perceptions of German banks as opposed to short to medium of most British financial institutions. The cultural dyad of long and short-term can be usefully illustrated by the differences between Japanese and British takeover practices. Executives from the latter are intent on the immediate value of the victim and thus make much use of accountants, while the former with a long-term view are not so interested in current values, but rather in future ones, and as a result tend to keep accountants in the background. This reflects the fact that the British have one of the highest proportions of accountants to general population in the world.

German bankers have a longer perspective than British financial institutions. This is due to the fact that German universal banks tend to lend money for longer periods than British commercial banks which concentrate upon short and middle-term lending. Long-term lending in Britain was, until recently, mainly the preserve of building societies. British banks entered the mortgage market in the 1980s. As building prices slumped soon afterwards, many British banks began edging out of this form of long-term lending. Unlike in Germany where long-term bank loans to companies are common, in Britain such corporate funding is normally obtained through the stock market.

The recent problems felt by British banks in the current recession is due to short-termism combined with the unduly optimistic view of the future that they held in the 1980s. They failed to consider the long-term potentials of their debtors. Neither did they realize the fragility of property values which underpinned many of their loans. British banks and investors' short-term responses are frequently attacked by British industrialists, who claim they cannot develop long-term plans which should produce good long-term results. If as a result there are short-term losses British companies are prone to takeovers and/or bank instigated liquidations. Short-termism also means that British bankers do not have a long memory of previously used practices. Thus the recently reintroduced transactional banking appears new to many younger bankers (Shreeve 1991a: 10). Short-termism is not, however, always detrimental. In the rapidly changing situation in Eastern Europe British financial institutions were more prepared to play a part than German universal banks. When the value of organizations is partially determined by past performances it is hard for bankers with a sense of history to estimate the value of institutions in rapidly changing circumstances. As a result valuations were based on equipment and other capital goods. From my interviews it appears that Italian, North American and British bankers and accountants were more prepared to operate in such circumstances. Not only was the past not useful, but the future was also murky. As a result investors (including universal banks) looking for long range investments were deterred. Only short-term futures were predictable and these are much more the specialization of British merchant banks.

One area where bankers' perspectives of the future have focused is "1992" and another is the eventual creation of fixed rates of exchange within Europe and/or a common European currency. In 1989 when I had any discussions with German and British bankers about the impact of 1992, there were three major areas of concern. The first was producing trans-European banking groups. This was mainly to be done by mergers and alliances with existing banks. In addition other banks were setting up branches in other major European cities. In this they frequently saw themselves as following their international customers. The mergers also provided indigenous clients. Compared with insurance executives who I also interviewed in the same year, bankers were relatively unconcerned about the differences of cultures concerned. The insurers felt there were major differences in marketing and in the types of product which were culturally acceptable in various parts of Europe.

One of the phrases most commonly used by British financiers in regard to the EC was the need for "a level playing field" (i.e., the need for equivalent conditions for banks based in other EC states). None felt that the field was level and all claimed they could manage 1992 successfully if it were. This was always explained in terms of local laws and practices and not cultural differences. No non-British bankers made any mention of such a problem.

The third major concern of bankers in 1989 was European currencies. They considered that few firms or individuals would want to borrow in foreign currencies unless there were fixed exchange rates. Thus for example the savings due to lower interest rates in Germany by having a house in Britain mortgaged in Deutsche marks could be easily lost by stirling falling relative to the mark (even if it were within narrow and permitted degrees of fluctuation).[2] In general it was felt that it was only worth having a loan in a particular currency if an income was also available in that currency. As a consequence in the late 1980s European financiers were all advocating Economic and Monetary Union (EMU). British bankers were not quite as enthusiastic in 1991, as they realized that they would lose the profits from exchange proceedings and the international transmission of funds if and when the EMU is introduced.

A fourth, less important, view of the future was also apparent among the bankers I interviewed. In the late 1980s European bankers were attempting to sell their services as advisors on the likely impact of 1992. In this they were joined by many accountants and other consultants. Other questions considered by bankers in 1989 included the impact of a Japanese banking invasion and whether London would retain its financial role. While Japanese banks head *The Banker's* lists of the top 1000 banks (July 1991) they appear to be less feared nowadays. The future of London persists, however, as a topic of debate. It is the largest financial center in Europe and a major center is needed to fill in the dealing time zone between Japan and the East coast of the USA. Unless the cost of office space in London becomes too prohibitive (and the property crash and new offices in the docklands have made this unlikely), or information technology replaces personal contact with offices spread throughout the EC (which is also unlikely), or sterling makes a spectacular crash (which is difficult in the Exchange Rate Mechanism), then London will probably retain a major role for as long as short-term investment pays off. If long-termism returns, the location of the European financial capital may well be Frankfurt or even Berlin. All the discussions of the future were seen in the context of the changing roles of the state and the EC in terms of globalization and centralization.

To sum up this section, concepts of m- and p-time differentiate banking in northern Europe from that in southern Europe while, short and long-termism divide British from German bankers. These different attitudes to time could cause problems for banks expanding from one cultural area to another in the EC. Thus while the concepts of banking were coming together concepts of time were still dividing regional approaches to banking.

The Globalization and Regulation of Banking

Globalization is another area where anthropology has a significant contribution to make to the economic and sociological studies of banking, in that it offers different theoretical foci (e.g., how meanings change with acculturation), and different comparative material (e.g., the globalization of religions; see Gullick and Crane 1992). At the organizational level the increasing influence of the EC and the globalization of Western style banking are rendering banks more uniform, while their relationships with their clients differentiate their regional practices.

Globalization of banking has accelerated during the last two decades. While social historians (e.g., Born 1983) differentiate globalization from centralization during the nineteenth and twentieth centuries, such a division is now more difficult. Information technology has had a similar role in both centralization and globalization. While centralization within a nation state involves fewer cultural conflicts than globalization, centralization within the EC produces just as many cultural clashes.

Much of the early expansion of banks into other European states in the nineteenth and early twentieth centuries was due to the attempts to follow expatriates.[3] This fashion has passed. A banker from one of the bigger British banks explained to me there was little point in being a major player in one country and a niche banker in another. His firm wished to be a major player in any country it entered. In contrast a Swiss banker suggested that his bank was seeking to find a niche in other countries. Its British niche was, however, not serving expatriates, but wealthy clients at home in Britain.

The first EC banking directive of 1977 made it easier for banks to move from one EC country to another. The second directive of 1989 was more important in that it sought to harmonize the essential supervisory rules of each member state by 1993 in such a way that a bank authorized in one state could operate in all member states without further bureaucracy. The second directive produced major changes in all European markets, most of which are thus undergoing the equivalent of the "Big Bang" of 1986 in Britain. The Big Bang stopped the segregation of financial roles in the stock market and opened the door for the acquisitions and mergers that paved the way for the formation of the current financial conglomerates. Some of these groups subsequently relinquished unprofitable financial activities by 1990 and specialized in just a few areas. The freedom to establish insurance businesses in other EC countries has also been simplified, though the rules for large industrial risks have been treated differently from those for the mass market (European Communities – Commission 1989).

While the development of many EC banks involved a mixture of growth and takeovers in their country of origin, their current perceptions of the future concentrate upon cross border alliances and mergers in the build up to 1993. That is to say they are less interested in developing from scratch in new areas or using hostile means to takeover concerns in the target areas. The use of alliances and mutually acceptable mergers is hoped to ease rapid expansion into the whole of the EC and (where thought relevant) gain the appropriate cultural expertise. The way in which banks are building financial bridges across Europe with mergers and special relations with other banks may have advantages in terms of information technology, but escalates the problems due to differing host cultures.

The cross cultural expansion of banking has resulted in changing systems of regulation. While historically banks were mainly regulated by national authorities, globalization nowadays means that regulation has, to a degree, to be undertaken by supranational bodies. At the national level of supervision, financial institutions are normally supervised by the central bank of their nation state which also acts as a lender of the last resort (in that it will act as a banker's bank), and are frequently nowadays the major banks of issue.[4] As deposits and loans have a major role in the money supply of a currency or state, central banks frequently oversee credit controls. Central banks vary in their degree of independence from state control. The German and Dutch are the least controlled in Europe. This issue, and the fear of a German-controlled Central Bank of Europe, are key concerns in the current British reluctance regarding EMU.

A major factor in the increasing role of the state during the 1980s was the impact of monetarism. Monetary supply is easier to measure than most other economic indicators. This meant that in areas where central banks were not as independent as the German and Dutch, politicians could more readily judge performances of their central banks. In the British case the control of money supply partially passed over to the more politically controllable Treasury. As a consequence the Bank of England lost many of its brokering roles between the financial institutions and the treasury. This meant that in the long term many informal methods of control lost their effectiveness and had to be replaced by more formal rules (Hilton 1987). Supranational administration is mainly through the Basle Agreement of 1987 which was signed by eleven countries as well as those of the EC. Banks operating in these countries will, by 1992, need to have capital equal to 8% of risk adjusted assets. With the recent crash in property values many banks have had difficulties in meeting this goal and have thus had to reduce their liquidity ratios.

In addition there are internal EC agreements. The European Monetary System was instituted by the EC in 1972 to stabilize the currencies of member states and to create a community reserve fund. The European Currency Unit (ECU) was created as a composite of the weighted values of members' currencies. National currencies could only diverge from each other by a fixed percentage. This merely formalized the economic reality by which the Italian, French, Danish, and Dutch currencies had become informally tied to the Deutsche mark. Britain joined in 1990 and thus restricted sterling's fluctuations with respect to other EC currencies. The present debate is about the EMU which would be a single European currency. This would halt all movements between national currencies and/or replace them and should render exchange systems unnecessary for any intra-EC deals.

At the organizational level, difficulties result from the use of foreign management methods, production systems, produce, etc., in host cultures. In practice marketing is normally most affected. Problems can, however, also occur with extraction (e.g., the cases of Aluminium in the Caribbean [Zamora and Reynolds 1988], and petroleum in the Middle East), production (e.g., Japanese tractors in Thailand [Titterud 1986]) and distribution (e.g., Securicor's initial difficulties on the European mainland). Changing values can, however, affect the whole range of deals. For example, while French financial managers are mainly concerned with solvency, their North American counterparts consider return on investment. Similarly North American executives are individuals competing for power, while Japanese managers seek harmony and cooperation within the working group. Some cultures tend to dislike change, while others welcome it (Terpstra and David 1985:126-200). Conflicting cultural pressures may be overcome by differentiating central processing facilities from regional marketing in the new Europe.

To sum up, in spite of increasing globalization, states continue to be major factors in banking, but mainly as part of supranational organizations such as the EC. In addition politicians have reorganized the financial service industries of Europe, increasing competition between different types of financial institutions and between nationally based concerns. However changes have also resulted from economic management (and/or mismanagement) with economic booms and recessions and the introduction of new perspectives like monetarism. Such changes have given the banks roles as advisors to clients similarly engaged in adapting to the administrative and business changes of the New Europe

The Relationship Between Banks and Their Clients

Friends and friends of friends form networks. Anthropologists and sociologists have long studied social networks as key factors in the operation of organizations. Studies of the successful anthropological application of networks to management include Fadiman (1984) and Sik (1988); Shapira (1988), in contrast, discusses the consequences of the failure to develop appropriate social networks in a firm in Israel. In Britain there are few of the complex networks found in Italy (Eisenstadt and Roniger 1984). Even in the city of London networks are declining in importance (Hilton 1987: 26-7). Despite this bankers and financiers still need personal contact with one another. While information technology can supply data to most areas with digital telephone exchanges, financiers still feel the need to work close to one another in financial centers such as London, Frankfurt and Paris. This is partially to obtain hints not put on the wires. This is legitimate as long as insider dealing is not involved. In northern Europe the patron/client relationship is not as strong as it is in the Mediterranean and as a result action sets are frequently more important. Action sets are social groups that are brought together for one purpose only and not for the multiple purposes of networks. British banks have recently emphasized the importance of outsiders and action sets. Thus for example Barclays Bank, which in the 1960s and 1970s left branch managers in post for decades, nowadays moves them every three years, so that they do not develop close ties with clients and colleagues.[5] Similarly some other networks within financial institutions are officially discouraged. As a consequence of the development of financial conglomerates, different branches within one may have very different relationships with other institutions and/or individuals. Thus for example when a client is intending a takeover bid with the aid of the organization, other sections which hold shares in the target would love to know about the potential bid. This is officially stopped by "Chinese walls," where information is not permitted to permeate between sections of the organization. This can strain networks and does not always work. In contrast universal banks like those in Germany have representatives on the boards of companies in which they have large holdings. These representatives are officially there as individuals, but in practice are links between the institutions and thus reinforce networks and maintain relational banking systems.

Bankers talk about the action set/network dyad with clients in terms of transaction banking versus relationship banking. In the 1980s there was a tendency for corporations to deal with many more banks than they did previously. This was partially due to foreign banks attempting to set up in major European cities. As they had no long-standing relationships with local firms, they had to undercut the local bankers in one-off deals. While initially useful to their clients, as terms were advantageous, this produced long-term problems when the recession set in. There were fewer connections between banks and corporate clients and as a result the banks were more ready to call in the liquidators when problems arose. This was complicated by the fact that many firms had numerous similar transactions with a multitude of banks, all of whom had to agree on any new terms under which a firm in trouble might be permitted to continue trading.

Banks in addition devolved functions to different groups and individual employees. As a consequence corporate treasurers had to deal with a considerable number of different banking officials, and relationships failed to develop, or where they had existed, broke down. With the return to relationship banking the number of personnel dealing with a particular corporate client was reduced and bankers who have little memory of the previous relationship phases are amazed how it produces more communication and trade.

Transaction and relationship banking differ in the degree of autonomy given to local branches. In Britain in contrast to the rest of Europe, the power to make decisions was generally removed from local branches. Instead major decisions were made centrally and mainly upon set criteria and equations and not upon knowledge of the clients per se. As a consequence most German, French, Spanish and Italian branch managers know their clients better, and can do more for them, with less reference to headquarters than in Britain.[6]

Relationships were also downplayed in dealings with the private clients of British commercial banks. They were treated as part of a mass market and the bank officials concerned became sales-people rather than advisors (many British branch officials have their salaries determined by their sales). This often results in unsuitable services being sold. There has been a tendency to lend on short-term conditions for long-term purposes which means that clients frequently have problems repaying loans when trade declines.

Relationships with mass consumers were also modified by competition from the building societies in Britain which could offer similar services at lower cost. As a result banks followed them in offering interest on checking accounts, but simultaneously introduced or increased bank charges for other services. Shopping around by clients has thus increased. A major consequence of the change from networks to action sets was that an increasing number of private individuals opened accounts with more than one financial institution and wealthier individuals moved to specialist banks who gave them more services.[7] As a result the major British banks like Barclays have had to introduce "private" or "personal banking services" for their wealthier clients, who then have access to one (or sometimes two) manager who oversees their affairs. One such manager explained to me that they were attempting to rebuild relationships so that the selected clients would be treated by their manager in a way analogous to that practiced in the 1960s, before banks moved their focus from well-off clients to a mass market in which virtually everyone had to have some form of checking account.

The expansion of retail banking to more clients occurred at the same time as the development of computers for keeping records and more recently for dealing with clients direct. This has reduced the need for personal contact and as a consequence many small branches of the major banks are being closed down in Britain. This accordingly renders personal contacts even less possible. As Spain has more branches per customer than any other EC member, British bankers expect there to be a similar decimation of small branches in Spain. While this may occur I suspect that the closures will not be as numerous as expected because of the greater importance of social networks in Spain. The increasing use of information technology is one of the major reasons put forward by bankers to explain why their institutions should increase in size and this may possibly override such social factors. In Britain where these changes have been most extreme, there have been major alterations to the image of bankers. While they were once seen as professionals akin to, but not as "nice" as lawyers, accountants and even medical doctors, they are now perceived as more villainous. British bankers have gained images similar to that of the North American banker, whilst German bankers are still considered comradely and high status.[8] It is with such a background that in 1991 the draft code of conduct produced by bankers was attacked by, amongst others, the British banking ombudsman who warned that it would do nothing to raise banks' low standing in the eyes of their clients (*Financial Times* 21 May 1991: 6).

The action set /social network divide between the business cultures of Europe can cause problems when banks operate transculturally. This is demonstrated by the problems raised by banks which had to undertake transactional banking even when they preferred relational banking, so as to obtain a foothold with major firms in other European countries. These difficulties were exacerbated by the recent recession. More difficulties occur in making contacts in network oriented cultures at the retail end of the market.

To sum up, networks and action sets can be seen as factors in both the success of financial institutions and in their failures. There was a tendency towards action sets in the 1980s which has been partially replaced by the use of networks during the early 1990s. Britain was more extreme in its oscillations than other European financial institutions. This factor thus serves to separate British banking from both southern European and Germanic practices. These differences also cause problems when expanding into areas with differing views about appropriate relationships between bankers and clients.

Historically many banks expanded internationally to follow their clients. Despite this many international travellers still have to operate a range of nationally based banks in the EC. This can cause intercultural problems. For example when I was investigating the difficulties met by expatriate executives on sojourns overseas[9] several interviewees listed banks. For instance a German company director working in the UK was horrified by the inefficiency, as he saw it, of his British bank and was amazed by the difficulties experienced when opening an account in England. Though he never realized it, much of this was due to British legal constraints.[10] Other quandaries concerning the British/German divide also result from cultural differences. Other expatriates complained of poor communications between their banks in their host and home countries and the cost of transferring funds across boundaries within the EC. The gap between debiting funds in one country and crediting them in another can give the banks concerned an interest free loan (Monk 1986), but this is only a partial explanation of delays. Small (and/or branch) banks have a tendency not to know which section of the other bank deals with such international transfers and items can thus become genuinely mislaid. When the expatriate comes from a major city or goes to one, this can sometimes be overcome by using branches of the same bank in both countries. The EC is now attempting to reduce the official bank charges on transfers between currencies.

The majority of banks attempt to sell their intercultural expertise to corporate clients. They will thus assist with different financial systems, mergers and acquisitions. The various bankers, with whom I discussed their role as transcultural advisors, emphasized financial, legal and political factors and did not rate other cultural items as important. This contrasts with the insurers who were asked about international problems. Those at the retail end were all too aware of cultural variations amongst their mass consumers in different countries and regions. For example in southern Europe there were problems with selling life insurance because of local concepts about fate and death. Values are similarly important for banking. These range from beliefs about usury (e.g., among clients from Islamic minorities in England and France) to beliefs on saving (or not, as the case may be).

Conclusions

Executives are not the only expatriates to find new banking systems a problem. Most anthropologists who undertake field research or take up employment outside their home country have to contend with alien banking systems. During my period of field research in Europe I have had to contend with a wide range of financial systems. This paper is a consequence of my attempts to explain my problems from an anthropological perspective.

Anthropology tends to have a particular set of perspectives on organizations. The anthropology of organizations tends to emphasize relationships from the bottom up. It is all too easy in both European society and social science to consider hierarchies as operating from the top down. Anthropological studies demonstrate that in many ways they are run from the bottom up and that there is a fair degree of reciprocity between the elite of organizations and the rest. Accordingly this study had its origins in an attempt to see banks from the customer/fieldworker up.

The anthropological perspective also differs in that it tends to have a wider awareness of cultural context, including the symbolic nature of time, space, wealth, banks in folklore etc., and different comparative material. For example, this chapter has shown how, while the ways in which banks are building financial bridges across Europe with mergers and special relations with other banks may have advantages in terms of information technology, globalization escalates integration problems due to differing host cultures. The breakdown of customer relations with the change from bank/client networks to financial action sets is also connected with centralization within a culture. These conflicting pressures could, however, be overcome by differentiating central processing facilities from regional marketing in the New Europe.

The investigation of time and networks in this chapter also leads to the hypothesis that non-verbal communication with all its levels of cultural meaning is as important, if not more so, than just speaking the appropriate languages. A major lacunae in the advice offered to British firms prior to 1992 is the virtual failure to mention the non-verbal aspects of communication. Many executives will probably use the linguistic skills which they are acquiring for use in an EC internal market to make cultural mistakes.[11]

This chapter has sought, like its companions, to make some predictions about the New Europe of the EC. The four trends discussed above will continue. Centralization will accordingly continue beyond the conventional bounds of banking. Similarly the influence of the state will have a major role to play, but in many ways as part of supra-state groupings (e.g., in the EC and among the signatories of the Basle Accord). Other changes will continue to devolve from the reorganization of the financial service industries of Europe with increasing competition between different types of financial institutions and between institutions with differing national bases. In addition states will continue to play a role in the affairs of banking through their own economic management (including changing theories of monetarism, the production of economic booms and recessions, and modifying the rules under which the banks operate). Such changes will continue to give the banks roles as advisors to clients similarly enmeshed in administrative changes (e.g., assisting clients in building bridges across Europe prior to 1993). The transnationality or globalization of banks continue, but the areas of expansion have changed. British banks for instance are less interested in Commonwealth and Third World banking and are reorienting themselves towards Europe. Similarly non-EC banks have set up offices in EC countries (especially in London) so as to be able to partake of the post-1992 financial climate in Europe. As a consequence of the continuation of these trends, which have spanned almost two centuries, there will undoubtedly be a major shake-out in European banking during the 1990s, but it is unlikely that it will be any better run (Shreeve 1991b: 1).

Other long term trends are also likely to continue. Thus German banks may continue to take a relatively long-term view in their operations, and to be slightly less enthusiastic about current banking fashions. Southern European bankers are more likely to continue to develop personal relationships with their clients than the Anglo Saxon north. British banks will probably persist in importing fashionable ideas from North America. Thus, while it is probable that acquaintance with any set of organizations makes one cynical about their survival, my research suggests that British bankers will continue to chase the short-term goals of British banking. Seen from an EC perspective, this may have disastrous results for the culture of British banking.

Notes

1. My main research into the financial service sector was undertaken in 1989-1991. I have attempted to restrict banking jargon to a minimum in this chapter and give explanations of most terms. More detailed explanations can be found in specialist dictionaries such as Bannock and Manser (1989).

2. These discussions were held before the United Kingdom was committed to joining such a system. The argument was not, however, totally convincing as it could be argued that one consequence of Danish farmers taking out German loans was to force their national currencies together.

3. Historically, the expansion of some financial services (especially insurance and commercial banking) similarly followed corporate clients abroad, but once they were there they sought to assist other clients to go transnational.

4. That is to say central banks issue the notes which form the national currency. It should, however, be noted that some commercial banks (e.g., those in Scotland) can also issue notes. In Luxembourg the banks are supervised by the Institut Monetaire and not by a central bank. This means that there is no bank of last resort for Luxembourg based banks.

5. The role of employment can become a major factor in some networks and be unimportant in others. While in Britain we do not go as far as, Sweden (where, for example, an advocate when telephoning about something unrelated to his work will introduce himself with "This is Advocate A"), British ranking is more work-based than in the Caribbean, where Afro-Caribbean ranking depends on ability in play not work (Abrahams 1983).

6. Despite the centralization of British banking it is noteworthy that in the recent disputes about the failure of British banks to pass on cuts in interest rates to small business clients, there was a major variation between statements by chairmen and actions by local management.

7. As a consequence stores and restaurants catering to the elite have accordingly noticed an increasing use by their clients of checks drawn on specialist banks. The amount of use of accounts by the wealthy differs from country to country. One major variable is the amount of data that bankers have to give to tax authorities. Banks in Germany and Luxembourg are the most secretive in the EC. The Maltese tax authorities appear to have the most data, and as a result, I met one professional who admitted that he virtually never used his account. Malta has applied to join the EC and its banking system will have to be modified before accession.

8. As a consequence when small businessmen outline their careers in business school training sessions in Durham University (England), I have noticed how in their personal narratives they make use of two kinds of intermediaries. Propp (1968) would have called them assistants and/or donors. These are the unhelpful bankers who have to be overcome or persuaded to assist the hero and the helpful business school personnel. Caulkins (1988) has made similar observations about the role of bankers in entrepreneurial life histories.

9. The main period during which I investigated expatriates was 1987-90 (Gullick 1990 a, b).

10. If the bank does not bother to obtain references from potential customers they lose the protection of the Cheques Act 1957 (Klein and Lambert 1987: 37).

11. Certainly some North American studies show that in South and Central America acting Latin American is more important than speaking good Spanish.

References

Abrahams, Roger D. 1983. *Man of Words in the West Indies*. Baltimore: Johns Hopkins Press.

Bannock, Graham, and William Manser. 1989. *International Dictionary of Finance*. London: The Economist Books.

Born, Karl E. 1983. *International Banking in the 19th and 20th Centuries*. Stuttgart: Berg.

Caulkins, Douglas. 1988. *Networks and Narratives: An Anthropological Perspective for Small Business Research*. Scottish Enterprise Foundation, Stirling University, Occasional Paper Series, no. 01/88.

Chapman, Stanley. 1984. *The Rise of Merchant Banking*. London: Unwin Hyman.

Clay, C. J. J., and B. S. Wheble. 1976. *Modern Merchant Banking*. Cambridge: Cambridge University Press.

Condon, John C. 1985. *Good Neighbors*. Yarmouth, Maine: Intercultural Press.

Eisenstadt, S .N., and L. Roniger. 1984. *Patrons, Clients and Friends*. Cambridge: Cambridge University Press.

European Communities – Commission. 1989. *Completing the Internal Market*. Luxembourg: Office for Official Publications of the European Communities.

Fadiman, J. A. 1984. "Forming business relations in Bantu Africa," in H. Serrie, ed., *Anthropology and International Business*. Pp. 89-111. Williamsburg: William and Mary.

Fairchild, H .P. 1975. *Immigration: A World Movement*. New York: Macmillan.

Greener, Michael. 1987. *The Penguin Business Dictionary*. London: Penguin.

Gullick, Charles J.M.R. 1990a. *British Expatriate Managers and their Families: A Study of Their Problems When Moving Abroad, Working Abroad, and Returning to Britain*. Unpublished M.A. thesis. Leeds University.

____. 1990b. "Expatriate British executives and culture shock," in Tomoko Hamada and Ann Jordan, eds., *Cross-cultural Management and Organizational Culture*. Williamsburg: William and Mary.

Gullick, Charles J.M.R., and J. Crane. 1992. "Myths in politics and politics in religion," in Mart Bax, Peter Kloss and Adrianus Koster, eds., *Faith and Polity*. Pp. 173-201. Amsterdam: VU Press.

Hall, Edward T. 1959. *The Silent Language*. New York: Doubleday.

____. 1966. *The Hidden Dimension*. New York: Doubleday.

Harrison, P.A. 1983. *Behaving Brazilian*. Rowley, MA: Newbury House.

Hilton, Anthony. 1987. *City Within a State*. London: Taurus.

221

Klein, Gerald, and Janice Lambert. 1987. *The Business of Banking*. London: Methuen.

Maidment, P. 1990. "Question of Definition: A Survey of International Banking." *The Economist* 7 April.

Minoura, Y. 1988. Growing up abroad and its impact upon cultural identity. Unpublished paper. 12th International Congress of Anthropological and Ethnological Sciences, Zagreb.

Mitchie, Ronald. 1992. *The City of London: Continuity and Change*. London: Macmillan.

Monk, Keith. 1986. *Go International*. London: McGraw Hill.

Norrington, H. 1989. Strategies for competitive advantage: banking. Unpublished paper. Economist Conference: 1992 and Beyond: Restructuring Europe's Financial Services. London

Propp, Vladimir. 1968 (2nd ed.). *Morphology of the Folktale*. (trans. S. Lawrence). American Folklore Society: University of Texas Press.

Serrie, Hendrix, ed. 1984. *Anthropology and International Business*. Studies in Third World Societies. Williamsburg: William and Mary.

Shapira, R. 1988. Ill management by alien managers. Unpublished paper. 12th International Congress of Anthropological and Ethnological Sciences, Zagreb.

Shreeve, Gavin. 1991a. "Re-inventing the wheel." *The Banker* May: 10-14.

_____. 1991b. "This Month." *The Banker* July: 1.

Sik, E. 1988. Reciprocal exchange of labour in Hungary. Unpublished paper. 12th International Congress of Anthropological and Ethnological Sciences, Zagreb.

Terpstra, Vern, and Kenneth David, 1985. *The Cultural Environment of International Business*. Cincinnati: Southwestern Publishing.

Titterud, Todd V. 1986. Japanese multinationals and the development of Thailand's farm machinery industry. Unpublished paper. 87th Annual Meeting of the American Anthropological Association, Phoenix.

Zamora, Mario D., and R. Reynolds. 1988. Cultural values in cross-national management: the case of the Reynolds International Corporation. 12th International Congress of Anthropological and Ethnological Sciences, Zagreb.

12

The Question of European Nationalism

Hervé Varenne

Twenty years ago, at the University of Chicago, when I announced that I would be going "downstate Illinois" to look at "American culture," the reaction was nearly unanimous: "what? America? culture? downstate Illinois?" In corridors, bars and such places, the gut reaction of my anthropological community, at least when we were not quite playing at anthropology, was that there couldn't be any culture to America, and that, should there be one, it would certainly not be found in any downstate Illinoises. Happily, this reaction was not consequential. When my professors assumed the mantle of anthropology they agreed that all this could be argued and they let me go. Ever since I have been telling in all sorts of forums, that one cannot take a practical step in the United States that is not sensitive to, and thereby reproductive of, America.

Fifteen years later, I decided that it was time to expand my comparative perspectives and, for many reasons, landed on Ireland. The reaction was quite unanimous this time: "Ireland? great! my grandfather came from County Clare! I went there once and we had such a great time! You are interested in the Irish character? Let me tell you all about it and then you must go on to the West, there you will find the real Ireland." From colleagues, to friends and students in the United States, to the Irish I met in Dublin, the chorus spoke with one voice: there is an Ireland, there is an Irish culture, and it is to be found in the Western counties. In consequence, I settled in a new suburb of Dublin, rented a semi-detached house, rarely visited pubs and spent time listening to people worrying about mortgages and the cost of food or private education. I hoped that I would thus find more about the forces that point to the West as the reality of the East, and may hide what people all over Ireland also have to deal with.

Still, I sometimes wondered whether I could just as well have stayed in New Jersey. In fact, to live in the suburbs of Dublin is not at all the same thing as living in the suburbs of New York. It may be the case that, in suburbs, whether of Dublin or New York City, people have to deal with close variations on "modernity." But the people of Dublin also have to deal with "Ireland" – an altogether cantankerous woman (mother? mistress?) as various poets of Irishness identify her. "America," even when represented as a woman in New York Bay, is something else altogether, and anthropologists must investigate the difference.

When I started looking around me in Dublin, I realized that something other than "Ireland" concerned my neighbors. It is something, a thing of some kind, that no one who now works in the geographical space of Western Eurasia,[1] can now ignore: "Europe." The nature of this "Europe" is no easy matter to ascertain. Much of it is quite concrete. There are dramatic performances (voting for the European Parliament); regulations and their justifications (subsidies for farmers, or the rate of maximum taxation); new tools and constraints in the construction of ordinary everyday life ("do I need a work permit to get a job in England? how do I preserve health insurance?" – questions that an 18 year old woman from the rural parts of Southern France can ask herself as she seizes opportunities that were not quite open to her parents). These practices have in fact made for further complexity since they are most concretely the products of the evolution of a "Common Market," the common name of a "European *Economic Community*," that transformed itself into the "European Community," and now is popularly known simply as "Europe." This Europe has its "European Parliament," a flag originally designed by a broader body, the "European Council," which, until recently, did not include any of the nations attached to the Soviet Union. The EC, in a complex way, is a "fiction" of Europe. It is now also an overwhelming social "fact" – in the Durkheimian sense – that is still in the process of being made – in the constructivist sense.

One aspect of this social fact is a set of discourses both affirming and denying the "reality" of Europe for certain purposes. Quite common in conversations with my neighbors in Dublin or when reading the Irish, British or French press are statements to the effect that "Europe" is only a matter of interest for businessmen and bureaucrats, that nobody really cares whether something or somebody is European or not. In such conversations, the talk then proceeds to a reaffirmation of the reality of "Ireland," "Wales," "Scotland," "England," "France" and such more or less traditional symbols on a stage that the people of Western Eurasia would probably consider a "world" (universal) stage.

There is also talk asserting the reality of Europe as a *cultural* entity of some sort. This is an intellectual discourse, or more precisely a conversation, which has built something that balances in the interpretive realm what politicians and bureaucrats have been doing "in Brussels." This conversation is interesting to anthropologists not only because of its existence as a curiosity. It is also interesting because its central theme is the central theme of anthropology: given the evidence for the local specification of practices that generate a phenomenological experience of "difference" when one moves from one locality to the next, what is one to do next about it? For anthropology, the problem is an academic one and concerns the proper understanding of "culture" as it relates to human beings in any locality. For the people with whom we will be concerned, as it has been for philosophers and other political thinkers since at least the 18th century, the concern is with the institutional expression of this difference, its affirmation on some broader stage, and its rationalization. The concern is with "nationalism."

The Political Culture of European Nationalism

There is not much reason to rehearse the arguments for the mythical association of the ideas, rituals, and practices of nationality with the people of Western Eurasia. They appear to have, if not invented, at least developed them into what Yeats once qualified, when writing about the 1916 uprising in Dublin ([1921] 1962), terribly beautiful theater: On its stage *peuples* (the French is most evocative here) forge, express, and defend collective identities grounded in a unique substance and a common position in a current history.[2] Since the French and American revolutions, this ideology has been a constituent aspect of everyday life in every part of Western Eurasia. Through the process of decolonization, it appears to have spread to the whole world, and perhaps to have thus escaped Europe. In any event, at the height of classical European nationalism (say, in June 1914), from Co. Clare on the West Coast of Ireland, and for a long way eastward, "nationality" was a matter of local concern. As the people of the centers knew, in Paris, London, or Berlin, one could never be sure that the people of the periphery would draw the practical consequences of the identity earlier dramatic performances of nationality were supposed to have built for them. Thus, everywhere, even in the remotest of villages, one had become accountable to the many apparatuses of centralized states administering local communities, imposing – violently if necessary – languages, educational systems, and, most concretely perhaps, universal conscription into huge armies. In the process people who may never have had any consciousness of their participation in wider systems were projected unto an international stage. There, as they killed each other, they were expected to complete positive and negative identifications with various fatherlands, one of them "theirs," and the others not.[3]

One does not have to be a Marxist to recognize that this association of people with national identities was made by human hands; that it is a cultural, rather than natural, product, and that it may be resisted. We now have many good histories of nationalism and its relationship to European culture or ideology (Anderson [1983] 1991; Dumont 1991; Gellner 1987; Hobsbawm 1990) that have demonstrated how nationalism evolved, and how it may be changing. Except for Dumont, this literature has not, however, recognized the relevance of the concurrent resistance against nationalism in the name of the universality of humanity. The origin of this resistance is inscribed in 18th century enlightenment, and, of those of the 19th century Europe who resisted, many worked for a supranational Europe, and for various "Internationales." Many more escaped across the Atlantic to a land where they hoped they would indeed be free from various tyrants.

There is not much anthropological research on this great debate, perhaps because anthropologists were not trained to notice its echoes at the local levels where they prefer to work, and perhaps also because to focus on these debates would lead them back on their own activity as participants in either the justification, or the critique, of nationalistic claims. Throughout his career, Louis Dumont has claimed, and, to my mind, demonstrated, that the refusal to consider overarching ideologies as context for local action is mistaken both in that it limits our ethnographic understanding of this action, and in that it prevents us from noticing how our own ideological framework shapes our theoretical understanding of the conditions of human action. Through the acceptance of the relevance of Cliffords' work (1988), there has been some advance on the latter front. Still it is easier for the historians or anthropologists of nationalism to highlight the contribution of their forefathers to the justification of a particular ideology,[4] then it is to place themselves in the ideological debate – perhaps because the nature of this debate as a conversation between identifiable persons in particular situations is not yet well understood.[5]

Let us, then, look at ourselves in the work of the intellectuals who have produced major expressions of "Europe." They are people like Benda, de ˙Rougemont, Monnet, etc., who are involved in a kind of applied anthropology where theoretical ideologies encounter historical happenstance.

The Question of European Nationality

It is easy to caricature the structure of the nationalistic ideology. One can state it as a recipe so perhaps as to preserve its processual characteristic: get yourself a geographical area; get yourself a population within this area; seize on something arguably characteristic about this population and survalue it; seize upon something arguably different from this characteristic in a neighboring population and devalue it; arrange it to demonstrate the antiquity of the characteristic of national focus; organize yourself with the neighbor (either through wars or support of its own development as a nation) to recognize your claim. For the past 200 years, even when the local conditions would seem to make the attempt a rather difficult one, when the calls to nationhood are made up according to the recipe, there is a good chance that the struggle will succeed if it can get some foreign help. There is something fascinating about the claims to nationhood of so many of the administrative areas that followed the collapse of empires, starting with the Austrian empire and moving on to the British or Russian empires. As centers lose their grip, smaller and smaller groups attempt to cook themselves into something that can claim the rights and privileges attached by other nations to the status of nation.

There is something equally fascinating – or is it frightening? – in seeing how some people in Western Eurasia are attempting to cook Europe itself into a nation of sorts. This effort can be traced to various moments. For the ideological reasons that give legitimacy to what can be traced through complex roots to a distant past, one can quote a 1306 project for the administrative unification of Christendom (geographically co-extensive then with Europe).[6] Many other such projects followed over the centuries.

It is only since the Second World War however that intellectual activity has had to keep pace with an administrative evolution which shows promise of inscribing in institutional history what had until then always been dismissed as impractical dreams. The beginning of the search for a representation of Europe can thus be dated to a 1946 conference in Geneva where Benda and de Rougemont[7] – who were and remained the prime movers of the effort – met with intellectuals like Karl Jaspers, Georg Lukacs, Maurice Merleau-Ponty, Jean Wahl and others, to talk about "l'esprit européen." Both the speeches and the following discussion were published (Benda et al. 1946) and this constitutes a fascinating document that catches a moment in the attempt to make something, the time for which seems to have come but which does not yet have a very clear outline.

A few years before the war, Benda had written something that he must have felt was still another in a long list of utopian calls (1933). It may thus not be surprising that, in his introductory remarks, he struck the sober note: "a consciousness of Europe has never existed" (1946: 9). Indeed the only history of Europe that could be written would be one that would be titled "A history of the Europeans in their will not to make Europe" (1946: 15). As he sees it, every time historical conditions made it possible for a consciousness of Europe to realize itself institutionally, from Charlemagne to Napoleon, the result was a further boost for the institutionalization of various parts of Europe as independent units. From the earliest, philosophers, kings, bourgeois and others who could speak at the center of the arena talked about what social philosophers eventually expressed as "national" units. Resistance to nationalism remained a phenomenon without consequences. When it moved closer to the center – as it started doing in the 18th century – the talk was made to center around "men" and "human nature."[8] It was absolutely generalized and no serious thinker stopped to consider the possibility that there might be "Europeans." For Benda, this failure is a major problem: None of "us" (he mentions the French, German, Italian, English, Scandinavian, Russian) talk about ourselves as "Europeans." There is no European consciousness of itself, no European will.[9] Europe must arise out of Europe as, he claims, France arose out of France and Germany out of Germany.

In the conference, Benda was distinctly in the minority. The other participants just assumed the existence of Europe and worked at determining what Europe was and in what ways it was distinct from various neighbors. In this setting these neighbors were mostly Russia and America, the two which are still built up as the relevant ones in more recent discussions – though they are now being joined by "the Arab world," "Japan," "the Third World." In his contribution to the conference, Merleau-Ponty answers Benda by arguing that while Europe may not have a *representation* of itself, while in fact such a *representation* might be dangerous since it would define itself against neighbors, there is an *Europe en acte*, ideological acts in fact, "un comportement typiquement Européen, et qui serait à peu près le suivant: une relation entre l'homme et la nature, d'abord qui n'est pas confusion, une distinction du moi et du monde; correlativement, l'idée de l'objectivité ou de la verité" (Benda et al. 1946: 74-5).[10] This idea is developed by de

Rougemont in a little book significantly titled *The meaning of Europe* (1963). For de Rougemont, it makes no doubt that there is something specific about Europe, something good (nationalism *oblige*), something that must be preserved, antagonistically against the relevant others if necessary but, eventually, for the good of whole world as an earth-wide federation is created, on European grounds of course. After all, as he claims unapologetically, "Europe discovered the whole of the earth, and nobody ever came and discovered Europe" (1963: 12).

The most fascinating part of this book may be the beginning when de Rougemont, in a process which anthropologists who have read Lévi-Strauss (or is it Malinowski?) will recognize, tells two myths of the origin of Europe. First, there is the Greek myth of Europa, the Tyrian princess who was abducted by Zeus and produced the beginning of the Westward movement which culminated with the settling of America. And then there is the Jewish myth of Noah's sons in which the Christian Church Fathers saw God giving Japheth "Europe and arms with the promise of boundless expansion" (1963: 19). From there de Rougemont goes on to tell us what Europe has been, what it is, and what it can be if it transforms the self that is already there into an institution of some sort on the international scene.

In his great compendium of the texts which reveal how Europe was conceived (1961), de Rougemont is content with just telling the myths. He does not move to abstract the "pattern" of these myths – perhaps because so many of them are self-analytical. Still, he stops just at the edge of the nationalistic affirmation of Europe as a substance. The image of Europe that emerges might be analogized to the image of the Americas as a setting for the affirmation of individuality, that is as a place without culture that is thus particularly open to the building of new cultures. Americans, Margaret Mead once wrote, "are all third generation" ([1942] 1965: Chapter III). They are not "native." Perhaps the same thing could be said of Europeans. In the myth of origin it says that the Greek goddess Europa was not a native of Europe either. She was born in Asia. Europe was the land given to her children.

A small group of intellectuals who have put themselves at the extreme right of political ideologies have gone further. They do claim unabashedly that there is an actual substantial "difference" to Europe, one that is grounded – not too surprisingly given the history of European nationalisms – on a myth of original common history (though a different one from those de Rougemont cited). For them, the "really" European becomes the Indo-European ideology of the three functions as sketched by Dumézil, an ideology of duty, strength and tolerance of multiplicity which Judeo-Christian, monotheistic (or mono-ideological) civilizations have attempted, unsuccessfully, to smother. They delight in finding evidence of the survival of pre-Christian myths and rituals in the modern world. They like the "pagan" Santa Claus, they like Soviet ritualism where the social world seems always to be divided into three orders: The Communist party in charge of ideological purity (the first "priestly" function), the army in charge of defense (the second "warrior" function), and the workers in charge of concrete survival (the third function); they give their children names drawn from Germanic mythology. They are particularly angry at Hitler for having used some of these ideas in such a way as to insure the imperial success of two versions of the anti-European Judeo-Christian civilization – the theistic "Protestant" version in the United States, and the atheistic "Communist" version in Russia. They seem to suspect that these two are hiding a deep agreement of purpose under the guise of a life threatening conflict, the purpose of keeping Europe militarily occupied so that it cannot organize itself into a threat to either empire. And they now fear the rise of the third major ideology to emerge out of the Bible: Islam.

The strong version of this argument has only been articulated intellectually – in France particularly – by a miniscule group, the *Groupement de recherche et d'études pour la civilisation européenne*, G.R.E.C.E. for short (obviously, the name derived from the acronym). This group emerged briefly in the late 1970s and then sank back into obscurity. Most French, and most Europeans, are unaware of its existence. The insistence on the need to reject Christianity in all its forms, including conservative Catholicity, insures that the group will remain a fringe event. Still, its argument is the most internally consistent with the fundamental myth of nationalism: The myth of the ethnic roots which, in Europe, served France, Germany, Italy, etc., and may still serve all those that want to ritualize a perceived difference as a State of some sort. It is the myth that has presided over the break-down of colonialist empires, the Myth of the "auto-determination" which may also be the Myth of anthropology: The myth that a "culture" is always the culture *of a particular people* attached to a particular land, and that it must be preserved in the name of their rights.

The last clause in the preceding sentence highlights the problem. The myth of nationalism is not simply about origins and characteristics, it also includes a prescription for its own incorporation in historical institutions. It is an interpretive model *of* behavior. It is also a model *for* behavior – to use Geertz's summary of the properties of culture ([1966] 1973). For a reminder let us look briefly at one unabashed statement of what is involved here:

La philosophie européenne que je defends est celle de l'autoaffirmation d'un peuple, de sa recherche de la puissance et du rayonnement, de sa specificité et de son homogénéité culturelle, de la reconquète de ses racines (Faye 1985: 13).[11]

Faye was writing here as a member of the G.R.E.C.E. and for him the reference to a "quest for power" is not empty. Power, will, struggle, these are key terms in all theories of nationalism. Nations, as we in fact know, do not peacefully emerge like some flower in early spring. As Patrick Pearse knew well, nations are baptized in blood.

The Consciousness of Europe

Whether "Europe" is primarily (Indo-)European, whether it is fundamentally Judeo-Christian, whether it is best characterized by the pattern of the philosophical arguments that developed from the Renaissance through the 18th and even the 19th century, whether one should rather look to the more local manifestations of character, ethos, or anything else, Europeans – that is people who assume the mantle of Europe – can read history and construct something that makes some sense. How much sense it does make remains a matter of discussions that are having practical consequences. For nationalism, particularly in that part of the world where it originated and was first inscribed in history, is not only an academic question for social scientists wondering about its applicability as a model of or for human behavior, in Europe or anywhere else. It is also a political question among those who wonder whether they should struggle for the further institutionalization of Europe. Many have resisted and continue to resist[12] both in the name of the old nations whose symbolic grounding would be devalued, and in the name of various universalisms and humanisms. The Europeanness of Europe, geographically and ideologically, is still up for grabs, and the answers to be given will make a lot of difference.

These matters were disputed at the beginning of the modern construction of Europe. Forty years later, the argument continues. Another French intellectual, Edgar Morin (1987), tries to clarify his position as one who opposed the economic and political construction of Europe through the 1950s and 1960s in the name of resistance to capitalism, and of construction of socialism. Still, he maintains that it is difficult to see Europe from Europe and that it is only through his travels in the United States that he finally understood what others had been talking about. Above all he remains afraid of what certain kinds of

European affirmation could bring, and he builds his whole argument around the denial of a European substance:

> Il faut abandonner toute Europe une, claire, distincte, harmonieuse, réfuter toute idée d'une essence ou substance européenne première qui précède la division et l'antagonisme. . . . C'est effectivement dans l'éclatement de la Chrétienté qu'ont put émerger ces réalités originellement européenne que sont les Etats-Nations, l'humanisme et la science, et c'est dans les divisions et antagonismes entre Etats-Nations que va se propager et s'imposer la notion d'Europe (1987: 27).[13]

In order for Europe not to become Europe the way Germany became Germany, there cannot have been a Europe, though there may be one in the future – as long as it does not institutionalize itself into anything like what nations were made to be. There is a question of faith here, though a very particular kind of faith:

> [La foi nouvelle] subit en elle la présence du Néant. Le recours à une pensée qui affronte courageusement le Néant, voilà le message vivant du nihilisme, ultime produit de l'aventure de l'esprit européen, voilà l'ultime conséquence de la perte des fondements, terme final de la recherche éperdue d'une Certitude première (1987: 192)[14]

Thus ends Morin's attempt to "Think Europe." Europe must be created out of Nothingness into Nothingness – the capital letters are his. No irony is permitted.

European Others

Morin, of course, has not escaped nationalism. He still speaks of "l'esprit européen" as of a particular set of understandings, a characteristic ideology. And so he remains puzzled, like de Rougemont and all the others professional thinkers we have looked at, by the fact that something, Europe, that has some level of historical existence, has in fact never had the *particular* kind of existence that traditional nations have had. The kind of existence that it does appear to have gained is that of a common "market," a soulless place where merchants exploit their customers.[15]

It is not surprising that no intellectual would see beauty in administrative regulations and custom agreements. Only Jean Monnet would title a little book on the European Coal and Steel Community *The United States of Europe have begun* (1955). Morin fails to see that this may be the only practical form that a non-imperialistic Europe can take.

What Monnet fails to see is that a "Europe" reduced to a market is indeed nothing. Thus the first major success and the first major failure in the construction of Europe took place within the first five years of the movement we are tracing: in 1951, politicians in France and Germany could agree to give up separate control over their coal and steel industries. In 1954, the French Parliament refused a "European Defense Community" that would have created a joint command structure for French and German troops. Discussions have continued on the matter of a joint defense, along with discussions of a joint currency, but they have yet to produce something. As some fear, "Europe" may remain a place for a self-satisfied comfortable middle-class quite content to leave the thinking, and the dirty work, including the fighting, to others – America and Africa particularly.

The positive side of this absence of the major symbols of a triumphant European nationalism is that it leaves room for the constituent nations of Europe to continue to symbolize themselves as different and independent on a universal stage. Several of the writers we mentioned saw the construction of Europe not as the autodetermination of a people so much as a step in the construction of pan-human world where the universal values developed in Europe could finally institutionalize themselves fully. This may in fact be typical of French intellectuals whose ideology Dumont summarized in the following terms:

> Côté français, je suis homme par nature et français par accident. Comme dans la philosophie des Lumières en général, la nation comme telle n'a pas de statut ontologique: à ce plan il n'y a rien, qu'un grand vide, entre l'individu et l'espèce, et la nation est simplement la plus vaste approximation empirique de l'humanité qui me soit accessible au plan de la vie réelle (1991: 129).[16]

The symbolic "absence" of Europe may thus satisty the French, more perhaps than it may satisfy the Germans, particularly if Dumont is right in his contrastive analysis of German ideology, an ideology that stresses the fundamentally social (cultural) constitution of the individual (1991).

This issue does not however concern only the people of Western Eurasia. There has always been, in the consciousness of Europe a recognition of various others. The new problem for Europe is that many of these others are getting to construct Europe in ways that cannot be ignored. Another quote from Benda may serve to outline the issue:

> Nous parlons couramment d'un romancier américain, un Hemingway, un Faulkner, un Miller, nous ne parlons pas d'un romancier «européen», mais d'un romancier français, anglais, russe. Les Américains, eux, parlent d'un romancier européen, ils assurent qu'il y a pour eux quelque chose de

commun (que d'ailleurs ils ne définissent pas) entre les littérateurs de nos diverses nations par opposition aux leurs; *mais ce qui importerait pour notre sujet, ce serait que ce soit nous qui parlions d'un littérateur européen.* Or, nous ne le faisons pas (my emphasis 1946: 21).[17]

Benda, like all who write from Europe about the place of America, distinguish what "they" do – which "is not important" – from what "we" do. America is not European.

In practice, Europe has had two inescapable Others: Russia, which may really belong to an orientalist Asia, and America, which was born out of Europe but whose cultural evolution has made it distinct. For me, the case of America is indeed the more interesting because, by all accounts America was constructed by Europeans taking to the New World what, in the nationalistic European literature, are generally cited as European traits, such as the stress on the separate constitution of the individual, the division of the self from the world which allows for scientific development and the capitalistic exploitation of the land, and restless expansionism.

This expansion did not stop at the Atlantic Ocean, but something has apparently happened in the crossing of this ocean that people on either side persist in constructing as a fundamental divide. There is no evidence however that this divide existed from the beginning. Not surprisingly, one of the projects for the construction of Europe de Rougemont quotes is one by William Penn who, after having organized his Sylvania in an American territory, eventually returned to Europe with a project that was neither the first not the last but which was filed away as just another of what would later be qualified as an "American" utopia.[18]

Penn's project is, however, in a different position from these others because it was developed out of a successful experience with institutionalizing something that appeared to resolve what those Europeans who crossed the Atlantic for ideological reasons disliked about the states of their birth: the very problem of nationalism. Penn did not talk about his American utopia as a "melting pot." One had to wait another 100 years for Crèvecoeur's triumphal affirmation that there was at least one place on the earth where Europeans could meet and transcend what were altogether insignificant differences.

If we were to continue talking like Benda or de Rougemont, we might talk of America as the Europe which Europeans lacked the will to make. Or perhaps the will was always there, but not the occasion. Certainly, those who, like Penn, willed Europe found it easier to build it across the ocean. On the Eastern side of this ocean, the argument that local units should self-determine was institutionalized in the nationalism that American ideology challenges.

Still, the successful making of America, and its entry on the European stage, made something which, by the end of WWII, could not be ignored any further: there, on the back of tanks and other military and industrial hardware, were people altogether indifferent to the very divisions that had appeared so real to those who had played their life on the Western Eurasian stage. William Penn was dismissed, and so was Woodrow Wilson, but Franklin Roosevelt, as he divided Europe with Stalin and installed America as protector of the Western "Atlantic" part, had to be dealt with. It may not be insignificant that the first institutionalization of Europe coincided with the first military occupation of Europe by non-Europeans.[19]

Inescapably now, America is present in Europe – as an army, as a popular culture (in music and life style products), but also as an ideology constituting the legitimacy of various types of nationalisms and defining the stages where the claims can be made. For America, Europe is both the "old country" of nostalgic remembrances, and the source of all the ills that plague the United States and possibly the earth. In some contexts at least Europe finds itself in the position of the West of Ireland and must deal with pressures to look more like itself than it ever did. In other contexts, Europe has to deal with the relative success of those who fight "Euro-centrism" in the United States for every step in this struggle does involve a definition of Europe. One can read such an instant classic in this struggle as Said's book on orientalism to see how this construction proceeds – in ways that one not so different as those that were used to construct an "Orient" for Europeans. Typically, Said opens his book with a quote from a "*French* journalist" and then, in a breath-taking short-cut writes "He was right about the place, of course, especially so far as a *European* was concerned. The Orient was almost a European invention" (my emphasis, 1978: 1). By a stroke of his pen he does to the various nations of Western Eurasia what he accuses "Europe" of having done to the people of the Middle East and thereby performs something which the various writers I have quoted would see as American cultural hegemony in the act.

The issue here is not the historical validity of any of these claims. The issue is that they are being made on all sorts of stages, with all sorts of practical consequences. The intellectual conversations among philosophers and politicians that shaped nationalism in the 18th and 19th centuries were no mere idle talk even if they were not always immediately transformed into the speech acts which started wars and signed peace treaties. These conversations produced a context where the president of France, when making certain official televised pronouncements, can do so framed not only by the flag of France, but also by that of Europe. One can notice the ever-expanding normalization of travel to countries that are identified as less and less "foreign." In still not quite a popular stage, one can notice the flowering of European flags over the gas stations that service superhighways. Given the centrality of language, it is interesting to note the development of an ideographic script on the dash boards of cars, or on highway signs, with the concomitant downplaying of alphabet based signs. Such signs must always be in a particular language, or in a particular order of messages if the sign is printed in several languages.

These are not mere curiosities. They are the concrete statements that historical persons have to make in the current context. They are fundamentally "cultural" acts in the transformative sense emphasized by Lévi-Strauss ([1947] 1969). They may or may not be the signs that would allows us (anthropologists and natives of any part of the world) to state that there is a European culture – in the American sense of "culture." This identification is, above all, a political problem since it concerns the type of legitimacy to be claimed by the institutional unit. Over the past several hundred years at least, in geographical areas now bounded as Ireland, France, Germany, Italy, and many others, some groups have had their claim to difference and independence internationally recognized as legitimate. In the process, the "nation" that they made acquired a "surfeit" of culture. By contrast, Europe is undercoded. We cannot even say of Europe that it is a "new nation" as it was said of the decolonized states, and as it might be used to understand the United States (Lipset 1963). To say of America that it was "conceived in liberty" by the agency of a people who formed a union is not simply to fall prey to an extended metaphor of biological reproduction. It expresses, reveals and inscribes something that was and remains fundamental to America. By contrast, it is fundamental to "France" that it did not begin, even though it took many kings and emperors many centuries to build. European nations are "eternal" quasi "metaphysical beings" (Benda 1932: 41). Europe itself – except for the small minority of speakers who are simply trying to displace the discourse of nationalism to a new stage – is neither new nor old and it thus presents a singular problem for the collective imagination of humanity.

Thoreau's quip about the relevance of the State in his everyday life may apply here too: "[Europe] does not concern me much and I shall bestow the fewest possible thoughts on it" ([1854] 1965). There is little evidence that the major political issues that have called for a response by local centers in the last ten years, say the reunification of Germany, the breakup of the Russian empire, the troubles in Northern Ireland, the civil wars in Yugoslavia, have produced any response specifically symbolized as a "European" one. The institutions that would allow for this to happen have precisely not been put in place. At the national level, this is equivalent to the almost complete absence of awareness of Europe in the suburbs of Dublin where I spent ten months. Europe was just not there in any way even remotely approaching the way America is there in the suburbs of New York.

Eventually, personal identification is not the issue. Whether the people of Dublin ever identify passionately with Europe, whether they are ever given institutional spaces to perform this identification, it remains that something major is being built that is transforming the stage on which private lives inscribe themselves. It may be that the local presence of Europe is mostly felt through the sceptical grumbling of people who do not quite recognize what has actually been achieved as what they expected. Still, we cannot ignore these grumblings and must take them for what they are: evidence that new constraints and possibilities have appeared while old ones are disappearing. The intellectuals who are giving voice to the many versions of these grumblings are only some of those who are participating in the making, building, constructing, perhaps even creating or inventing (the architectural or artistic metaphors may not be misplaced here) of Europe. We have here a large scale experiment in the culturing (cultivation?) of history which will certainly stretch our understanding of what human beings can do.

Notes

1. I explain elsewhere (1986) the analytical usefulness of distinguishing geographically or administratively bounded spaces from cultural patterns that may be dominant there.

2. When talking about the "New States" which Europe spawned around the world, Geertz talks about these two poles as "essentialism" and "epochalism" ([1971] 1973:240-241), and may have missed the way in which the language of nationalism is itself a cultural language with very specific roots. Schneider can help us clarify these roots if we follow his argument that "nationalism" has a lot in common with "kinship" as a (European more than American) cultural system (1969) – all the metaphors that build "nationalism" are centered on common descent ("blood") and a shared condition ("code for conduct").

3. Whether they did or not is another matter: World War I was interpreted very differently by the peasants/workers turned soldiers of, say, France, Russia, or Ireland.

4. See Herzfeld on Greece (1987) or Varenne on Ireland (1989), among others.

5. In this vain, I would place my own work within the traditions of resistance to "nationalism" as a particular institutionalization of cultural difference. Its

roots must have something to do with the French universalism that Dumont talks about, as it must be modified when one has become convinced of the supra-individual reality of social systems and cultures. Milton Singer once said that there was something "Catholic" about all this (personal communication). I am still somewhat puzzled about this identification, but it may be appropriate.

6. All the details about the history of the building of Europe as a distinct geo-political area come from de Rougemont's fascinating "chronique des prises de conscience successives de notre unité de culture, des temps homériques ànos jours" (1961: 7). Note the use of the first person plural pronoun, and its association with "unité de culture."

7. De Rougemont, best known in the United States for this writings on the cultural history of love ([1939] 1956, [1961] 1963), wrote abundantly about the possibility of Europe and, for many years, was the President of the European Cultural Center in Geneva. His role may be best evoked by a quip from Morin who writes that "L'idée de fédération européenne ne fleurit que dans la banlieue de Genève, avec la prédiction de Denis de Rougemont" (1987: 139).

8. Hobsbawm illustrates this in his account of French revolutionary discourse (1990: 18ff).

9. I emphasize this notion of "will" because it plays a major role in Benda's writings about the source of nationality and plays a comparatively small role in the more traditional American handling of nationality. A notion of will to power may be implicit in the newer writing about the deliberate making of nations, and the "hegemony" of certain forms. Such authors appear, when talking about this aspect of nationalism, that their reader will join in their moral judgment of such acts of will. Benda however belonged to another generation when to refer to "will" was positive indeed.

10. "A typically European comportment that would be more or less characterized by a relationship between man and nature that does not confuse them, by the distinction between the self and the world; correlatively, by the idea of objectivity or truth" (my translation).

11. "The European philosophy I defend is that of the self-determination of a people, of its search for power and expression, of its specificity and cultural homogeneity, of the reclaiming of its roots" (my translation).

12. This resistance is certainly much weaker than it used to be, particularly with the collapse of the old socialist orders which, for various tactical reasons having to do with the position of the Soviet Union in the Cold War, became the staunchest supporters of "national independence." The remaining resistance may now be mostly expressed in the ironic skepticism of those who claim that "Europe" only has to do with the mass marketing of consumer goods (Enzensberger 1988).

13. "One must abandon any clear, distinct, harmonious Europe. One must refute any idea of a primordial European essence or substance that would have precedence over division and antagonism. . . . It is in the bursting of Christiandom that these originally European realities that are the Nation-States could emerge, along with humanism and science. It in the divisions and antagonisms between Nation-States that the notion of Europe propagated and imposed itself" (my translation).

14. "[The new faith] carries in itself the presence of Nothingness. The use of a thought which faces courageously Nothingness, here is the living message of nihilism, ultimate product of the adventure of the European spirit, here is the ultimate consequence of the loss of foundations, end point of the desperate search for a primordial certainty" (my translation).

15. In French, as in English, the adjective "common" which is officially supposed to refer to "community" has also a pejorative connotation that associates what it qualifies with the uncouth, the basely material, the uneducated lower classes, and, by extension to the *bourgeois*.

16. "From the French point of view, I am a man by nature and French by accident. As in enlightenment in general, the nation has no ontological status: at this level there is nothing, a big emptiness between the individual and the species. The nation is simply the largest empirical approximation of humanity that I can have access to in real life" (my translation).

17. "We speak commonly of an american novelist, a Hemingway, a Faulkner, a Miller, we do not speak of an "European" novelist, but of a French, English, Russian novelist. Americans do speak of a European novelist. They affirm that there is for them something common (that they do not quite specify) among the literary authors from our diverse nations by opposition to theirs; but what would be importnat for what we are dealing with, is that we ourselves spoke of a European literary author. In fact, we do not" (my translation).

18. For a summary of this project and its place within contemporary ones, see de Rougemont (1961: 100-105).

19. Note that the experiences of Europeans in South America, or Australia, is not so much dismissed as irrelevant as it is radically ignored. They are neither Self nor Other.

References

Anderson, Benedict. 1991 [1983]. *Imagined Communities*. Revised Edition. New York: Verso.

Benda, Julien. 1932. *Esquisse d'une histoire des Français dans leur volonté d'être une nation*. Paris: Gallimard.

_____. 1933. *Discours à la nation européenne*. Paris: Gallimard.

_____. 1946. "Conférence," In J. Benda et al., eds., *L'esprit européen*. Pp. 9-36. Neuchâtel: Editions de la Baconnière.

Benda, Julien, et al. 1946. *L'esprit européen*. Textes des conferences et des entretiens organisés par les Rencontres Internationales de Genève. Neuchâtel: Editions de la Baconnière.

Clifford, James. 1988. *The Predicament of Culture*. Cambridge: Harvard University Press.

Dumont, Louis. 1991. *L'idéologie allemande: France-Allemagne et retour*. Paris: Gallimard.

Enzensberger, Hans. 1988 [1987]. *Europe, Europe!* Tr. from the German by P. Gallissaires and C. Orsoni. Paris: Gallimard.

Fabian, Johannes. 1983 *Time and the other: How anthropology makes its object.* New York: Columbia University Press.

Faye, Guillaume. 1985. *Nouveau discours à la nation européenne.* Paris: Editions Albatros.

Geertz, Clifford. 1973 [1966] "Religion as a cultural system," in *The Interpretation of Cultures.* New York: Basic Books.

———. 1973 [1971]. "After the revolution: The fate of nationalism in the new states," in *The Interpretation of Cultures.* New York: Basic Books.

Gellner, Ernest. 1987. *Culture, Identity and Politics.* Cambridge: Cambridge University Press.

Herzfeld, Michael. 1987. *Anthropology Through the Looking Glass: Critical ethnography in the margins of Europe.* New York: Cambridge University Press.

Hobsbawm, E.J. 1990. *Nations and Nationalism since 1780.* New York: Cambridge University Press.

Lévi-Strauss, Claude. 1969 [1947]. *The Elementary Structures of Kinship.* Tr. by J. Bell and J. von Sturmer. Boston: Beacon Press.

Lipset, Seymour. 1963. *The First New Nation: The United States in historical and comparative perspective.* New York: Basic Books.

Mead, Margaret. 1965 [1942]. *And Keep Your Powder Dry: An anthropologist looks at America.* New York: W. Morrow & Co.

Merleau-Ponty, Maurice. 1946. "Commentary," In J. Benda et al., eds., *L'esprit européen* Pp. 74-77. Neuchâtel: Editions de la Baconnière.

Monnet, Jean. 1955. *Les Etats-Unis d'Europe ont commencé.* Paris: Robert Laffont.

Morin, Edgar. 1987. *Penser l'Europe.* Paris: Gallimard.

Rougemont, Denis de. 1956 [1939]. *Love in the Western World.* New York: Pantheon Books.

———. 1961. *Vingt-huigt siècles d'Europe: La conscience européenne à travers les textes.* Paris: Payot.

———. 1963 [1961] *Love Declared: Essays on the myth of love.* Tr. from the French by R. Howard. Boston: Beacon Press.

———. 1965 [1963]. *The Meaning of Europe.* Tr. by A. Braley. New York: Stein and Day.

Said, Edward. 1978. *Orientalism.* New York: Pantheon Books.

Schneider, David. 1969. "Kinship, nationality and religion in American culture: Toward a definition of kinship," in V. Turner, ed., *Forms of Symbolic Action.* Pp. 116-125. Proceedings of the American Ethnological Society.

Thoreau, Henry. 1965 [1854]. *Walden and On the duty of civil disobedience.* New York: Harper and Row.

Varenne, Hervé. 1986. *Symbolizing America.* Lincoln, NE: The University of Nebraska Press.

———. 1989. "A confusion of signs: The semiosis of anthropological Ireland," in B. Lee and G. Urban, eds., *Semiotics, Self and Society.* Pp. 121-152. New York: Mouton de Gruyter.

Williams, Raymond. 1977. *Marxism and Literature.* Oxford: Oxford University Press.

Yeats, W.B. 1962 [1921]. "Easter 1916," in *Selected poems.* New York: Collier Books.

Index